M

Moment's Notice

JAZZ IN POETRY & PROSE

EDITED BY ART LANGE & NATHANIEL MACKEY

COFFEE HOUSE PRESS :: MINNEAPOLIS :: 1993

Acknowledgments to the publishers and authors for the work published in this book appear on page 359, following the text, and shall constitute a continuation of this acknowledgments page.

Cover photograph of Thelonious Monk by Jim Marshall. Used with permission from the photographer.

The publishers thank the following organizations for assistance that helped make this book possible: the Bush Foundation, Cowles Media/ Star Tribune, the McKnight Foundation, the Minnesota State Arts Board, and the Andrew W. Mellon Foundation.

Coffee House Press books are distributed to the trade by our primary distributor, Consortium Book Sales and Distribution, 1045 Westgate Drive, St. Paul, MN 55114. Our books are also available through all major library distributors and jobbers, and through most small press distributors, including Bookpeople, Bookslinger, Inland, and Small Press Distribution. For catalogs or other information write to:
Coffee House Press
27 North Fourth Street, Suite 400, Minneapolis, MN 55401

Library of Congress Cataloging in Publication Data
Moment's Notice: jazz in poetry and prose / edited by
Art Lange and Nathaniel Mackey.
        p. cm.
    ISBN 1-56689-001-2 (pbk.) : $17.50
    1. Jazz–Literary collections. 2. American literature–20th century.
    i. Lange, Art, 1952- . ii Mackey, Nathaniel, 1947- .
PS509.J33M66 1993
810.8'0357–DC20   93-10151
                                CIP

Contents

Editors' Note

That jazz is the United States' best known indigenous art form all but goes without saying by now. The reception jazz has garnered and the influence it has exercised have extended not only far beyond the geographic boundaries of its country of origin but far beyond the boundaries of music itself. Jazz is at the same time a musicians' music, considered the most demanding, quintessentially musical of musical idioms by its practitioners (who typically sacrifice material security in order to pursue their art), and a music which, much more than most, is more than music. It has become a widely deployed symbol, a signifier freighted with a panoply of meanings, attitudes and associations which are variously and sometimes conflictingly aesthetic, religious, racial, political, epistemic, individual, social, philosophic, visceral, idiosyncratic, collective, utopic, dyspeptic—on and on. It has become, that is, iconic, its own often iconoclastic impulses notwithstanding.

It is not surprising, then, that jazz has attracted the attention of artists working in other media, iconographers who, as such, are also adept interpreters of icons, readers of icons. It is particularly unsurprising that a music which so frequently and characteristically aspires to the condition of speech, reflecting critically, it seems, upon the limits of the sayable, should have provoked and proved of enormous interest to practitioners of the art of the word—writers. There exists a unique body of literature inspired by and concerned with jazz, as was made abundantly clear, for anyone who had not already noticed, by the publication in 1990 and 1991 of three anthologies: Richard N. Albert's *From Blues to Bop: A Collection of Jazz Fiction*, Marcela Breton's *Hot and Cool: Jazz Short Stories* and Sascha Feinstein and Yusef Komunyakaa's *The Jazz Poetry Anthology*. That this body of literature is even larger than the publication of these anthologies indicates, a fact their respective editors point out, is further attested by the publication of yet a fourth, the present volume. Which is to say, in part at least, that we have endeavored, while inevitably including work which is also included in these three previous collections, to bring forth a good deal of the work which is not—other work by authors represented in them as well as work by authors who are not represented.

The most readily evident way in which this anthology differs from others is that we have chosen to bring together poetry and prose, making this the first major collection of jazz-influenced literature to do so. The significance of this extends beyond its being a first however. The literary registration of jazz's impact and importance looks considerably different if one takes a multi-genre view rather than confining oneself to a single genre. Just as musical instruments differ in the tasks they can perform and the tonal and timbral contributions they can make, literary genres differ in the expressive possibilities they afford. To fully sample the range of what writers have done under jazz's influence requires the inclusion of poems, stories, excerpts from novels and more—and by more we mean writings which blur the line between genres, bending genre in ways which are analogous to a musician bending notes.

We have sought to make this collection as representative as possible, given space constraints and prohibitive permission-to-reprint fees, of the range and variety of styles in which jazz has moved writers to write. We have been especially concerned to better represent the experimental end of the spectrum than have previous anthologies, to include a good deal more of the work in which writers, consistent with jazz's emphasis on invention and the "sound of surprise," have challenged conventional expectations regarding structure, language, character, voice and other components of literary form. In addition to offering tributes to and portraits of individual musicians, depictions of and meditations upon the social and cultural milieu in which the music exists, evocations of the music's import for specific audiences and so forth, writers have been moved to inspect, as artists witnessing other artists wrestling with the limits of their particular medium, the possibilities and resistances peculiar to writing. Mack Thomas once wrote, in liner notes, of Eric Dolphy confronting "the barrier that begins with what the horn will not do." Writers, tracking what John Clellon Holmes calls "the unnameable truth of music," have had to deal with a similar confrontation. Charles Lloyd, asked to comment on a piece of his music by a radio interviewer, answered, "Words don't go there." Writers influenced by jazz have been variously rising to the challenge of proving him wrong.

— Art Lange and Nathaniel Mackey

Mu

[An excerpt from *Harlem Gallery*]

Hideho Heights
and I, like the brims of old hats,
slouched at a sepulchered table in the Zulu Club.
Frog Legs Lux and his Indigo Combo
spoke with tongues that sent their devotees
out of this world!

Black and brown and yellow fingers flashed,
like mirrored sunrays of a heliograph,
on clarinet and piano keys, on cornet valves.

Effervescing like acid on limestone,
Hideho said:
"Oh White Folks, O Black Folks,
the dinosaur imagined its extinction meant
the death of the piss ants."

Cigarette smoke
—opaque veins in Carrara marble—
magicked the habitués into
humoresque and grotesques.
Lurid lights
spraying African figures on the walls
ecstasied maids and waiters,
pickups and stevedores—
with delusions
of Park Avenue grandeur.

Once, twice,
Hideho sneaked a swig.
"On the house," he said, proffering the bottle
as he lorded it under the table.
Glimpsing the harpy eagle at the bar,
I grimaced,
"I'm not the house snake of the Zulu Club."

A willow of a woman,
bronze as knife money,
executed, near our table, the Lenox Avenue Quake.
Hideho winked at me and poked
that which
her tight Park Avenue skirt vociferously advertised.
Peacocking herself, she turned like a ballerina,
her eyes blazing drops of rum on a crepe suzette.
"Why, you—"
A sanitary decree, I thought. "Don't *you* me!" he fumed.
The lips of a vixen exhibited a picadill flare.
"*What* you smell isn't cooking," she said.
Hideho sniffed.
"Chanel No. 5," he scoffed,
"from Sugar Hill."
I laughed and clapped him on the shoulder.
"A bad metaphor, *poet.*"
His jaws closed
like an alligator squeezer.
"She's a willow," I emphasized,
"a willow by a cesspool."
Hideho mused aloud,
"Do I hear The Curator rattle Eliotic bones?"

Out of the Indigo Combo
flowed rich and complex polyrhythms.
Like surfacing bass,
exotic swells and softenings
of the veld vibrato
emerged.

* * *

Was that Snakehips Briskie
gliding out of the aurora australis of the Zulu Club
into the kaleidoscopic circle?

* * *

Etnean gasps!
Vesuvian acclamations!

* * *

Snakehips poised himself—
Giovanni Gabrieli's
single violin against his massed horns.

* * *

The silence of the revelers was the arrested
hemorrhage of an artery
grasped by bull forceps.
I felt Hideho's breath against my ear.
"The penis act in the Garden of Eden," he confided.

* * *

Convulsively, unexampledly,
Snakehips' body and soul
began to twist and untwist like a gyrating rawhide—
began to coil, to writhe
like a prismatic-hued python
in the throes of copulation.

Eyes bright as the light
at Eddystone Rock,
an ebony Penthesilea

grabbed her tiger's-eye yellow-brown
beanpole Sir Testiculus of the evening
and gave him an Amazonian hug.
He wilted in her arms
like a limp morning-glory.
"The Zulu Club is in the groove," chanted Hideho,
"and the cats, the black cats, are *gone!*"

In the *ostinato*
of stamping feet and clapping hands
the Promethean bard of Lenox Avenue became a
lost loose-leaf
as memory vignetted
Rabelaisian I's of the Boogie-Woogie dynasty
in barrel houses, at rent parties,
on riverboats, at wakes:
The Toothpick, Funky Five, and Tippling Tom!
Ma Rainey, Countess Willie V., and Aunt Harriet!
Speckled Red, Skinny Head Pete, and Stormy Weather!
Listen, Black Boy.
Did the High Priestess at 27 rue de Fleurus
assert, "The Negro suffers from nothingness"?
Hideho confided like a neophyte on The Walk,
"Jazz is the marijuana of the Blacks."
In the *tribulum* of dialectics, I juggled the idea;
then I observed,
"Jazz is the philosophers' egg of the Whites."

Hideho laughed from below the Daniel Boone rawhide belt
he'd redeemed, in a Dallas pawn shop,
with part of the black-market
loot set loose
in a crap game
by a Yangtze ex-coolie who,
in a Latin Quarter dive below Telegraph Hill,
out-Harvarded his Alma Mater.

Frog Legs Lux and his Indigo Combo
let go
with a wailing pedal point
that slid into
Basin Street Blues
like Ty Cobb stealing second base:
Zulu,
King of the Africans,
arrives on Mardi Gras morning;
the veld drum of Baby Dodds'
great-grandfather
in Congo Square
pancakes the first blue note
in a callithump of the USA.
And now comes the eve of Ash Wednesday.
Comus on parade!
All God's children revel
like a post-Valley Forge
charivari in Boston celebrating the nuptials of
a gay-old-dog minuteman with a lusty maid.

★ ★ ★

Just as
the bourgeois adopted
the lyric-winged piano of Liszt in the court at Weimar
for the solitude of his
aeried apartment,
Harlem chose
for its cold-water flat
the hot-blues cornet of King Oliver
in his cart
under the
El pillars of the Loop.

The yanking fishing rod
of Hideho's voice
jerked me out of my bird's-foot violet romanticism.
He mixed Shakespeare's image with his own
and caricatured me:
"Yonder Curator has a lean and hungry look;
he thinks too much.
Such blackamoors are dangerous to
the Great White World!"

***

With a dissonance
from the Weird Sisters,
the jazz diablerie
boiled down and away
in the vacuum pan
of the Indigo Combo.

—MELVIN TOLSON

Projection

On the day when the Savoy
leaps clean over to Seventh Avenue
and starts jitterbugging
with the Renaissance,
on that day when Abyssinia Baptist Church
throws her enormous arms around
St. James Presbyterian
and 409 Edgecombe
stoops to kiss 12 West 133rd,
on that day—
Do, Jesus!
Manhattan Island will whirl
like a Dizzy Gillespie transcription
played by Inez and Timme.
On that day, Lord,
Sammy Davis and Marian Anderson
will sing a duet,
Paul Robeson
will team up with Jackie Mabley,
and Father Divine will say in truth,
Peace!
It's truly
wonderful!

Flatted Fifths

Little cullud boys with beards
re-bop be-bop mop and stop.

Little cullud boys with fears,
frantic, kick their draftee years
into flatted fifths and flatter beers
that at a sudden change become
sparkling Oriental wines
rich and strange
silken bathrobes with gold twines
and Heilbroner, Crawford,
Nat-undreamed-of Lewis combines
in silver thread and diamond notes
on trade-marks inside
Howard coats.
Little cullud boys in berets
    oop pop-a-da
horse a fantasy of days
    ool ya koo
and dig all plays.

Jam Session

Letting midnight
out on bail
pop-a-da
having been
detained in jail
oop-pop-a-da
for sprinkling salt
on a dreamer's tail
pop-a-da

Be-Bop Boys

Imploring Mecca
to achieve
six discs
with Decca.

1. Billie Holiday. Photograph by William P. Gottlieb, © 1979.

Song for Billie Holiday

What can purge my heart
   Of the song
     And the sadness?
What can purge my heart
   But the song
   Of the sadness?
What can purge my heart
   Of the sadness
   Of the song?

Do not speak of sorrow
With dust in her hair,
Or bits of dust in eyes
A chance wind blows there.
The sorrow that I speak of
Is dusted with despair.

Voice of muted trumpet,
Cold brass in warm air.
Bitter television blurred
By sound that shimmers—
   Where?

—LANGSTON HUGHES

Soledad

(And I, I am no longer of that world)

Naked, he lies in the blinded room
chainsmoking, cradled by drugs, by jazz
as never by any lover's cradling flesh.

Miles Davis coolly blows for him:
O pena negra, sensual Flamenco blues;
the red clay foxfire voice of Lady Day

(lady of the pure black magnolias)
sobsings her sorrow and loss and fare you well,
dryweeps the pain his treacherous jailers

have released him from for a while.
His fears and his unfinished self
await him down in the anywhere streets.

He hides on the dark side of the moon,
takes refuge in a stained-glass cell,
flies to a clockless country of crystal.

Only the ghost of Lady Day knows where
he is. Only the music. And he swings
oh swings: beyond complete immortal now.

JULIO CORTÁZAR

Hopscotch

[An excerpt]

Guy Monod decided to wake up when Ronald and Etienne agreed to listen to Jelly Roll Morton; opening one eye he decided that the back outlined in the light of the green candles must belong to Gregorovius. He shuddered, the green candles seen from a bed made a bad impression on him, the rain on the skylight was strangely mixed with the remnants of his dream-images, he had been dreaming about an absurdly sunny place, where Gaby was walking around nude and feeding crumbs to a group of stupid pigeons the size of ducks. "I have a headache," Guy said to himself. He was not in the least interested in Jelly Roll Morton although it was amusing to hear the rain on the skylight as Jelly Roll sang: "Stood on a corner, an' she was soakin' wet . . ." Wong would certainly have come up with a theory about real and poetic time, but was it true that Wong had mentioned making coffee? Gaby feeding the pigeons crumbs and Wong, the voice of Wong going in between Gaby's nude legs in a garden with brightly colored flowers, saying: "A secret I learned in the casino at Menton." Quite possible, after all, that Wong would appear with a pot full of coffee.

Jelly Roll was at the piano beating the time softly with his foot for lack of a better rhythm section. Jelly Roll could sing "Mamie's Blues" rocking a little, staring up at some decoration on the ceiling, or it was a fly that came and went or a spot that came and went in Jelly Roll's eyes. "Eleven twenty-four took my baby away-ay . . ." That's what life had been, trains bringing people and taking them away while you stood on the corner with wet feet, listening to a nickelodeon and laughing and cussing out the yellow windows of the saloon where you didn't always have enough money to go in. "Eleven twenty-four took my baby away-ay . . ." Babs had taken so many trains in her life, she liked to go by train if in the end there was some friend waiting for her, if Ronald softly put his hand on her hip the way he was doing now, sketching out the music on her skin, "Eleven-thirteen'll carry her back one day," obviously some train would bring her back again, but who knows if Jelly Roll was going to be on that platform, at that piano, that time he sang the blues about Mamie Desdume, the rain on a Paris skylight at one o'clock in the morning, wet feet, and a whore who muttered "If you can't hand me a dollar then hand me a rotten dime," Babs had said things like that in Cincinnati, every woman had said things like that somewhere, even in the bed of a king, Babs had a very special idea of what the bed of a king was like but in any case some woman must have said something like, "If you can't give me a million, gimme a lousy grand," a matter of proportions, and why was Jelly Roll's piano so sad, so much that rain that woke Guy up, that was making La Maga cry, and Wong who wasn't coming with the coffee.

"It's too much," Etienne said, sighing. "I don't know why I stand for that garbage. It's moving, but it's garbage."

"It's no Pisanello medal, of course," Oliveira said.

"Or opus whatever-you-want by Schoenberg," said Ronald. "Why did you want to hear it? Besides intelligence you also lack charity. Have you ever stood with your feet in a puddle at midnight? Jelly Roll has, you can tell when he sings, it's something you learn, man."

"I can paint better if my feet are dry," Etienne said. "And don't come around with any Salvation Army arguments. Why don't you put on something more intelligent, like those Sonny Rollins solos. At least those modern guys make you think of Jackson Pollock or Tobey, it's easy to see that they've left the age of the pianola and the box of watercolors."

"He's capable of believing in progress in art," Oliveira said yawning. "Don't pay any attention to him, Ronald, and with that hand you have free dig out that little record of the "Stack O'Lee Blues," when all's said and done I think it has a fine piano solo on it."

"That business about progress in art is ancient nonsense," Etienne said, "but in jazz as in any art there's always a flock of fakers. Music that can be translated into emotion is one thing, but emotion which pretends to pass as music is another. Paternal grief in F sharp, sarcastic laughter in yellow, violet, and black. No, my boy, it's hard to say where art begins, but it's never that stuff."

No one seemed disposed to contradict him because Wong had quietly appeared with the coffee and Ronald, shrugging his shoulders, had turned loose Fred Waring and his Pennsylvanians and after a terrible scratching they reached the theme that fascinated Oliveira, an anonymous trumpet followed by the piano, all wrapped up in the smoke of an old phonograph and a bad recording, of a corny prejazz band, all in all like those old records, showboats, Storyville nights, where the old only really universal music of the century had come from, something that brought people closer together and in a better way than Esperanto, UNESCO, or airlines, a music which was primitive enough to have gained such universality and good enough to make its own history, with schisms, abdications, and heresies, its Charleston, its Black Bottom, its Shimmy, its Fox Trot, its Stomp, its Blues, to label its forms, this style and the other one, swing, bebop, cool, a counterpoint of romanticism and classicism, hot and intellectual jazz, human music, music with a history in contrast to stupid animal dance music, the polka, the waltz, the *zamba*, a music that could be known and liked in Copenhagen as well as in Mendoza or Cape Town, a music that brings adolescents together, with records under their arms, that gives them names and melodies to use as passwords so they can know each other and become intimate and feel less lonely surrounded by bosses, families, and bitter love affairs, a music that accepts all imaginations and tastes, a collection of instrumental 78's with Freddie Keppard or Bunk Johnson, the reactionary cult of Dixieland, an academic specialization in Bix Beiderbecke, or in the adventures of Thelonious Monk, Horace Silver, or Thad Jones, the vulgarities of Erroll Garner or Art Tatum, repentance and rejection, a preference for small groups, mysterious recordings with false names and strange titles and labels made up on the spur of the moment, and that whole freemasonry of Saturday nights in a student's room or in some basement café with girls who would rather dance to "Stardust" or "When Your Man Is Going to Put You Down," and have a sweet slow smell of perfume and skin and heat, and let themselves be kissed when the hour is late and somebody has put on the "The Blues with a Feeling" and hardly anybody is really dancing, just standing up together, swaying back and forth, and everything is hazy and dirty and lowdown and every man is stroking shoulders and the girls have their mouths half-opened and turn themselves to delightful fear and the night, while a trumpet comes on to possess them in the name of all men, taking them with a single hot phrase that drops them like a cut flower into the arms of their partners, and there comes a motionless race, a jump up into the night air, over the city, until a miniature piano brings them to again, exhausted, reconciled, and still virgins until next Saturday, all of this from a kind of music that horrifies solid citizens who think that nothing is true unless there are programs and ushers, and that's the way things are and jazz is like a bird who migrates or emigrates or immigrates or transmigrates, roadblock jumper, smuggler, something that runs and mixes in and tonight in Vienna Ella Fitzgerald is singing while in Paris Kenny Clarke is helping open a new *cave* and in Perpignan Oscar Peterson's fingers are dancing around and Satchmo, everywhere, with that gift of omnipresence given him by the Lord, in Birmingham, in Warsaw, in Milan, in Buenos Aires, in Geneva, in the whole world, is inevitable, is rain and bread and salt, something completely beyond national ritual, sacred traditions, language and folklore: a cloud without frontiers, a spy of air and water, an archetypal form, something from before, from below, that brings Mexicans together with Norwegians and Russians and Spaniards, brings them back into that obscure and forgotten central flame, clumsily and badly and precariously he delivers them back to a betrayed origin, he shows them that perhaps there have been other paths and that the only one they took was maybe not the only one or the best one, or that perhaps there have been other paths and that the one they took was the best, but that perhaps there were other paths that made for softer walking and that they had not taken those, or that they only took them in a halfway sort of way, and that a man is always more than a man and always less than a man, more than a man because he has in himself all that jazz suggests and lies in wait for and even anticipates, and less than a man because he has made an aesthetic and sterile game out of this liberty, a chessboard where one must be bishop or knight, a definition of liberty which is taught in school, in the very schools where the pupils are never taught ragtime rhythm or the first notes of the blues, and so forth and so on.

I set right here and think
　　　　three thousand miles away,
set right here and think
　　　　three thousand miles away,
can't remember the night
had the blues this bad any-way . . .

Louis, Super-Cronopio

Louis Armstrong concert
Paris, 9 November 1952

It seems that the imperious bird known as God breathed into the side of the first man to animate him and give him soul. If Louis instead of the little bird had been there for that breath, man would have turned out much better. Chronology, history, and other concatenations are a total disaster. A world that began with Picasso instead of ending with him would be a world exclusively for Cronopios, and the Cronopios would dance Tregua and dance Catalan on every corner, and perched on a lamppost Louis would blow for hours, making huge chunks of raspberry syrup stars fall from the sky to be eaten by children and dogs.

These are the things you think of while taking your seat at the Champs Élysées Theater when Louis is about to appear, since he arrived in Paris this afternoon like an angel, in other words on Air France, and you imagine the tremendous confusion in the cabin of the plane, with innumerable Famas clutching briefcases full of documents and balance sheets, and Louis among them dying of laughter, waving his finger at passengers the Famas would rather not see because they have just finished vomiting, poor things. And Louis eating a hot dog that the girl on the plane had brought to make him happy and because if she hadn't Louis would have chased her all over the plane until he got it. While all this was going on, the airplane landed in Paris and the journalists flocked around, and as a result I already have a *France-Soir* photo of Louis surrounded by white faces, and without prejudice I can say that in this photo his face is the only human one among so many faces of reporters.

Now you see how things are in this theater. Here, where the great Cronopio Nijinsky once discovered secret swings and stairs in the air that lead to happiness, Louis will appear any moment and the end of the world will begin. Of course, Louis does not have the slightest idea that he will plant his yellow shoes in the spot Nijinsky's dancer slippers once were set, but one virtue of Cronopios is the way they don't dwell on what happened in the past or whether the gentleman in the box is the

Prince of Wales. Nor would Nijinsky have attached any importance to the fact that Louis would play the trumpet in his theater. These things are left to the Famas, and also the Esperanzas, who occupy themselves in recording the chronicles and fixing the dates and putting it all in moroccan leather and cloth bindings. Tonight the theater is copiously furnished with Cronopios who, not satisfied with lining the hall and climbing up to the lights, have invaded the stage and seated themselves there, have curled up in all the free spaces and the spaces that are not free, to the great indignation of the ushers who only the day before at a flute and harp recital had a public so well educated that it was a pleasure, not to mention that these Cronopios do not tip well and seat themselves whenever possible without consulting an usher. Most of the ushers are Esperanzas, who are clearly depressed by the Cronopios' behavior, and sigh heavily, flicking their penlights on and off, which in Esperanzas is a sign of great melancholy. Another thing the Cronopios immediately do is whistle and shout, calling for Louis who splits his sides with laughter making them wait just a moment longer, so the Champs Élysées Theater swells like a mushroom as the Cronopios yell for Louis, and paper airplanes rain down from all sides, landing in the eyes and down the necks of the Famas and Esperanzas, who twist around indignantly, and also of the Cronopios, who rise up furious, grab the airplanes, and hurl them off with terrible force, and so things go from bad to worse in the Champs Élysées Theater.

Now a man comes out to say a few words into the microphone, but since the public is waiting for Louis and this gentleman is going to stand in the way, the Cronopios are outraged and they protest vociferously, completely drowning out the speech of the gentleman who can be seen opening and closing his mouth, looking remarkably like a fish in a tank.

Since Louis is a Super-Cronopio, he regrets missing the speech and suddenly appears through a side entrance, and the first thing that appears is his great white handkerchief floating in the air, and behind it a stream of gold also floating in the air, which is Louis's trumpet, and behind that, emerging from the darkness of the entrance, is another darkness full of light, and this is Louis himself, advancing onto the stage, and everyone falls silent, and what occurs next is the total and definitive collapse of the bookshelves and all their hardware.

2. Louis Armstrong. Photograph by William P. Gottlieb, © 1979.

Behind Louis come the guys in the band, and there is Trummy Young, who plays the trombone as if he were holding a nude woman of honey, and Arvel Shaw, who plays the bass as if he were holding a nude woman of smoke, and Cozy Cole, who sits over the drums like the Marquis de Sade over the buttocks of eight bound and naked women, and then come two other musicians whose names I don't wish to recall and who I think are there through an impresario's error or because Louis ran into them on the Pont Neuf and saw their hungry faces, and besides, one of them was named Napoleon, which would be an irresistible inducement for a Cronopio as Super as Louis.

And now the apocalypse is loosed, Louis merely raises his golden sword and the first phrase of "When It's Sleepy Time Down South" falls upon the audience like a leopard's caress. From Louis's trumpet the music unfurls like the enribboned speeches of primitive saints, his hot yellow writing is drawn in the air, and after this first sign "Muskrat Ramble" is unleashed, and in our chairs we hang on tightly to everything there is to hang on to, including our neighbors, so that the hall appears to contain a horde of crazed octopuses, and in the middle is Louis with his eyes white behind his trumpet, with his handkerchief waving in a continuous farewell to something unknown, as if Louis always has to say goodbye to the music that he makes and unmakes in a moment, as if he knows the terrible price of his marvelous freedom. Of course, after every number, when Louis laughs the laugh of his final phrase and the gold ribbon is cut as if by a shining shears, the Cronopios on the stage jump several yards in every direction, while the Cronopios in the hall writhe enthusiastically in their seats, and the Famas attending the concert by mistake or because they have to or because it costs a lot regard each other with polite reserve, but of course they haven't understood a thing, their heads ache horribly, and in general they wish they were at home listening to good music selected and explained by good announcers, or any place else so long as it was miles from the Champs Élysées Theater.

One thing you shouldn't miss is that not only does an avalanche of applause fall on Louis the moment he finishes his chorus, but he is obviously just as delighted with himself, he laughs through his great teeth, waves his handkerchief, and comes and goes about the stage, exchanging words of approval with his musicians, quite pleased by the proceedings. Then he takes advantage of Trummy Young hoisting his trombone and blowing a phenomenal succession of staccato and gliding masses of sound to dry his face carefully with his handkerchief, and not just his face but also his throat, and even the insides of his eyes to judge from the way he rubs them. And now we realize that Louis brings his sidemen with him because he enjoys them and they make him feel at home on the stage. Meanwhile, he uses the platform where Cozy Cole sits like Zeus dispensing supernatural quantities of rays and stars to hold a dozen white handkerchiefs that he picks up one after another as the preceding one turns to soup. But this sweat naturally comes from somewhere and in a few minutes Louis feels he is getting dehydrated, so while Arvel Shaw is locked in terrible amorous combat with his dark lady, Louis pulls from Zeus's platform an extraordinary, mysterious red vessel, tall and narrow, which appears to be either a dicebox or the container of the Holy Grail, and when he takes a drink it provokes the wildest speculations from the Cronopios in the audience: some maintain that Louis is drinking milk, while others flush with indignation at this theory, declaring that such a vessel could only contain the blood of a bull or wine from

Crete, which amounts to the same thing. Meanwhile, Louis has hidden the vessel, he has a fresh handkerchief in his hand, and now he feels the urge to sing, so he sings, but when Louis sings the established order of things is suspended and from his mouth that had been writing pennants of gold now rises the lowing of a lovesick deer, the cry of an antelope toward the stars, the buzz of honeybees in sleepy plantations. Lost in the immense cavern of his song, I close my eyes, and with the voice of the Louis of today all his voices from other days come to me, his voice from old records lost forever, his voice singing "When Your Lover Has Gone," singing "Confessin'," singing "Thankful," singing "Dusky Stevedore." And although I'm lost in the perfect uproar of the crowd, which is swinging like a pendulum from Louis's voice, for a moment I return to myself and think of 1930 when I met Louis through a first record, and of 1935 when I bought my first Louis, the "Mahogany Hall Stomp" from Polydor. And I open my ears and he is there, after twenty-two years of South American love he is there singing, laughing with his whole unreformed child's face, Cronopio Louis, Louis Super-Cronopio, Louis joy of those who are worthy of him.

Now Louis has learned that his friend Hughes Panassié is in the house, and this naturally makes him very happy, so he runs to the microphone and dedicates his music to him, and he and Trummy Young begin a counterpoint of trombone and trumpet that makes you tear your shirt to pieces and fling them—one by one or all together—into the air. Trummy Young attacks like a bison, with falls and rebounds that make you prick up your ears, but now Louis fills in the holes and you begin to hear nothing but his trumpet, to understand once again that when Louis blows, everybody falls in and lends an ear. Afterwards comes the reconciliation, Trummy and Louis grow together like two poplars, and the air is split from top to bottom by a final slash that leaves us all sweetly dumb. The concert has ended, already Louis is changing his shirt and thinking of the hamburger they're going to make him in the hotel and the bath he's going to take, but the hall remains full of Cronopios lost in their dreams, multitudes of Cronopios who slowly, unconcernedly, start for the exit, each one still with his dream, and at the center of each dream a little Louis is blowing and singing.

—Julio Cortázar

Giuffre's Nightmusic

There is moonrise under your fingernail—
Light broken from a black stick
Where your hands in darkness are sorting the probables.

Hunger condenses midnight on the tongue . . .
Journeys . . . Blues . . . ladder of slow bells,
Toward the cold hour of lunar prophecy:

A scale-model city, unlighted, in a shelf
In the knee of the Madonna; a barbwire fence
Strummed by the wind: dream-singing emblems.

—The flags that fly above the breakfast food
     Are not your colors.
                              The republic of the moon
Gives no sleepy medals. Nor loud ornament.

He Don't Plant Cotton

Spring entered the black belt in ashes, dust, and drabness, without benefit of the saving green. The seasons were known only by the thermometer and the clothing of the people. There were only a few nights in the whole year when the air itself told you. Perhaps a night in April or May might escape the plague of smells, achieve a little of the enchantment, be the diminished echo of spring happening ardently in the suburbs, but it was all over in a night and the streets were filled with summer, as a hollow mouth with bad breath, and even the rain could not wash it away. And winter . . .

The beginning snow swirled in from the lake, dusting the streets with white. Baby squinted down the lonesome tracks. The wind twisted snow into his eyes, the flakes as sharp as sand, grinding, and his eyeballs were coated with cold tears. Baby worked his hands in his overcoat pockets to make heat. He saw a woman cross the street to catch the Big Red, which was coming now, but the woman refused stiffly to run for it. The wind went off hooting down the tracks ahead. Baby got on. The conductor held out one hand for the fare and yanked a cord twice with the other, prodding the red monster into motion.

Baby sat down inside. A cold breeze swept the floor, rattling old transfers and gum wrappers. Baby placed his feet uneasily on the heater to make the meager warmth funnel up his pants' legs. The dark flesh beneath the tuxedo was chilled to chalky gray at the joints. He listened to the wheels bump over the breaks in the track, and the warmth from the heater rose higher on his legs. He became warm and forgetful of the weather, except as scenery. The streets were paved evenly with snow twinkling soft and clean and white under the lights, and velvet red and green from the neon signs.

New York may be all right, he hummed to himself, but Beale Street's paved with gold. That's a lie, he thought; I been down on Beale. And Chicago, same way. All my life playing jobs in Chicago, and I still got to ride the Big Red. And that's no lie. Jobs were getting harder and harder to find. What they wanted was Mickey Mouse sound effects, singing strings, electric guitars, neon violins, even organs and accordions and harmonica teams. Hard to find a spot to play in, and when you did it was always a white place with drunken advertising men wanting to hear "a old song"—"My Wild Irish Rose" or "I Love You Truly." So you played it, of course, and plenty of schmaltz. And the college kids who wanted swing—any slick popular song. So you played that, too. And always you wanted to play the music you were born to, blue or fast, music that had no name. You managed somehow to play that, too, when there was a lull or the place was empty and you had to stay until 4 A.M. anyway.

Baby got off the streetcar and walked the same two blocks he saw every night except Tuesday. The wind had died down almost entirely and the snow whirled in big flakes end over end. Padding along, Baby told himself he liked winter better than summer. Then he came to the place, said, "How's it, Chief?" to the doorman, an Indian passing for Negro, went down three steps, and forgot all about winter and summer. It was always the same here. It was not so much a place of temperatures as a place of lights and shades of chromium, pastel mirrors, the smell of beer, rum, whisky, smoke—a stale blend of odors and shadows, darkness and music. It was a place of only one climate and that was it.

Baby's overcoat, hat, and scarf went into a closet and settled familiarly on hooks. His old tuxedo walked over to the traps. Its black hands rubbed together briskly, driving out the chill. One hand fumbled in the dark at the base of the big drum, and a second later a watery blue light winked on dully and flooded the drumhead, staring like a blind blue eye. Immediately the tuxedo sat down and worked its feet with a slight rasping noise into the floor. The fingers thumped testingly on the hide, tightened the snare. They knew, like the ears, when it was right. Gingerly, as always, the right foot sought the big drum's pedal. The tuxedo was not ready yet. It had to fidget and massage its seat around on the chair, stretch out its arms, and hug the whole outfit a fraction of an inch this way and that. Then the eyes glanced at the piano player, signaling ready. The drumsticks paused a moment tensely, slid into the beat, barely heard, accenting perfectly the shower of piano notes. Everything worked together for two choruses. Then the piano player tapered his solo gently, so that at a certain point Baby knew it was his. He brought the number to a lifeless close, run down. Too early in the evening.

"Dodo," Baby said to the piano player, "Libby come in yet?"

Dodo sent a black hand up, slow as smoke, toward the ceiling. "Upstairs," he said, letting the hand fall to the keyboard with a faint, far-off chord. It stirred there, gently worming music from the battered upright. Notes drew nearer, riding on ships and camels through a world of sand and water, till they came forthright from the piano, taking on patterns, as the other black hand came to life on the bass keys, dear to Dodo. Baby picked up his sticks, recognizing the number. He called it "Dodo's Blues," though he knew Dodo called it nothing. Every night about this time, when there was no crowd and Dodo hadn't yet put on the white coat he wore servicing the bar, they would play it. Baby half closed his eyes. With pleasure he watched Dodo through the clouds of rhythm he felt shimmering up like heat from his drums. Baby's eyes were open only enough to frame Dodo like a picture; everything else was out. It was a picture of many dimensions; music was only one of them.

Here was a man, midgety, hunchbacked, black, and proud—mostly all back and music. A little man who, when he was fixing to play, had to look around for a couple of three-inch telephone directories. Piling them on top of the piano bench, he sat down, with all their names and streets and numbers and exchanges under him. He had very little of thighs and stomach—mostly just back, which threw a round shadow on the wall. When he leaned farther away from the piano, so the light slanted through his hands, his shadow revealed him walking on his hands down the keyboard, dancing on the tips of fingery toes. Sometimes it seemed to Baby through half-closed eyes, when Dodo's body was bobbing on the wall and his hands were feet dancing on the keyboard, as though the dim light shaped him into a gigantic, happy spider. When he became a spider you could forget he was a man, hunchbacked, runtish, black; and he, too, could forget perhaps that he had to be careful and proud. Perhaps he could be happy always if his back and size and color and pride were not always standing in the way. The piano made him whole. The piano taught him to find himself and jump clean over the moon. When he played, his feet never touched the pedals.

People were beginning to fill the place. They finished off the number, Baby smiling his admiration, Dodo scrupulously expressionless.

"For a young man . . ." Baby said.

Dodo got down off the telephone directories and threw them under the piano at the bass end, beyond the blue glow of the big drum. He had seen Libby come down the steps from the dressing room—a red dress, a gardenia. Dodo went behind the bar and put on his white service coat. Libby sat down at the piano.

Helplessly attracted, several men came over from the bar and leaned on the piano. They stared, burdening Libby's body with calculations. Singly at first and then, gathering unity, together. Libby sang a popular song. The men went back to the bar to get their drinks, which they brought over and set on top of the upright. Libby sang the words about lost love, and the men licked their lips vacantly. At the end of the song they clapped fiercely. Libby ignored them with a smile.

"Say, that was just fine," one man said. "Where you from anyhow?"

With a little grin Libby acknowledged Baby. Baby, beaming his veteran admiration of a fine young woman, nodded.

"Where you from? Huh?"

"New Orleans."

"Well, you don't say!" the man blurted out joyfully. "We're from down South, too . . . Mississippi, matter of fact!"

Icily, Libby smiled her appreciation of this coincidence. She looked at Baby, who was also registering appropriately. Just think of that! Small world! And welcome to our city!

"Well, what do you know!" crowed the gentleman from Mississippi. "So you're from down South!" He was greatly pleased and already very drunk. He eyed his friends, four or five of them, distributing his discovery equally among them.

"You never know," he explained. Then he appeared to suffer a pang of doubt. He turned quickly to Libby again, as though to make sure she was still there. His eyes jellied blearily and in them an idea was born.

"I know," he said. "Sing . . . sing—sing 'Ol' Man River' for the boys. They all'd sure like that."

Without responding, Libby looked down at her hands, smiling. She measured chords between her thumbs and little fingers, working her amusement into the keys. Baby stared at the mottled hide of his snare drum, at the big one's rim worn down from playing "Dixieland." The gentleman from Mississippi got worried.

"Aw, sing it," he pleaded. So Libby sang a chorus. The gentlemen from Mississippi were overwhelmed. They loved the song, they loved the

South, the dear old Southland. Land of cotton, cinnamon seed, and sandy bottom. Look away! Look away! They loved themselves. Look away! Look away! There was the tiniest touch of satire in Libby's voice, a slightly overripe fervor. Baby caught it and behind the bar Dodo caught it, but the gentlemen did not. Dodo had put down the martini glass he was polishing and look away! look away!—good.

At the bridge of the second chorus, Libby nodded "Take it!" to Baby. He stood up, staggering from the heat of the fields, clenching his black, toilworn fists. In profound anguish, he hollered, giving the white folks his all, really knocking himself out.

> *"Tote dat barge*
> *Lift dat bale*
> *Git a little drunk—"*

Baby grimaced in torment and did his best to look like ol' Uncle Tom out snatchin' cotton.

Behind the bar, unnoticed, Dodo's sad black face had turned beatific. "—And you land in jail!" Dodo could not see the other faces, the big white ones, but he could imagine them, the heads fixed and tilted. It was too dark in the place, and he could make out only blurrily the outlines of the necks. Ordinarily he was capable only of hating them. Now he had risen to great unfamiliar heights and was actually enjoying them. Surprised at this capacity in himself, yet proud he could feel this way, he was confused. He went further and started to pity them. But his memory stood up outraged at his forgetfulness and said, Kill that pity dead. Then he remembered he was really alone in the place. It was different with Libby and Baby, though they were black, too. He did not understand why. Say their skin was thicker—only that was not why. Probably this was not the first time they had jived white folks to death and them none the wiser. Dodo was not like that; he had to wait a long time for his kicks. From his heart no pity went out for the white men. He kept it all to himself, where it was needed. But he had to smile inside of him with Libby and Baby. Only more. Look at that fool Baby! Jam up!

> *"Bend yo'r knees!*
> *An' bow yo'r head!*

An' pull dat rope
Until yo're dead."

Baby sat down with a thud, exhausted. The gentlemen from Mississippi brayed their pleasure. My, it was good to see that black boy all sweatin' and perspirin' that way. They clapped furiously, called for drinks, gobbled . . .

"And bring some for the darkies!"

Baby swallowed some of his drink. He looked at the beaten rim of the big drum, than at the sticks. He took out his pocketknife and scraped the rough, splintery places smooth. He glanced at Libby and ventured the kind of smile he felt and knew she did. He finished his drink. The gentlemen from Mississippi hung around the piano, getting drunker, shouting in one another's faces. Nervously Libby lighted a cigarette. A college boy tried to make conversation with her while his honey-haired girl assumed an attitude of genuine concern.

"Can you play 'Hot Lips'?" He was the real American Boy.

"Don't know it," Libby lied. She wished she didn't.

"Can you play 'Sugar Blues'?" Right back.

"Don't know it."

One of the Mississippi gentlemen, who had been hanging back, crowded up to the piano, making his move. He drained his drink and pushed closer to the piano so as to brush Libby's left hand with the front of his trousers. Libby moved her hand, sounding a chord that Baby caught. The gentleman, grinning lewdly, tried to follow her hand up the keyboard.

"That's all right," he snickered. "Play lots of bass, honey."

The first gentleman from Mississippi, drink in hand, stumbled over from the bar. He told Libby to play that "Ol' Man River" song some more. Libby hesitated. Then she lit into it, improvising all around it, and it was a pleasure for Baby, but the first gentleman from Mississippi was not happy. He said if that was the best she could do she had better try singing. Libby sang only one chorus. The gentlemen from Mississippi, though they applauded, were not gratified. There was an air of petulance among them. They remembered another time they had heard the song, but it was not clear now what had made it different and better. They saw Baby all right, but they did not remember that he was the one who had sung before, the good one that toted their bars, lifted their bales, and landed drunk in their jails. Something was wrong, but they saw no remedy. Each gentleman suspected the fault was personal, what with him drinking so heavy and all.

Dodo, behind the bar, had not enjoyed the song the last time, hating the coercion the white men worked on Libby and Baby, and feared his advantage was slipping away. In a minute he would be hating them to pieces again.

"Can you play 'Tiger Rag'?" The American Boy was back.

"No." Libby made a face and then managed to turn it into a smile for him. He held his drink up for the world to see on the night before the big game.

The honey-haired girl wrenched her face into a winning smile and hit the jackpot. "Can you play 'St. Louis Blues'?"

"How you want it?" Libby said. She put out her cigarette. "Blues, rhumba . . . what kind a way?"

"Oh, play it low down. The way *you people* play it." So Libby would understand, she executed a ponderous wink, narrowed her eyes, and made them glitter wantonly behind the lashes. "*You* know," she said.

Libby knew. She played "St. Louis," losing herself in it with Baby. She left the college boy and the honey-haired girl behind. She forgot she knew. She gazed at Baby with her eyes dreamy, unseeing, blind with the blue drum, her head nodding in that wonderful, graceful way. Baby saw his old tuxedo in the mirror, its body shimmying on the chair, and he was pleased. The drums, beating figures, rocked with a steady roll. They were playing "Little Rock Getaway" now, the fine, young-woman music.

And Libby was pleased, watching Baby. And then, somehow, he vanished for her into the blue drum. The sticks still danced at an oblique angle on the snare, but there were no hands to them and Libby could not see Baby on the chair. She could only feel him somewhere in the blue glow. Abandoning herself, she lost herself in the piano. Now, still without seeing him, she could feel him with a clarity and warmth beyond vision. Miniature bell notes, mostly blue, blossomed ecstatically, perished *affettuoso,* weaving themselves down into the dark beauty of the lower keys, because it was closer to the drum, and multiplied. They came back to "St. Louis" again.

"Stop." The first gentleman from Mississippi touched Libby on the arm. "When I do that to you, that means 'Stop,'" he said. Libby chorded easily. "Some of the boys like to hear that 'Ol' Man River' some more." He straightened up, turning to the other gentleman, his smile assuring them it would not be long now.

"Kick off," Baby sighed.

But Libby broke into "St. Louis" again. Baby, with a little whoop, came clambering after, his sticks slicing into the drum rim, a staccato "Dixieland."

The first gentleman frowned, touching Libby's arm, "Remember what that means? Means 'Ol' Man River,'" he said calmly, as though correcting a slight error. "Toot sweet. Know what that means? That's French. Means right now." No harm done, however. Just that his friends here, a bunch of boys from down South, were dying to hear that song again—up to him to see that they got satisfaction—knew there would be no trouble about it.

"We'll play it for you later on," Libby said quickly. "We got some other requests besides yours. How many you got now, Baby?"

Baby held up eight fingers, very prompt.

"Coming up," he said.

The first gentleman was undecided. "Well . . ." he drawled. Libby began a popular song. The first gentleman faced his friends. His eyes more or less met theirs and found no agreement. The boys looked kind of impatient, like a bunch of boys out for a little fun and not doing so well. He turned to Libby again.

"We just gotta have that 'Ol' Man River' some more. Boys all got their hearts set on it," he said. "Right away! Toot sweet! Toot—away!" There he'd gone and made a joke, and the boys all laughed and repeated it to each other. Libby played on, as though she had not heard. The first gentleman took hold of her arm. She gazed steadily up into his bleary eyes.

"Not now. Later."

"No, you don't. You gotta play it right now. For a bunch of boys from down South. They all got a hankerin' to hear that 'Ol' Man River' some more."

"So you best play it," another gentleman said, leaning down hard on the old upright piano. "On account of I'm gonna take and give ear. We kinda like how that old song sounds up North. Whatcha all need. The drummer will sing," he said, and looked at Baby. Baby looked back, unsmiling.

Libby chorded lightly, waiting for the gentlemen from Mississippi to get tired. They could not see how it was with her and Baby—never.

"You ain't gonna play?"

Baby's eyes strained hard in their sockets.

"We ain't comin'," Libby said.

Baby's eyes relaxed and he knew the worst part was over. They felt the same way about it. They had made up their minds. The rest was easy. Baby was even a little glad it had happened. A feeling was growing within him that he had wanted to do this for a long time—for years and years, in a hundred different places he had played.

Secretly majestic, Baby sat at his drums, the goal of countless uplifted eyes—beseeching him. For it seemed that hordes of white people were far below him, making their little commotions and noises, asking favors of him, like Lord, please bring the rain, or Lord, please take it away. Lord Baby. Waves of warm exhilaration washed into him, endearing him to himself. No, he smiled, I am sorry, no favors today. Yes, Lord, they all said, if that's the way it is, so be it.

But somebody objected. The manager's voice barked, far below, scarcely audible to Baby in his new eminence. ". . . honoring requests," he heard, and ". . . trouble with the local," and ". . . wanting to get a sweet-swing trio in this place a long time now." And the manager, strangely small, an excited, pale pygmy, explaining to the gentlemen from Mississippi, also small, how it was, "That's all I can do in the circumstances," and them saying "Well, I guess so; well, I guess so all right; don't pay to pamper 'em, to give 'em an inch."

Baby noticed Libby had got up from the piano and put on her coat, the long dress hanging out at the bottom, red.

"I won't change," she said, and handed Baby the canvas cover for the snare drum.

"Huh?" Baby said foggily. He set about taking his traps apart. Dodo, not wearing his white service coat, came over to help.

"You don't have to," Baby said.

Chief, freezing outside in his long, fancy maroon coat, opened the door for them. "You all through, Baby?"

"Yeah, Chief. You told that right."

They walked down the street toward the car line. Baby, going first, plowed a path for Libby and Dodo in the snow. Window sills, parked cars, and trees were padded with it. The wind was dead and buried. Baby bore the big drum on his shoulder and felt the sticks pressing tight and upright in his vest pockets, two on each side. Libby had her purse and street clothes rolled up under one arm. Dodo carried the snare drum.

Softly as snow, Libby laughed, "That's all I can do in the circumstances," she said.

"I got your old circumstances," Baby said.

Then they were silent, tramping in the snow.

At the corner they waited in a store entrance for a southbound streetcar. Libby raised a foot now and then, shuddering with cold. Dead still, Dodo breathed down inside the collar of his overcoat, retarding his breath, frowning at the little smoke trickling out, as though it were the only thing left in the world to remind him he was alive. Baby talked of taking a cab and finally did go out into the street to hail one approaching. It slowed up, pulled over to the curb, hesitated . . . and lurched away, with Baby's hand reaching for the door. Baby watched the cab speed down the snowy street, following it for a few steps, speechless. There was nothing to do. Without looking, he saw Libby and Dodo shivering in the store entrance. They had seen the cab come and go. They had not moved an inch. They waited unfooled, as before, for the Big Red.

"What's wrong with you, Baby?" Libby called out. A tiny moment of silence, and she was laughing, gradually louder, mellow octaves of it, mounting, pluming . . .

Like her piano, it seemed to Baby—that fine, young-woman laughter.

"Why you laugh so much, woman?" he inquired plaintively from the street. Then he moved to join them, a few steps only, dallying at the curb to temper the abruptness of his retreat. Like her piano on "Little Rock"—that fine, young-woman laughter.

—J. F. POWERS

Clock

for Albert Ayler

At last   that night   the pounding
in his dark released a flower

electricity of nerve   a blue
serrated fire   the scent

blooming through years of glass
wounded him   he

unfolded e.
rect   a wrecked

calyx   what disasters unhinged
from his glowing   what

impinges of pain   he
stood still   still

unable to move   his roots
moored in water   mirrored

through mud   anchored
him

.

un
    til the

clock

ground up
  to tick

    the time
round.
ed the rook.   skill

of the
horn

in its cradle of   alarms

      tell
ing what

ever tale
was

    tocked

it threw rick.
ets into the

blood.   it flew
crick

ets into every quar.   ter
tone

&
quaver   till an eye

O

pened on the moon
&

blue notes flick.
ered flick.

ered flick.
ered from the three.

corners of the womb

.

when the clicks

            close

the

clock

        stopp.

.

& the rock   of his skull   fall down

                        —Kamau Brathwaite

Freedom and Discipline

Saint Harmony, many
years I have stript

naked in your service
under the lash. Yes,

I believe the first
I heard (living, there

aloud in the hall) was
Sergei Rachmaninoff

set at the keys like a
great dwarf, a barrel

on three spindles,
megalocephalus, hands

with fourteen fingers,
ugly as Merlin, with whom

I was in love, a boy and
an old man; a boy nodding

and an old man sorrowing
under the brushfire of the

people's heart, until he
coolly knocked out the

"Prelude in C# Minor." Second
was Coleman Hawkins

in about 1933 perhaps.
I, stript and bleeding,

leapt to the new touch,
up and over the diminished

in a full-voiced authority
of blue-gold blues. I

would do nothing, locked
in discipline, sworn to

freedom. The years shrieked
and smothered, like billboards

beside a road at night.
I learnt how Catlett

drove the beat without
harming it, how Young

sped between the notes,
how Monk reconstructed

a broken chord to make
my knuckles rattle, and much

from oblivion: Newton,
Fasola, Berigan, my

inconsolable Papa Yancey.
Why I went to verse-making

is unknowable, this
grubbing art. Trying.

Harmony, to fix your beat
in things that have none

and want none—absurdity!
Let that be the answer

to any hope of statecraft.
As Yeats said, *Fal de rol.*

Freedom and discipline concur
only in ecstacy, all else

is shoveling out the muck.
Give me my old hot horn.

Three Paragraphs

A day   very solid   February 12th, 1944
cheerless in New York City
                         (while I kneedeep
elsewhere in historical war
was wrecking Beauty's sleep
and her long dream)
                         a day (blank, gray) at four
in the afternoon, overheated in the w.o.r.
Recording Studios. Gum wrappers *and* dust
and a stale smell. A day. The cast
was Albert Ammons, Lips Page, Vic Dickenson,
Don Byas, Israel
Crosby, and Big Sid Catlett. (*And* it was Abe Linkhorn's

birthday.) And Milt Gabler
presided beyond the glass with a nod, a sign. Ammons
counted off

        a-waaaaan . . .   *tu!*

    and went feeling
his way on the keys gently,
        while Catlett summoned

the exact beat from—
    say from the sounding depths, the universe . . .
When Dickenson came on it was all established,
no guessing, and he started with a blur
as usual, smears, brays—Christ
the dirtiest noise imaginable
        belches, farts
            curses
but it was music
      music now
        with Ammons trilling in counterpoise.
Byas next, meditative, soft/
        then Page
with that tone like the torn edge
of reality:
      and so the climax, long dying riffs—
groans, wild with pain—
and Crosby throbbing *and* Catlett riding stiff
yet it was music   music.
            (Man, doan
fall in that bag.
    you caint describe it.)
          Piano & drum.
Ammons & Catlett drove the others. *And* it was done
and they listened *and* heard themselves
    better than they were, for they had come

high above themselves. Above everything, flux, ooze,

loss, need, shame, improbability/ the awfulness
of gut-wrong,   sex-wrack,   horse & booze,
the whole goddamn mess,
And Gabler said "We'll press it"   *and* it was
     "Bottom Blues"
BOTTOM BLUES five men knowing it well   blacks
     & jews
yet music, music   high
in the celebration of fear, strange joy
of pain: blown out, beaten out
                              a moment ecstatic
in the history
of creative mind *and* heart/   not singular, not the
     rarity
we think, but real and a glory
our human shining, shekinah . . .   Ah,
                    holy spirit, ninefold
I druther've bin a-setting there, supernumerary
cockroach i' th' corner, a-listenin, a listenin . . .
          than be the Prazedint ov the Wuurld.

                                        —HAYDEN CARRUTH

The Subterraneans

[An excerpt]

While they ate in the kitchen I pretended to read. I pretended to pay no attention whatever. We went out for a walk the three of us and by now all of us vying to talk like three good friends who want to get in and say everything on their minds, a friendly rivalry—we went to the Red Drum to hear the jazz which that night was Charlie Parker with Honduras Jones on drums and others interesting, probably Roger Beloit too, whom I wanted to see now, and that excitement of softnight San Francisco bop in the air but all in the cool sweet unexerting Beach—so we in fact ran, from Adam's on Telegraph Hill, down the white street under lamps, ran, jumped, showed off, had fun—felt gleeful and something was throbbing and I was pleased that she was able to walk as fast as we were—a nice thin strong little beauty to cut along the street with and so striking everyone turned to see, the strange bearded Adam, dark Mardou in strange slacks, and me, big gleeful hood.

So there we were at the Red Drum, a tableful of beers a few that is and all the gangs cutting in and out, paying a dollar quarter at the door, the little hip-pretending weasel there taking tickets, Paddy Cordavan floating in as prophesied (a big tall blond brakeman type subterranean from Eastern Washington cowboy-looking in jeans coming in to a wild generation party all smoky and mad and I yelled "Paddy Cordavan?" and "Yeah?" and he'd come over)—all sitting together, interesting groups at various tables, Julien, Roxanne (a woman of 25 prophesying the future style of America with short almost crewcut but with curls black snaky hair, snaky walk, pale pale junky anemic face and we say junky when once Dostoevski would have said what? if not ascetic or saintly? but not in the least? but the cold pale booster face of the cold blue girl and wearing a man's white shirt but with the cuffs undone untied at the buttons so I remember her leaning over talking to someone after having slinked

3. Charlie Parker with Tommy Potter. Photograph by William P. Gottlieb, © 1979.

across the floor with flowing propelled shoulders, bending to talk with her hand holding a short butt and the neat little flick she was giving it to knock ashes but repeatedly with long long fingernails an inch long and also orient and snake-like)—groups of all kinds, and Ross Wallenstein, the crowd, and up on the stand Bird Parker with solemn eyes who'd been busted fairly recently and had now returned to a kind of bop dead Frisco but had just discovered or been told about the Red Drum, the great new generation gang wailing and gathering there, so here he was on the stand, examining them with his eyes as he blew his now-settled-down-into-regulated-design "crazy" notes—the booming drums, the high ceiling—Adam for my sake dutifully cutting out at about 11 o'clock so he could go to bed and get to work in the morning, after a brief cutout with Paddy and myself for a quick ten-cent beer at roaring Pantera's, where Paddy and I in our first talk and laughter together pulled wrists—now Mardou cut out with me, glee eyed, between sets, for quick beers, but at her insistence at the Mask instead where they were fifteen cents, but she had a few pennies herself and we went there and began earnestly talking and getting hightingled on the beer and now it was the beginning—returning to the Red Drum for sets, to hear Bird, whom I saw distinctly digging Mardou several times also myself directly into my eye looking to search if really I was that great writer I thought myself to be as if he knew my thoughts and ambitions or remembered me from other night clubs and other coasts, other Chicagos—not a challenging look but the king and founder of the bop generation at least the sound of it in digging his audience digging his eyes, the secret eyes him-watching, as he just pursed his lips and let great lungs and immortal fingers work, his eyes separate and interested and humane, the kindest jazz musician there could be while being and therefore naturally the greatest—watching Mardou and me in the infancy of our love and probably wondering why, or knowing it wouldn't last, or seeing who it was would be hurt, as now, obviously, but not quite yet, it was Mardou whose eyes were shining in my direction, though I could not have known and now do not definitely know—except the one fact, on the way home, the session over the beer in the Mask drunk we went home on the Third Street bus sadly through night and throb knock neons and when I suddenly leaned over her to shout something further (in her secret self as later confessed) her heart leapt to smell the "sweetness of my breath" (quote) and suddenly she almost loved me—I not knowing this, as we found the Russian dark sad door of Heavenly Lane a great iron gate rasping on the sidewalk to the pull, the insides of smelling garbage cans sad-leaning together, fish heads, cats, and then the Lane itself, my first view of it (the long history and hugeness of it in my soul, as in 1951 cutting along with my sketch-book on a wild October evening when I was discovering my own writing soul at last I saw the subterranean Victor who'd come to Big Sur once on a motorcycle, was reputed to have gone to Alaska on same, with little subterranean chick Dorie Kiehl, there he was in striding Jesus coat heading north to Heavenly Lane to his pad and I followed him awhile, wondering about Heavenly Lane and all the long talks I'd been having for years with people like Mac Jones about the mystery, the silence of the subterraneans, "urban Thoreaus" Mac called them, as from Alfred Kazin in New York New School lectures back East commenting on all the students being interested in Whitman from a sexual revolution standpoint and in Thoreau from a contemplative mystic and antimaterialistic as if existentialist or whatever standpoint, the *Pierre*-of-Melville goof and wonder of it, the dark little beat burlap dresses, the stories you'd heard about great tenormen shooting junk by broken windows and starting at their horns, or great young poets with beats lying high in Rouault-like saintly obscurities, Heavenly Lane the famous Heavenly Lane where they'd all at one time or another the beat subterraneans lived, like Alfred and his little sickly wife something straight out of Dostoevski's Petersburg slums you'd think but really the American lost bearded idealistic—the whole thing in any case), seeing it for the first time, but with Mardou, the wash hung over the court, actually the back courtyard of a big 20-family tenement with bay windows, the wash hung out and in the afternoon the great symphony of Italian mothers, children, fathers BeFinneganing and yelling from stepladders, smells, cats mewing, Mexicans, the music from all the radios whether bolero of Mexican or Italian tenor of spaghetti eaters or loud suddenly turned-up KPFA symphonies of Vivaldi harpsichord intellectuals performances boom blam the tremendous sound of it which I then came to hear all the summer wrapt in the arms of my love—walking in there now, and going up the narrow musty stairs like in a hovel, and her door.

—JACK KEROUAC

Let's All Hear It for Mildred Bailey!

The men's can at Café Society Uptown
was need I say it? Upstairs
and as I headed for the stairs I
stumbled slightly
not about to fall
and Mildred Bailey
swept by in a nifty outfit:
off-brown velvet
cut in a simple suit-effect
studded with brass nail heads
(her hair dressed with stark simplicity)
"Take it easy, Sonny," she
advised me and passed on to the supper-club
(surely no supper was
served at Café you-know-which?)
A star spoke to me
in person! No one
less than Mildred Bailey!

Downstairs I nursed one drink
(cheap is cheap)
and Mildred Bailey got it on
and the boys all stood up and shouted
"Mama Won't You Scrap Your Fat?"
a lively number
during the brown-out
in war-haunted, death-smeared
NY

Then things got better, greater:
Mildred Bailey sang immortal hits
indelibly
permanently
marked by that voice
with built-in laughter
perfect attack: always
on the note
not behind or above it
and the extra something nice
that was that voice
a quality, a sound she had
on a disc, a waxing
you know it: Mildred Bailey

The night progressed:
a second drunk—oops—drink
(over there, boys, in what seemed
like silence boxcars rolled on
loaded with Jews, gypsies, nameless
forever others: The Final Solution
a dream of
Adolf Hitler:
Satan incarnate)
Mildred Bailey winds up the show
with a bouncy
number: when she gets back
to Brooklyn
from cheapo cruise ship
visitation:
Havana, Cuba
(then the door stood wide
to assorted thrills)
the next one in her life
ain't gonna be no loser, a clerk
oh no
"You can bet that he'll be Latin"

And Mildred Bailey, not
quite alone
in her upstate farmhouse
the rain is falling
she listens to another voice
somehow sadly
it is singing a song:
music
in a world gone wrong.

—James Schuyler

Sonny's Blues

I read about it in the paper, in the subway, on my way to work. I read it, and I couldn't believe it, and I read it again. Then perhaps I just stared at it, at the newsprint spelling out his name, spelling out the story. I stared at it in the swinging lights of the subway car, and in the faces and bodies of the people, and in my own face, trapped in the darkness which roared outside.

It was not to be believed and I kept telling myself that, as I walked from the subway station to the high school. And at the same time I couldn't doubt it. I was scared, scared for Sonny. He became real to me again. A great block of ice got settled in my belly and kept melting there slowly all day long, while I taught my classes algebra. It was a special kind of ice. It kept melting, sending trickles of ice water all up and down my veins, but it never got less. Sometimes it hardened and seemed to expand until I felt my guts were going to come spilling out or that I was going to choke or scream. This would always be at a moment when I was remembering some specific thing Sonny had once said or done.

When he was about as old as the boys in my classes his face had been bright and open, there was a lot of copper in it; and he'd had wonderfully direct brown eyes, and great gentleness and privacy. I wondered what he looked like now. He had been picked up, the evening before, in a raid on an apartment downtown, for peddling and using heroin.

I couldn't believe it: but what I mean by that is that I couldn't find any room for it anywhere inside me. I had kept it outside me for a long time. I hadn't wanted to know. I had had suspicions, but I didn't name them, I kept putting them away. I told myself that Sonny was wild, but he wasn't crazy. And he'd always been a good boy, he hadn't ever turned hard or evil or disrespectful, the way kids can, so quick, so quick, especially in Harlem. I didn't want to believe that I'd ever see my brother going down, coming to nothing, all that light in his face gone out, in the condition I'd already seen so many others. Yet it had happened and here I was, talking about algebra to a lot of boys who might, every one of them for all I knew, be popping off needles every time they went to the head. Maybe it did more for them than algebra could.

I was sure that the first time Sonny had ever had horse, he couldn't have been much older than these boys were now. These boys, now, were living as we'd been living then, they were growing up with a rush and their heads bumped abruptly against the low ceiling of their actual possibilities. They were filled with rage. All they really knew were two darknesses, the darkness of their lives, which was now closing in on them, and the darkness of the movies, which had blinded them to that other darkness, and in which they now, vindictively, dreamed, at once more together than they were at any other time, and more alone.

When the last bell rang, the last class ended, I let out my breath. It seemed I'd been holding it for all that time. My clothes were wet—I may have looked as though I'd been sitting in a steam bath, all dressed up, all afternoon. I sat alone in the classroom a long time. I listened to the boys outside, downstairs, shouting and cursing and laughing. Their laughter struck me for perhaps the first time. It was not the joyous laughter which—God knows why—one associates with children. It was mocking and insular, its intent to denigrate. It was disenchanted, and in this, also, lay the authority of their curses. Perhaps I was listening to them because I was thinking about my brother and in them I heard my brother. And myself.

One boy was whistling a tune, at once very complicated and very simple, it seemed to be pouring out of him as though he were a bird, and it sounded very cool and moving through all that harsh, bright air, only just holding its own through all those other sounds.

I stood up and walked over to the window and looked down into the courtyard. It was the beginning of the spring and the sap was rising in the boys. A teacher passed through them every now and again, quickly, as though he or she couldn't wait to get out of that courtyard, to get those boys out of their sight and off their minds. I started collecting my stuff. I thought I'd better get home and talk to Isabel.

The courtyard was almost deserted by the time I got downstairs. I saw this boy standing in the shadow of a doorway, looking just like Sonny. I almost called his name. Then I saw that it wasn't Sonny, but somebody we used to know, a boy from around our block. He'd been Sonny's friend. He'd never been mine, having been too young for me, and, anyway, I'd never liked him. And now, even though he was a grown-up man, he still hung around that block, still spent hours on the street corners, was always high and raggy. I used to run into him from time to time and he'd often work around to asking me for a quarter or fifty cents. He always had some real good excuse, too, and I always gave it to him, I don't know why.

But now, abruptly, I hated him. I couldn't stand the way he looked at me, partly like a dog, partly like a cunning child. I wanted to ask him what the hell he was doing in the school courtyard.

He sort of shuffled over to me, and he said, "I see you got the papers. So you already know about it."

"You mean about Sonny? Yes, I already know about it. How come they didn't get you?"

He grinned. It made him repulsive and it also brought to mind what he'd looked like as a kid. "I wasn't there. I stay away from them people."

"Good for you." I offered him a cigarette and I watched him through the smoke. "You come all the way down here just to tell me about Sonny?"

"That's right." He was sort of shaking his head and his eyes looked strange, as though they were about to cross. The bright sun deadened his damp dark brown skin and it made his eyes look yellow and showed up the dirt in his kinked hair. He smelled funky. I moved a little away from him and I said, "Well, thanks. But I already know about it and I got to get home."

"I'll walk you a little ways," he said. We started walking. There were a couple of kids still loitering in the courtyard and one of them said good-night to me and looked strangely at the boy beside me.

"What're you going to do?" he asked me. "I mean, about Sonny?"

"Look. I haven't seen Sonny for over a year, I'm not sure I'm going to do anything. Anyway, what the hell *can* I do?"

"That's right," he said quickly, "ain't nothing you can do. Can't much help old Sonny no more, I guess."

It was what I was thinking and so it seemed to me he had no right to say it.

"I'm surprised at Sonny, though," he went on—he had a funny way of talking, he looked straight ahead as though he were talking to himself—"I thought Sonny was a smart boy, I thought he was too smart to get hung."

"I guess he thought so too," I said sharply, "and that's how he got hung. And how about you? You're pretty goddamn smart, I bet."

Then he looked directly at me, just for a minute. "I ain't smart," he said. "If I was smart I'd have reached for a pistol a long time ago."

"Look. Don't tell *me* your sad story, if it was up to me, I'd give you one." Then I felt guilty—guilty, probably, for never having supposed that the poor bastard *had* a story of his own, much less a sad one, and I asked, quickly, "What's going to happen to him now?"

He didn't answer this. He was off by himself some place. "Funny thing," he said, and from his tone we might have been discussing the quickest way to get to Brooklyn, "when I saw the papers this morning, the first thing I asked myself was if I had anything to do with it. I felt sort of responsible."

I began to listen more carefully. The subway station was on the corner, just before us, and I stopped. He stopped, too. We were in front of a bar and he ducked slightly, peering in, but whoever he was looking for didn't seem to be there. The juke box was blasting away with something black and bouncy and I half watched the barmaid as she danced her way from the juke box to her place behind the bar. And I watched her face as she laughingly responded to something someone said to her, still keeping time to the music. When she smiled one saw the little girl, one sensed the doomed, still-struggling woman beneath the battered face of the semi-whore.

"I never *give* Sonny nothing," the boy said finally, "but a long time ago I come to school high and Sonny asked me how it felt." He paused, I couldn't bear to watch him, I watched the barmaid, and I listened to the music which seemed to be causing the pavement to shake. "I told him it felt great." The music stopped, the barmaid paused and watched the juke box until the music began again. "It did."

All this was carrying me some place I didn't want to go. I certainly didn't want to know how it felt. It filled everything, the people, the houses, the music, the dark, quicksilver barmaid, with menace; and this menace was their reality.

"What's going to happen to him now?" I asked again.

"They'll send him away some place and they'll try to cure him." He shook his head. "Maybe he'll even think he's kicked the habit. Then they'll let him loose"—he gestured, throwing his cigarette into the gutter. "That's all."

"What do you mean, that's *all?*"

But I knew what he meant.

"I *mean*, that's *all*." He turned his head and looked at me, pulling down the corners of his mouth. "Don't you know what I mean?" he asked, softly.

"How the hell *would* I know what you mean?" I almost whispered it, I don't know why.

"That's right," he said to the air, "how would *he* know what I mean?" He turned toward me again, patient and calm, and yet I somehow felt him shaking, shaking as though he were going to fall apart. I felt that ice in my guts again, the dread I'd felt all afternoon; and again I watched the barmaid, moving about the bar, washing glasses, and singing. "Listen. They'll let him out and then it'll just start all over again. That's what I mean."

"You mean—they'll let him out. And then he'll just start working his way back in again. You mean he'll never kick the habit. Is that what you mean?"

"That's right," he said, cheerfully. "*You* see what I mean."

"Tell me," I said at last, "why does he want to die? He must want to die, he's killing himself, why does he want to die?"

He looked at me in surprise. He licked his lips. "He don't want to die. He wants to live. Don't nobody want to die, ever."

Then I wanted to ask him—too many things. He could not have answered, or if he had, I could not have borne the answers. I started walking. "Well, I guess it's none of my business."

"It's going to be rough on old Sonny," he said. We reached the subway station. "This is your station?" he asked. I nodded. I took one step down. "Damn!" he said, suddenly. I looked up at him. He grinned again. "Damn it if I didn't leave all my money home. You ain't got a dollar on you, have you? Just for a couple of days, is all."

All at once something inside gave and threatened to come pouring out of me. I didn't hate him any more. I felt that in another moment I'd start crying like a child.

"Sure," I said. "Don't sweat." I looked in my wallet and didn't have a dollar, I only had a five. "Here," I said. "That hold you?"

He didn't look at it—he didn't want to look at it. A terrible closed look came over his face, as though he were keeping the number on the bill a secret from him and me. "Thanks," he said, and now he was dying to see me go. "Don't worry about Sonny. Maybe I'll write him or something."

"Sure," I said. "You do that. So long."

"Be seeing you," he said. I went on down the steps.

And I didn't write Sonny or send him anything for a long time. When I finally did, it was just after my little girl died, he wrote me back a letter which made me feel like a bastard.

Here's what he said:

Dear brother,

You don't know how much I needed to hear from you. I wanted to write you many a time but I dug how much I must have hurt you and so I didn't write. But now I feel like a man who's been trying to climb up out of some deep, real deep and funky hole and just saw the sun up there, outside. I got to get outside.

I can't tell you much about how I got here. I mean I don't know how to tell you. I guess I was afraid of something or I was trying to escape from something and you know I have never been very strong in the head (smile). I'm glad Mama and Daddy are dead and can't see what's happened to their son and I swear if I'd known what I was doing I would never have hurt you so, you and a lot of other fine people who were nice to me and who believed in me.

I don't want you to think it had anything to do with me being a musician. It's more than that. Or maybe less than that. I can't get anything straight in my head down here and I try not to think about what's going to happen to me when I get outside again. Sometime I think I'm going to flip and *never* get outside and sometime I think I'll come straight back. I tell you one thing, though, I'd rather blow my brains out than go through this again. But that's what they all say, so they tell me. If I tell you when I'm coming to New York and if you could meet me, I sure would appreciate it. Give my love to Isabel and the kids and I was sure sorry to hear about little Gracie. I wish I could be like Mama and say the Lord's will be done, but I don't know it seems to me that trouble is the one thing that never does get stopped and I don't know what good it does to blame it on the Lord. But maybe it does some good if you believe it.

Your brother,
Sonny

Then I kept in constant touch with him and I sent him whatever I could and I went to meet him when he came back to New York. When I saw him many things I thought I had forgotten came flooding back to me. This was because I had begun, finally, to wonder about Sonny, about the life that Sonny lived inside. This life, whatever it was, had made him older and thinner and it had deepened the distant stillness in which he had always moved. He looked very unlike my baby brother. Yet, when he smiled, when we shook hands, the baby brother I'd never known looked out from the depths of his private life, like an animal waiting to be coaxed into the light.

"How you been keeping?" he asked me.

"All right. And you?"

"Just fine." He was smiling all over his face. "It's real good to see you again."

"It's good to see you."

The seven years' difference in our ages lay between us like a chasm: I wondered if these years would ever operate between us as a bridge. I was remembering, and it made it hard to catch my breath, that I had been there when he was born; and I had heard the first words he had ever spoken. When he started to walk, he walked from our mother straight to me. I caught him just before he fell when he took the first steps he ever took in this world.

"How's Isabel?"

"Just fine. She's dying to see you."

"And the boys?"

"They're fine too. They're anxious to see their uncle."

"Oh, come on. You know they don't remember me."

"Are you kidding? Of course they remember you."

He grinned again. We got into a taxi. We had a lot to say to each other, far too much to know how to begin.

As the taxi began to move, I asked, "You still want to go to India?"

He laughed. "You still remember that. Hell, no. This place is Indian enough for me."

"It used to belong to them," I said.

And he laughed again. "They damn sure knew what they were doing when they got rid of it."

Years ago, when he was around fourteen, he'd been all hipped on the idea of going to India. He read books about people sitting on rocks, naked, in all kinds of weather, but mostly bad, naturally, and walking barefoot through hot coals and arriving at wisdom. I used to say that it sounded to me as though they were getting away from wisdom as fast as they could. I think he sort of looked down on me for that.

"Do you mind," he asked, "if we have the driver drive alongside the park? On the west side—I haven't seen the city in so long."

"Of course not," I said. I was afraid that I might sound as though I were humoring him, but I hoped he wouldn't take it that way.

So we drove along, between the green of the park and the stony, lifeless elegance of hotels and apartment buildings, toward the vivid, killing streets of our childhood. These streets hadn't changed, though housing projects jutted up out of them now like rocks in the middle of a boiling sea. Most of the houses in which we had grown up had vanished, as had the stores from which we had stolen, the basements in which we had first tried sex, the rooftops from which we had hurled tin cans and bricks. But houses exactly like the houses of our past yet dominated the landscape, boys exactly like the boys we once had been found themselves smothering in these houses, came down into the streets for light and air and found themselves encircled by disaster. Some escaped the trap, most didn't. Those who got out always left something of themselves behind, as some animals amputate a leg and leave it in the trap. It might be said, perhaps, that I had escaped, after all, I was a school teacher; or that Sonny had, he hadn't lived in Harlem for years. Yet, as the cab moved uptown through streets which seemed, with a rush, to darken with dark people, and as I covertly studied Sonny's face, it came to me that what we both were seeking through our separate cab windows was that part of ourselves which had been left behind. It's always at the hour of trouble and confrontation that the missing member aches.

We hit 110th Street and started rolling up Lenox Avenue. And I'd known this avenue all my life, but it seemed to me again, as it had seemed on the day I'd first heard about Sonny's trouble, filled with a hidden menace which was its very breath of life.

"We almost there," said Sonny.

"Almost." We were both too nervous to say anything more.

We live in a housing project. It hasn't been up long. A few days after it was up it seemed uninhabitably new, now, of course, it's already rundown. It looks like a parody of the good, clean, faceless life—God knows the people who live in it do their best to make it a parody. The beat-looking grass lying around isn't enough to make their lives green, the hedges will never hold out the streets, and they know it. The big windows fool no one, they aren't big enough to make space out of no space. They don't bother with the windows, they watch the TV screen instead. The playground is most popular with the children who don't play at jacks, or skip rope, or roller skate, or swing, and they can be found in it after dark. We moved in partly because it's not too far from where I teach, and partly for the kids; but it's really just like the houses in which Sonny and I grew up. The same things happen, they'll have the same things to remember. The moment Sonny and I started into the house I had the feeling that I was simply bringing him back into the danger he had almost died trying to escape.

Sonny has never been talkative. So I don't know why I was sure he'd be dying to talk to me when supper was over the first night. Everything went fine, the oldest boy remembered him, and the youngest boy liked him, and Sonny had remembered to bring something for each of them; and Isabel, who is really much nicer than I am, more open and giving, had gone to a lot of trouble about dinner and was genuinely glad to see him. And she's always been able to tease Sonny in a way that I haven't. It was nice to see her face so vivid again and to hear her laugh and watch her make Sonny laugh. She wasn't, or, anyway, she didn't seem to be, at all uneasy or embarrassed. She chatted as though there were no subject which had to be avoided and she got Sonny past his first, faint stiffness. And thank God she was there, for I was filled with that icy dread again. Everything I did seemed awkward to me, and everything I said sounded freighted with hidden meaning. I was trying to remember everything I'd heard about dope addiction and I couldn't help watching Sonny for signs. I wasn't doing it out of malice. I was trying to find out something about my brother. I was dying to hear him tell me he was safe.

"Safe!" my father grunted, whenever Mama suggested trying to move to a neighborhood which might be safer for children. "Safe, hell! Ain't no place safe for kids, nor nobody."

He always went on like this, but he wasn't, ever, really as bad as he sounded, not even on weekends, when he got drunk. As a matter of fact, he was always on the lookout for "something a little better," but he died before he found it. He died suddenly, during a drunken weekend in the middle of the war, when Sonny was fifteen. He and Sonny hadn't ever got on too well. And this was partly because Sonny was the apple of his father's eye. It was because he loved Sonny so much and was frightened for him, that he was always fighting with him. It doesn't do any good to fight with Sonny. Sonny just moves back, inside himself, where he can't be reached. But the principal reason that they never hit it off is that they were so much alike. Daddy was big and rough and loud-talking, just the opposite of Sonny, but they both had—that same privacy.

Mama tried to tell me something about this, just after Daddy died. I was home on leave from the army.

This was the last time I ever saw my mother alive. Just the same, this picture gets all mixed up in my mind with pictures I had of her when she was younger. The way I always see her is the way she used to be on a Sunday afternoon, say, when the old folks were talking after the big Sunday dinner. I always see her wearing pale blue. She'd be sitting on the sofa. And my father would be sitting in the easy chair, not far from her. And the living room would be full of church folks and relatives. There they sit, in chairs all around the living room, and the night is creeping up outside, but nobody knows it yet. You can see the darkness growing against the windowpanes and you hear the street noises every now and again, or maybe the jangling beat of a tambourine from one of the churches close by, but it's real quiet in the room. For a moment nobody's talking, but every face looks darkening, like the sky outside. And my mother rocks a little from the waist, and my father's eyes are closed. Everyone is looking at something a child can't see. For a minute they've forgotten the children. Maybe a kid is lying on the rug, half asleep. Maybe somebody's got a kid in his lap and is absentmindedly stroking the kid's head. Maybe there's a kid, quiet and big-eyed, curled up in a big chair in the corner. The silence, the darkness coming, and the darkness in the faces frightens the child obscurely. He hopes that the hand which strokes his forehead will never stop—will never die. He hopes that there will never come a time when the old folks won't be sitting around the living room, talking about where they've come from, and what they've seen, and what's happened to them and their kinfolk.

But something deep and watchful in the child knows that this is bound to end, is already ending. In a moment someone will get up and turn on the light. Then the old folks will remember the children and they won't talk any more that day. And when light fills the room, the child is filled with darkness. He knows that everytime this happens he's moved just a little closer to that darkness outside. The darkness outside is what the old folks have been talking about. It's what they've come from. It's what they endure. The child knows that they won't talk any more because if he knows too much about what's happened to *them*, he'll know too much too soon, about what's going to happen to *him*.

The last time I talked to my mother, I remember I was restless. I wanted to get out and see Isabel. We weren't married then and we had a lot to straighten out between us.

There Mama sat, in black, by the window. She was humming an old church song, *Lord, you brought me from a long ways off.* Sonny was out somewhere. Mama kept watching the streets.

"I don't know," she said, "if I'll ever see you again, after you go off from here. But I hope you'll remember the things I tried to teach you."

"Don't talk like that," I said, and smiled. "You'll be here a long time yet."

She smiled, too, but she said nothing. She was quiet for a long time. And I said, "Mama, don't you worry about nothing. I'll be writing all the time, and you be getting the checks. . . ."

"I want to talk to you about your brother," she said, suddenly. "If anything happens to me he ain't going to have nobody to look out for him."

"Mama," I said, "ain't nothing going to happen to you or Sonny. Sonny's all right. He's a good boy and he's got good sense.

"It ain't a question of his being a good boy," Mama said, "nor of his having good sense. It ain't only the bad ones, nor yet the dumb ones that gets sucked under." She stopped, looking at me. "Your Daddy once had a brother," she said, and she smiled in a way that made me feel she was in pain. "You didn't never know that, did you?"

"No," I said, "I never knew that," and I watched her face.

"Oh, yes," she said, "your Daddy had a brother." She looked out of the window again. "I know you never saw your Daddy cry. But *I* did—many a time, through all these years."

I asked her, "What happened to his brother? How come nobody's ever talked about him?"

This was the first time I ever saw my mother look old.

"His brother got killed," she said, "when he was just a little younger than you are now. I knew him. He was a fine boy. He was maybe a little full of the devil, but he didn't mean nobody no harm."

Then she stopped and the room was silent, exactly as it had sometimes been on those Sunday afternoons. Mama kept looking out into the streets.

"He used to have a job in the mill," she said, "and, like all young folks, he just liked to perform on Saturday nights. Saturday nights, him and your father would drift around to all different places, go to dances and things like that, or just sit around with people they knew, and your father's brother would sing, he had a fine voice, and play along with himself on his guitar. Well, this particular Saturday night, him and your father was coming home from some place, and they were both a little drunk and there was a moon that night, it was bright like day. Your father's brother was feeling kind of good, and he was whistling to himself, and he had his guitar slung over his shoulder. They was coming down a hill and beneath them was a road that turned off from the highway. Well, your father's brother, being always kind of frisky, decided to run down this hill, and he did, with that guitar banging and clanging behind him, and he ran across the road, and he was making water behind a tree. And your father was sort of amused at him and he was still coming down the hill, kind of slow. Then he heard a car motor and that same minute his brother stepped from behind the tree, into the road, in the moonlight. And he started to cross the road. And your father started to run down the hill, he says he don't know why. This car was full of white men. They was all drunk, and when they seen your father's brother they let out a great whoop and holler and they aimed the car straight at him. They was having fun, they just wanted to scare him, the way they do sometimes, you know. But they was drunk. And I guess the boy, being drunk, too, and scared, kind of lost his head. By the time he jumped it was too late. Your father says he heard his brother scream when the car rolled over him, and he heard the wood of that guitar when it give, and he heard them strings go flying, and he heard them white men shouting, and the car kept on a-going and it ain't stopped till this day. And, time your father got down the hill, his brother weren't nothing but blood and pulp."

Tears were gleaming on my mother's face. There wasn't anything I could say.

"He never mentioned it," she said, "because I never let him mention it before you children. Your Daddy was like a crazy man that night and for many a night thereafter. He says he never in his life seen anything as dark as that road after the lights of that car had gone away. Weren't nothing, weren't nobody on that road, just your Daddy and his brother and that busted guitar. Oh, yes. Your Daddy never did really get right again. Till the day he died he weren't sure but that every white man he saw was the man that killed his brother."

She stopped and took out her handkerchief and dried her eyes and looked at me.

"I ain't telling you all this," she said, "to make you scared or bitter or to make you hate nobody. I'm telling you this because you got a brother. And the world ain't changed."

I guess I didn't want to believe this. I guess she saw this in my face. She turned away from me, toward the window again, searching those streets.

"But I praise my Redeemer," she said at last, "that He called your Daddy home before me. I ain't saying it to throw no flowers at myself, but, I declare, it keeps me from feeling too cast down to know I helped your father get safely through this world. Your father always acted like he was the roughest, strongest man on earth. And everybody took him to be like that. But if he hadn't had *me* there—to see his tears!"

She was crying again. Still, I couldn't move. I said, "Lord, Lord, Mama, I didn't know it was like that."

"Oh, honey," she said, "there's a lot that you don't know. But you are going to find it out." She stood up from the window and came over to me. "You got to hold on to your brother," she said, "and don't let him fall, no matter how evil you gets with him. You going to be evil with him many a time. But don't you forget what I told you, you hear?"

"I won't forget," I said. "Don't you worry, I won't forget. I won't let nothing happen to Sonny."

My mother smiled as though she were amused at something she saw in my face. Then, "You may not be able to stop nothing from happening. But you got to let him know you's *there*."

Two days later I was married, and then I was gone. And I had a lot of things on my mind and I pretty well forgot my promise to Mama until I got shipped home on a special furlough for her funeral.

And, after the funeral, with just Sonny and me alone in the empty kitchen, I tried to find out something about him.

"What do you want to do?" I asked him.

"I'm going to be a musician," he said.

For he had graduated, in the time I had been away, from dancing to the jukebox to finding out who was playing what, and what they were doing with it, and he had bought himself a set of drums.

"You mean, you want to be a drummer?" I somehow had the feeling that being a drummer might be all right for other people but not for my brother Sonny.

"I don't think," he said, looking at me very gravely, "that I'll ever be a good drummer. But I think I can play a piano."

I frowned. I'd never played the role of the older brother quite so seriously before, had scarcely ever, in fact, *asked* Sonny a damn thing. I sensed myself in the presence of something I didn't really know how to handle, didn't understand. So I made my frown a little deeper as I asked: "What kind of musician do you want to be?"

He grinned. "How many kinds do you think there are?"

"Be *serious*," I said.

He laughed, throwing his head back, and then looked at me. "I *am* serious."

"Well, then, for Christ's sake, stop kidding around and answer a serious question. I mean, do you want to be a concert pianist, you want to play classical music and all that, or—or what?" Long before I finished he was laughing again. "For Christ's *sake*, Sonny!"

He sobered, but with difficulty. "I'm sorry. But you sound so—*scared!*" and he was off again.

"Well, you may think it's funny now, baby, but it's not going to be so funny when you have to make your living at it, let me tell you *that*." I was furious because I knew he was laughing at me and I didn't know why.

"No," he said, very sober now, and afraid, perhaps, that he'd hurt me, "I don't want to be a classical pianist. That isn't what interests me. I mean"—he paused, looking hard at me, as though his eyes would help me to understand, and then gestured helplessly, as though perhaps his hand would help—"I mean, I'll have a lot of studying to do, and I'll have to study *everything*, but, I mean, I want to play *with*—jazz musicians." He stopped. "I want to play jazz," he said.

Well, the word had never before sounded as heavy, as real, as it sounded that afternoon in Sonny's mouth. I just looked at him and I was probably frowning a real frown by this time. I simply couldn't see why on earth he'd want to spend his time hanging around nightclubs, clowning around on bandstands, while people pushed each other around a dance floor. It seemed—beneath him, somehow. I had never thought about it before, had never been forced to, but I suppose I had always put jazz musicians in a class with what Daddy called "good-time people."

"Are you *serious*?"

"Hell, *yes*, I'm serious."

He looked more helpless than ever, and annoyed, and deeply hurt.

I suggested, helpfully: "You mean—like Louis Armstrong?"

His face closed as though I'd struck him. "No. I'm not talking about none of that old-time, down-home crap."

"Well, look, Sonny, I'm sorry, don't get mad. I just don't altogether get it, that's all. Name somebody—you know, a jazz musician you admire."

"Bird."

"Who?"

"Bird! Charlie Parker! Don't they teach you nothing in the goddamn army?"

I lit a cigarette. I was surprised and then a little amused to discover that I was trembling. "I've been out of touch," I said. "You'll have to be patient with me. Now. Who's this Parker character?"

"He's just one of the greatest jazz musicians alive," said Sonny, sullenly, his hands in his pockets, his back to me. "Maybe *the* greatest," he added, bitterly, "that's probably why *you* never heard of him."

"All right," I said, "I'm ignorant. I'm sorry. I'll go out and buy all the cat's records right away, all right?"

"It don't," said Sonny, with dignity, "make any difference to me. I don't care what you listen to. Don't do me no favors."

I was beginning to realize that I'd never seen him so upset before. With another part of my mind I was thinking that this would probably turn out to be one of those things kids go through and that I shouldn't make it seem important by pushing it too hard. Still, I didn't think it would do any harm to ask: "Doesn't all this take a lot of time? Can you make a living at it?"

He turned back to me and half leaned, half sat, on the kitchen table. "Everything takes time," he said, "and—well, yes, sure, I can make a living at it. But what I don't seem to be able to make you understand is that it's the only thing I want to do."

"Well, Sonny," I said, gently, "you know people can't always do exactly what they *want* to do—"

"*No*, I don't know that," said Sonny, surprising me. "I think people *ought* to do what they want to do, what else are they alive for?"

"You getting to be a big boy," I said desperately, "it's time you started thinking about your future."

"I'm thinking about my future," said Sonny, grimly. "I think about it all the time."

I gave up. I decided, if he didn't change his mind, that we could always talk about it later. "In the meantime," I said, "you got to finish school." We had already decided that he'd have to move in with Isabel and her folks. I knew this wasn't the ideal arrangement because Isabel's folks are inclined to be dicty and they hadn't especially wanted Isabel to marry me. But I didn't know what else to do. "And we have to get you fixed up at Isabel's."

There was a long silence. He moved from the kitchen table to the window. "That's a terrible idea. You know it yourself."

"Do you have a *better* idea?"

He just walked up and down the kitchen for a minute. He was as tall as I was. He had started to shave. I suddenly had the feeling that I didn't know him at all.

He stopped at the kitchen table and picked up my cigarettes. Looking at me with a kind of mocking, amused defiance, he put one between his lips. "You mind?"

"You smoking already?"

He lit the cigarette and nodded, watching me through the smoke. "I just wanted to see if I'd have the courage to smoke in front of you." He grinned and blew a great cloud of smoke to the ceiling. "It was easy." He looked at my face. "Come on, now. I bet you was smoking at my age, tell the truth."

I didn't say anything but the truth was on my face, and he laughed. But now there was something very strained in his laugh. "Sure. And I bet that ain't all you was doing."

He was frightening me a little. "Cut the crap," I said. "We already decided that you was going to go and live at Isabel's. Now what's got into you all of a sudden?"

"*You* decided it," he pointed out. "*I* didn't decide nothing." He stopped in front of me, leaning against the stove, arms loosely folded. "Look, brother. I don't want to stay in Harlem no more, I really don't." He was very earnest. He looked at me, then over toward the kitchen window. There was something in his eyes I'd never seen before, some thoughtfulness, some worry all his own. He rubbed the muscle of one arm. "It's time I was getting out of here."

"Where do you want to *go*, Sonny?"

"I want to join the army. Or the navy, I don't care. If I say I'm old enough, they'll believe me."

Then I got mad. It was because I was so scared. "You must be crazy. You goddamn fool, what the hell do you want to go and join the *army* for?"

"I just told you. To get out of Harlem."

"Sonny, you haven't even finished *school*. And if you really want to be a musician, how do you expect to study if you're in the *army*?"

He looked at me, trapped, and in anguish. "There's ways. I might be able to work out some kind of deal. Anyway, I'll have the G.I. Bill when I come out."

"*If* you come out." We stared at each other. "Sonny, please. Be reasonable. I know the setup is far from perfect. But we got to do the best we can."

"I ain't learning nothing in school," he said. "Even when I go." He turned away from me and opened the window and threw his cigarette out into the narrow alley. I watched his back. "At least, I ain't learning nothing you'd want me to learn." He slammed the window so hard I thought the glass would fly out, and turned back to me. "And I'm sick of the stink of these garbage cans!"

"Sonny," I said, "I know how you feel. But if you don't finish school now, you're going to be sorry later that you didn't." I grabbed him by the shoulders. "And you only got another year. It ain't so bad. And I'll come back and I swear I'll help you do *whatever* you want to do. Just try to put up with it till I come back. Will you please do that? For me?"

He didn't answer and he wouldn't look at me.

"Sonny. You hear me?"

He pulled away. "I hear you. But you never hear anything *I* say."

I didn't know what to say to that. He looked out of the window and then back at me. "Okay," he said, and sighed. "I'll try."

Then I said, trying to cheer him up a little, "They got a piano at Isabel's. You can practice on it."

And as a matter of fact, it did cheer him up for a minute. "That's right," he said to himself. "I forgot that." His face relaxed a little. But the worry, the thoughtfulness, played on it still, the way shadows play on a face which is staring into the fire.

But I thought I'd never hear the end of that piano. At first, Isabel would write me, saying how nice it was that Sonny was so serious about his music and how, as soon as he came in from school, or wherever he had been when he was supposed to be at school, he went straight to that piano and stayed there until suppertime. And, after supper, he went back to that piano and stayed there until everybody went to bed. He was at the piano all day Saturday and all day Sunday. Then he bought a record player and started playing records. He'd play one record over and over again, all day long sometimes, and he'd improvise along with it on the piano. Or he'd play one section of the record, one chord, one change, one progression, then he'd do it on the piano. Then back to the record. Then back to the piano.

Well, I really don't know how they stood it. Isabel finally confessed that it wasn't like living with a person at all, it was like living with sound. And the sound didn't make any sense to her, didn't make any sense to any of them—naturally. They began, in a way, to be afflicted by this presence that was living in their home. It was as though Sonny were some sort of god, or monster. He moved in an atmosphere which wasn't like theirs at all. They fed him and he ate, he washed himself, he walked in and out of their door; he certainly wasn't nasty or unpleasant or rude, Sonny isn't any of those things; but it was as though he were all wrapped up in some cloud, some fire, some vision all his own; and there wasn't any way to reach him.

At the same time, he wasn't really a man yet, he was still a child, and they had to watch out for him in all kinds of ways. They certainly couldn't throw him out. Neither did they dare to make a great scene about that piano because even they dimly sensed, as I sensed, from so many thousands of miles away, that Sonny was at that piano playing for his life.

But he hadn't been going to school. One day a letter came from the school board and Isabel's mother got it—there had, apparently, been other letters but Sonny had torn them up. This day, when Sonny came in, Isabel's mother showed him the letter and asked where he'd been spending his time. And she finally got it out of him that he'd been down in Greenwich Village, with musicians and other characters, in a white girl's apartment. And this scared her and she started to scream at him and what came up, once she began—though she denies it to this day— was what sacrifices they were making to give Sonny a decent home and how little he appreciated it.

Sonny didn't play the piano that day. By evening, Isabel's mother had calmed down but then there was the old man to deal with, and Isabel herself. Isabel says she did her best to be calm but she broke down and started crying. She says she just watched Sonny's face. She could tell, by watching him, what was happening with him. And what was happening was that they penetrated his cloud, they had reached him. Even if their fingers had been a thousand times more gentle than human fingers ever are, he could hardly help feeling that they had stripped him naked and were spitting on that nakedness. For he also had to see that his presence, that music, which was life or death to him, had been torture for them and that they had endured it, not at all for his sake, but only for mine. And Sonny couldn't take that. He can take it a little better today than he could then but he's still not very good at it and, frankly, I don't know anybody who is.

The silence of the next few days must have been louder than the sound of all the music ever played since time began. One morning, before she went to work, Isabel was in his room for something and she suddenly realized that all of his records were gone. And she knew for certain that he was gone. And he was. He went as far as the navy would carry him. He finally sent me a postcard from some place in Greece and that was the first I knew that Sonny was still alive. I didn't see him any more until we were both back in New York and the war had long been over.

He was a man by then, of course, but I wasn't willing to see it. He came by the house from time to time, but we fought almost every time we met. I didn't like the way he carried himself, loose and dreamlike all the time, and I didn't like his friends, and his music seemed to be merely an excuse for the life he led. It sounded just that weird and disordered.

Then we had a fight, a pretty awful fight, and I didn't see him for months. By and by I looked him up, where he was living, in a furnished room in the Village, and I tried to make it up. But there were lots of people in the room and Sonny just lay on his bed, and he wouldn't come downstairs with me, and he treated these other people as though they were his family and I weren't. So I got mad and then he got mad, and then I told him that he might just as well be dead as live the way he was living. Then he stood up and he told me not to worry about him any more in life, that he *was* dead as far as I was concerned. Then he pushed me to the door and the other people looked on as though nothing were happening, and he slammed the door behind me. I stood in the hallway, staring at the door. I heard somebody laugh in the room and then the tears came to my eyes. I started down the steps, whistling to keep from crying, I kept whistling to myself, *You going to need me, baby, one of these cold, rainy days.*

I read about Sonny's trouble in the spring. Little Grace died in the fall. She was a beautiful little girl. But she only lived a little over two years. She died of polio and she suffered. She had a slight fever for a couple of days, but it didn't seem like anything and we just kept her in bed. And we would certainly have called the doctor, but the fever dropped, she seemed to be all right. So we thought it had just been a cold. Then, one day, she was up, playing, Isabel was in the kitchen fixing lunch for the two boys when they'd come in from school, and she heard Grace fall down in the living room. When you have a lot of children you don't always start running when one of them falls, unless they start screaming or something. And, this time, Grace was quiet. Yet, Isabel says that when she heard that *thump* and then that silence, something happened in her to make her afraid. And she ran to the living room and there was little

Grace on the floor, all twisted up, and the reason she hadn't screamed was that she couldn't get her breath. And when she did scream, it was the worst sound, Isabel says, that she'd ever heard in all her life, and she still hears it sometimes in her dreams. Isabel will sometimes wake me up with a low, moaning, strangled sound and I have to be quick to awaken her and hold her to me and where Isabel is weeping against me seems a mortal wound.

I think I may have written Sonny the very day that little Grace was buried. I was sitting in the living room in the dark, by myself, and I suddenly thought of Sonny. My trouble made his real.

One Saturday afternoon, when Sonny had been living with us, or, anyway, been in our house, for nearly two weeks, I found myself wandering aimlessly about the living room, drinking from a can of beer, and trying to work up the courage to search Sonny's room. He was out, he was usually out whenever I was home, and Isabel had taken the children to see their grandparents. Suddenly I was standing still in front of the living room window, watching Seventh Avenue. The idea of searching Sonny's room made me still. I scarcely dared to admit to myself what I'd be searching for. I didn't know what I'd do if I found it. Or if I didn't.

On the sidewalk across from me, near the entrance to a barbecue joint, some people were holding an old-fashioned revival meeting. The barbecue cook, wearing a dirty white apron, his conked hair reddish and metallic in the pale sun, and a cigarette between his lips, stood in the doorway, watching them. Kids and older people paused in their errands and stood there, along with some older men and a couple of very tough-looking women who watched everything that happened on the avenue, as though they owned it, or were maybe owned by it. Well, they were watching this, too. The revival was being carried on by three sisters in black, and a brother. All they had were their voices and their Bibles and a tambourine. The brother was testifying and while he testified two of the sisters stood together, seeming to say, amen, and the third sister walked around with the tambourine outstretched and a couple of people dropped coins into it. Then the brother's testimony ended and the sister who had been taking up the collection dumped the coins into her palm and transferred them to the pocket of her long black robe. Then she raised both hands, striking the tambourine against the air, and then against one hand, and she started to sing. And the two other sisters and the brothers joined in.

It was strange, suddenly, to watch, though I had been seeing these street meetings all my life. So, of course, had everybody else down there. Yet, they paused and watched and listened and I stood still at the window. "*Tis the old ship of Zion*," they sang, and the sister with the tambourine kept a steady, jangling beat, "*it has rescued many a thousand!*" Not a soul under the sound of their voices was hearing this song for the first time, not one of them had been rescued. Nor had they seen much in the way of rescue work being done around them. Neither did they especially believe in the holiness of the three sisters and the brother, they knew too much about them, knew where they lived, and how. The woman with the tambourine, whose voice dominated the air, whose face was bright with joy, was divided by very little from the woman who stood watching her, a cigarette between her heavy, chapped lips, her hair a cuckoo's nest, her face scarred and swollen from many beatings, and her black eyes glittering like coal. Perhaps they both knew this, which was why, when, as rarely, they addressed each other, they addressed each other as Sister. As the singing filled the air the watching, listening faces underwent a change, the eyes focusing on something within; the music seemed to soothe a poison out of them; and time seemed, nearly, to fall away from the sullen, belligerent, battered faces, as though they were fleeing back to their first condition, while dreaming of their last. The barbecue cook half shook his head and smiled, and dropped his cigarette and disappeared into his joint. A man fumbled in his pockets for change and stood holding it in his hand impatiently, as though he had just remembered a pressing appointment further up the avenue. He looked furious. Then I saw Sonny, standing on the edge of the crowd. He was carrying a wide, flat notebook with a green cover, and it made him look, from where I was standing, almost like a schoolboy. The coppery sun brought out the copper in his skin, he was very faintly smiling, standing very still. Then the singing stopped, the tambourine turned into a collection plate again. The furious man dropped in his coins and vanished, so did a couple of the women, and Sonny dropped some change in the plate, looking directly at the woman with a little smile. He started across the avenue, toward the house. He has a slow, loping walk, something like the way Harlem hipsters walk, only he's imposed on this his own half-beat. I had never really noticed it before.

I stayed at the window, both relieved and apprehensive. As Sonny disappeared from my sight, they began singing again. And they were still singing when his key turned in the lock.

"Hey," he said.

"Hey, yourself. You want some beer?"

"No. Well, maybe." But he came up to the window and stood beside me, looking out. "What a warm voice," he said.

They were singing *If I could only hear my mother pray again!*

"Yes," I said, "and she can sure beat that tambourine."

"But what a terrible song," he said, and laughed. He dropped his notebook on the sofa and disappeared into the kitchen. "Where's Isabel and the kids?"

"I think they went to see their grandparents. You hungry?"

"No." He came back into the living room with his can of beer. "You want to come some place with me tonight?"

I sensed, I don't know how, that I couldn't possibly say no. "Sure. Where?"

He sat down on the sofa and picked up his notebook and started leafing through it. "I'm going to sit in with some fellows in a joint in the Village."

"You mean, you're going to play, tonight?"

"That's right." He took a swallow of his beer and moved back to the window. He gave me a sidelong look. "If you can stand it."

"I'll try," I said.

He smiled to himself and we both watched as the meeting across the way broke up. The three sisters and the brother, heads bowed, were singing *God be with you till we meet again.* The faces around them were very quiet. Then the song ended. The small crowd dispersed. We watched the three women and the lone man walk slowly up the avenue.

"When she was singing before," said Sonny, abruptly, "her voice reminded me for a minute of what heroin feels like sometimes—when it's in your veins. It makes you feel sort of warm and cool at the same time. And distant. And—and sure." He sipped his beer, very deliberately not looking at me. I watched his face. "It makes you feel—in control. Sometimes you've got to have that feeling."

"Do you?" I sat down slowly in the easy chair.

"Sometimes." He went to the sofa and picked up his notebook again. "Some people do."

"In order," I asked, "to play?" And my voice was very ugly, full of contempt and anger.

"Well"—he looked at me with great, troubled eyes, as though, in fact, he hoped his eyes would tell me things he could never otherwise say— "they *think* so. And *if* they think so—!"

"And what do *you* think?" I asked.

He sat on the sofa and put his can of beer on the floor. "I don't know," he said, and I couldn't be sure if he were answering my question or pursuing his thoughts. His face didn't tell me. "It's not so much to *play*. It's to *stand* it, to be able to make it at all. On any level." He frowned and smiled: "In order to keep from shaking to pieces."

"But these friends of yours," I said, "they seem to shake themselves to pieces pretty goddamn fast."

"Maybe." He played with the notebook. And something told me that I should curb my tongue, that Sonny was doing his best to talk, that I should listen. "But of course you only know the ones that've gone to pieces. Some don't—or at least they haven't *yet* and that's just about all *any* of us can say." He paused. "And then there are some who just live, really, in hell, and they know it and they see what's happening and they go right on. I don't know." He sighed, dropped the notebook, folded his arms. "Some guys, you can tell from the way they play, they on something *all* the time. And you can see that, well, it makes something real for them. But of course," he picked up his beer from the floor and sipped it and put the can down again, "they *want* to, too, you've got to see that. Even some of them that say they don't—*some*, not all."

"And what about you?" I asked—I couldn't help it. "What about you? Do *you* want to?"

He stood up and walked to the window and remained silent for a long time. Then he sighed. "Me," he said. Then: "While I was downstairs before, on my way here, listening to that woman sing, it struck me all of a sudden how much suffering she must have had to go through—to sing like that. It's *repulsive* to think you have to suffer that much."

I said: "But there's no way not to suffer—is there, Sonny?"

"I believe not," he said and smiled, "but that's never stopped anyone from trying." He looked at me. "Has it?" I realized, with this mocking look, that there stood between us, forever, beyond the power of time or forgiveness, the fact that I had held silence—so long!—when he had needed human speech to help him. He turned back to the window. "No, there's no way not to suffer. But you try all kinds of ways to keep from drowning in it, to keep on top of it, and to make it seem—well, like *you*. Like you did something, all right, and now you're suffering for it. You know?" I said nothing. "Well you know," he said impatiently, "why *do* people suffer? Maybe it's better to do something to give it a reason, *any* reason."

"But we just agreed," I said, "that there's no way not to suffer. Isn't it better, then, just to—take it?"

"But nobody just takes it," Sonny cried, "that's what I'm telling you! *Everybody* tries not to. You're just hung up on the *way* some people try—it's not *your* way!"

The hair on my face began to itch, my face felt wet. "That's not true," I said, "that's not true. I don't give a damn what other people do, I don't even care how they suffer. I just care how *you* suffer." And he looked at me. "Please believe me," I said, "I don't want to see you—die—trying not to suffer."

"I won't," he said, flatly, "die trying not to suffer. At least, not any faster than anybody else."

"But there's no need," I said, trying to laugh, "is there? in killing your-self."

I wanted to say more, but I couldn't. I wanted to talk about will power and how life could be—well, beautiful. I wanted to say that it was all within; but was it? or, rather, wasn't that exactly the trouble? And I wanted to promise that I would never fail him again. But it would all have sounded—empty words and lies.

So I made the promise to myself and prayed that I would keep it.

"It's terrible sometimes, inside," he said, "that's what's the trouble. You walk these streets, black and funky and cold, and there's not really a living ass to talk to, and there's nothing shaking, and there's no way of getting it out—that storm inside. You can't talk it and you can't make love with it, and when you finally try to get with it and play it, you realize *nobody's* listening. So *you've* got to listen. You got to find a way to listen."

And then he walked away from the window and sat on the sofa again, as though all the wind had suddenly been knocked out of him. "Some-times you'll do *anything* to play, even cut your mother's throat." He laughed and looked at me. "Or your brother's." Then he sobered. "Or your own." Then: "Don't worry. I'm all right now and I think I'll *be* all right. But I can't forget—where I've been. I don't mean just the physical place I've been, I mean where I've *been*. And *what* I've been."

"What have you been, Sonny?" I asked.

He smiled—but sat sideways on the sofa, his elbow resting on the back, his fingers playing with his mouth and chin, not looking at me. "I've been something I didn't recognize, didn't know I could be. Didn't know anybody could be." He stopped, looking inward, looking helplessly young, looking old. "I'm not talking about it now because I feel *guilty* or anything like that—maybe it would be better if I did, I don't know. Anyway, I can't really talk about it. Not to you, not to anybody," and now he turned and faced me. "Sometimes, you know, and it was actually when I was most *out* of the world, I felt that I was in it, that I was with it, really, and I could play or I didn't really have to *play,* it just came out of me, it was there. And I don't know how I played, thinking about it now, but I know I did awful things, those times, sometimes, to people. Or it wasn't that I *did* anything to them—it was that they weren't real." He picked up the beer can; it was empty; he rolled it between his palms: "And other times—well, I needed a fix, I needed to find a place to lean, I needed to clear a space to *listen*—and I couldn't find it, and I—went crazy, I did terrible things to *me,* I was terrible *for* me." He began pressing the beer can between his hands, I watched the metal begin to give. It glittered, as he played with it, like a knife, and I was afraid he would cut himself, but I said nothing. "Oh well. I can never tell you. I was all by myself at the bottom of something, stinking and sweating and crying and shaking, and I smelled it, you know? *my* stink, and I thought I'd die if I couldn't get away from it and yet, all the same, I knew that everything I was doing was just locking me in with it. And I didn't know," he paused, still flattening the beer can, "I didn't know, I still *don't* know, something kept telling me that maybe it was good to smell your own stink, but I didn't think that *that* was what I'd been trying to do—and—who can stand it?" and he abruptly dropped the ruined beer can, looking at me with a small, still smile, and then rose, walking to the window as though it were the lodestone rock. I watched his face, he watched the avenue. "I couldn't tell you when Mama died—but the reason I wanted to leave Harlem so bad was to get away from drugs. And then, when I ran away, that's what I was running from—really. When I came back, nothing had changed, *I* hadn't changed, I was just—older." And he stopped, drumming with his fingers on the windowpane. The sun had vanished, soon darkness would fall. I watched his face. "It can come again," he said, almost as though speaking to himself. Then he turned to me. "It can come again," he repeated. "I just want you to know that."

"All right," I said, at last. "So it can come again, All right."

He smiled, but the smile was sorrowful. "I had to try to tell you," he said.

"Yes," I said. "I understand that."

"You're my brother," he said, looking straight at me, and not smiling at all.

"Yes," I repeated, "yes. I understand that."

He turned back to the window, looking out. "All that hatred down there," he said, "all that hatred and misery and love. It's a wonder it doesn't blow the avenue apart."

We went to the only nightclub on a short, dark street, downtown. We squeezed through the narrow, chattering, jam-packed bar to the entrance of the big room, where the bandstand was. And we stood there for a moment, for the lights were very dim in this room and we couldn't see. Then, "Hello, boy," said a voice and an enormous black man, much older than Sonny or myself, erupted out of all that atmospheric lighting and put an arm around Sonny's shoulder. "I been sitting right here," he said, "waiting for you."

He had a big voice, too, and heads in the darkness turned toward us.

Sonny grinned and pulled a little away, and said, "Creole, this is my brother. I told you about him."

Creole shook my hand. "I'm glad to meet you, son," he said, and it was clear that he was glad to meet me *there*, for Sonny's sake. And he smiled, "You got a real musician in *your* family," and he took his arm from Sonny's shoulder and slapped him, lightly, affectionately, with the back of his hand.

"Well. Now I've heard it all," said a voice behind us. This was another musician, and a friend of Sonny's, a coal-black, cheerful-looking man, built close to the ground. He immediately began confiding to me, at the top of his lungs, the most terrible things about Sonny, his teeth gleaming like a lighthouse and his laugh coming up out of him like the beginning of an earthquake. And it turned out that everyone at the bar knew Sonny, or almost everyone; some were musicians, working there, or nearby, or not working, some were simply hangers-on, and some were there to hear Sonny play. I was introduced to all of them and they were all very polite to me. Yet, it was clear that, for them, I was only Sonny's brother. Here, I was in Sonny's world. Or, rather: his kingdom. Here, it was not even a question that his veins bore royal blood.

They were going to play soon and Creole installed me, by myself, at a table in a dark corner. Then I watched them, Creole, and the little black man, and Sonny, and the others, while they horsed around, standing just below the bandstand. The light from the bandstand spilled just a little short of them and, watching them laughing and gesturing and moving about, I had the feeling that they, nevertheless, were being most careful not to step into that circle of light too suddenly: that if they moved into the light too suddenly, without thinking, they would perish in flame. Then, while I watched, one of them, the small, black man, moved into the light and crossed the bandstand and started fooling around with his drums. Then—being funny and being, also, extremely ceremonious—Creole took Sonny by the arm and led him to the piano. A woman's voice called Sonny's name and a few hands started clapping. And Sonny, also being funny and being ceremonious, and so touched, I think, that he could have cried, but neither hiding it nor showing it, riding it like a man, grinned, and put both hands to his heart and bowed from the waist.

Creole then went to the bass fiddle and a lean, very bright-skinned brown man jumped up on the bandstand and picked up his horn. So there they were, and the atmosphere on the bandstand and in the room began to change and tighten. Someone stepped up to the microphone and announced them. Then there were all kinds of murmurs. Some people at the bar shushed others. The waitress ran around, frantically getting in the last orders, guys and chicks got closer to each other, and the lights on the bandstand, on the quartet, turned to a kind of indigo. Then they all looked different there. Creole looked about him for the last time, as though he were making certain that all his chickens were in the coop, and then he—jumped and struck the fiddle. And there they were.

All I know about music is that not many people ever really hear it. And even then, on the rare occasions when something opens within, and the music enters, what we mainly hear, or hear corroborated, are personal, private, vanishing evocations. But the man who creates the music is hearing something else, is dealing with the roar rising from the void and imposing order on it as it hits the air. What is evoked in him, then, is of another order, more terrible because it has no words, and triumphant, too, for that same reason. And his triumph, when he triumphs, is ours. I just watched Sonny's face. His face was troubled, he was working hard, but he wasn't with it. And I had the feeling that, in a way, everyone on the bandstand was waiting for him, both waiting for him and pushing him along. But as I began to watch Creole, I realized that it was Creole who held them all back. He had them on a short rein. Up there, keeping the beat with his whole body, wailing on the fiddle, with his eyes half closed, he was listening to everything, but he was listening to Sonny. He was having a dialogue with Sonny. He wanted Sonny to leave the shoreline and strike out for the deep water. He was Sonny's witness that deep water and drowning were not the same thing—he had been there, and he knew. And he wanted Sonny to know. He was waiting for Sonny to do the things on the keys which would let Creole know that Sonny was in the water.

And, while Creole listened, Sonny moved, deep within, exactly like someone in torment. I had never before thought of how awful the relationship must be between the musician and his instrument. He has to fill it, this instrument, with the breath of life, his own. He has to make it do what he wants it to do. And a piano is just a piano. It's made out of so much wood and wires and little hammers and big ones, and ivory. While there's only so much you can do with it, the only way to find this out is to try; to try and make it do everything.

And Sonny hadn't been near a piano for over a year. And he wasn't on much better terms with his life, not the life that stretched before him now. He and the piano stammered, started one way, got scared, stopped; started another, panicked, marked time, started again; then seemed to have found a direction, panicked again, got stuck. And the face I saw on Sonny I'd never seen before. Everything had been burned out of it, and, at the same time, things usually hidden were being burned in, by the fire and fury of the battle which was occurring in him up there.

Yet, watching Creole's face as they neared the end of the first set, I had the feeling that something had happened, something I hadn't heard. Then they finished, there was scattered applause, and then, without an instant's warning, Creole started into something else, it was almost sardonic, it was "Am I Blue." And, as though he commanded, Sonny began to play. Something began to happen. And Creole let out the reins. The dry, low, black man said something awful on the drums, Creole answered, and the drums talked back. Then the horn insisted, sweet and high, slightly detached perhaps, and Creole listened, commenting now and then, dry, and driving, beautiful and calm and old. Then they all came together again, and Sonny was part of the family again. I could tell this from his face. He seemed to have found, right there beneath his fingers, a damn brand-new piano. It seemed that he couldn't get over it. Then, for a while, just being happy with Sonny, they seemed to be agreeing with him that brand-new pianos certainly were a gas.

Then Creole stepped forward to remind them that what they were playing was the blues. He hit something in all of them, he hit something in me, myself, and the music tightened and deepened, apprehension began to beat the air. Creole began to tell us what the blues were all about. They were not about anything very new. He and his boys up there were keeping it new, at the risk of ruin, destruction, madness, and death, in order to find new ways to make us listen. For, while the tale of how we suffer, and how we are delighted, and how we may triumph is never new, it always must be heard. There isn't any other tale to tell, it's the only light we've got in all this darkness.

And this tale, according to that face, that body, those strong hands on those strings, has another aspect in every country, and a new depth in every generation. Listen, Creole seemed to be saying, listen. Now these are Sonny's blues. He made the little black man on the drums know it, and the bright, brown man on the horn. Creole wasn't trying any longer to get Sonny in the water. He was wishing him Godspeed. Then he stepped back, very slowly, filling the air with the immense suggestion that Sonny speak for himself.

Then they all gathered around Sonny and Sonny played. Every now and again one of them seemed to say, amen. Sonny's fingers filled the air with life, his life. But that life contained so many others. And Sonny went all the way back, he really began with the spare, flat statement of the opening phrase of the song. Then he began to make it his. It was very beautiful because it wasn't hurried and it was no longer a lament. I seemed to hear with what burning he had made it his, with what burning we had yet to make it ours, how we could cease lamenting. Freedom lurked around us and I understood, at last, that he could help us to be free if we would listen, that he would never be free until we did. Yet, there was no battle in his face now. I heard what he had gone through, and would continue to go through until he came to rest in earth. He had made it his: that long line, of which we knew only Mama and Daddy. And he was giving it back, as everything must be given back, so that, passing through death, it can live forever. I saw my mother's face again, and felt, for the first time, how the stones of the road she had walked on must have bruised her feet. I saw the moonlit road where my father's brother died. And it brought something else back to me, and carried me past it. I saw my little girl again and felt Isabel's tears again, and I felt my own tears begin to rise. And I was yet aware that this was only a moment, that the world waited outside, as hungry as a tiger, and that trouble stretched above us, longer than the sky.

Then it was over. Creole and Sonny let out their breath, both soaking wet, and grinning. There was a lot of applause and some of it was real. In the dark, the girl came by and I asked her to take drinks to the bandstand. There was a long pause, while they talked up there in the indigo light and after a while I saw the girl put a Scotch and milk on top of the piano for Sonny. He didn't seem to notice it, but just before they started playing again, he sipped from it and looked toward me and nodded. Then he put it back on top of the piano. For me, then, as they began to play again, it glowed and shook above my brother's head like the very cup of trembling.

—James Baldwin

Chasing the Bird

The sun sets unevenly and the people
go to bed.

The night has a thousand eyes.
The clouds are low, overhead.

Every night it is a little bit
more difficult, a little

harder. My mind
to me a mangle is.

4. Sonny Rollins. Photograph by W. Patrick Hinely, © 1981.

Listening to Sonny Rollins at the Five Spot

There will be many other nights like
be standing here with someone, some
one
someone
some-one
some
some
some
some
some
some
one
there will be other songs
a-nother fall, another—spring, but
there will never be a-noth, noth
anoth
noth
anoth-er
noth-er
noth-er
        Other lips that I may kiss,
but they won't thrill me like
        thrill me like
              like yours
used to
        dream a million dreams
but how can they come
when there
        never be
a-noth—

Song for Bird and Myself

I am dissatisfied with my poetry.
I am dissatisfied with my sex life.
I am dissatisfied with the angels I believe in.
    Neo-classical like Bird,
    Distrusting the reality
    of every note.
    Half-real
    We blow the sentence pure and real
    Like chewing angels.

"Listen, Bird, why do we have to sit here dying
in a half-furnished room?
The rest of the combo
Is safe in houses
Blowing bird-brained Dixieland,
How warm and free they are. What right
Music."
    "Man,
    We
    Can't stay away from the sounds.
    We're *crazy*, Jack
    We gotta stay here 'til
    They come and get us."

Neo-classical like Bird.
Once two birds got into the Rare Book Room.
Miss Swift said,
"Don't
Call a custodian
Put crumbs on the outside of the window

Let them
Come outside."

      Neo-classical
The soft line strains
Not to be neo-classical.
But Miss Swift went to lunch. They
Called a custodian.
Four came.
Armed like Myrmidons, they
Killed the birds.
Miss Munsterberg
Who was the first
American translator of Rilke
Said
"Suppose one of them
Had been the Holy Ghost."
Miss Swift,
Who was back from lunch,
Said
"Which."
    But the poem isn't over.
    It keeps going
    Long after everybody
    Has settled down comfortably into laughter.
    The bastards
    On the other side of the paper
    Keep laughing.
    LISTEN.
    STOP LAUGHING.
    THE POEM ISN'T OVER. Butterflies.
I knew there would be butterflies
For butterflies represent the lost soul
Represent the way the wind wanders
Represent the bodies
We only clasp in the middle of a poem.
See, the stars have faded.

There are only butterflies.
Listen to
The terrible sound of their wings moving.
Listen,
The poem isn't over.

Have you ever wrestled with a bird,
You idiotic reader?
Jacob wrestled with an angel.
(I remind you of the image)
Or a butterfly
Have you ever wrestled with a single butterfly?
Sex is no longer important.
Colors take the form of wings. Words
Have got to be said.
A butterfly,
A bird,
Planted at the heart of being afraid of dying.
Blow,
Bird,
Blow,
Be,
Neo-classical.
Let the wings say
What the wings mean
Terrible and pure.

The horse
In Cocteau
Is as neo-classical an idea as one can manage.
Writes all our poetry for us
Is Gertrude Stein
Is God
Is the needle for which
God help us
There is no substitute
Or the Ace of Swords

When you are telling a fortune
Who tells death.
Or the Jack of Hearts
Whose gypsy fortune we clasp
In the middle of a poem.

"And are we angels, Bird?"
"That's what we're trying to tell 'em, Jack
There aren't any angels except when
You and me blow 'em."

So Bird and I sing
Outside your window
So Bird and I die
Outside your window.
This is the wonderful world of Dixieland
Deny
The bloody motherfucking Holy Ghost.
This is the end of the poem.
You can start laughing, you bastards. This is
The end of the poem.

—JACK SPICER

Streets of Gold

[An excerpt]

The bar was on Fordham Road, just off Jerome Avenue.

"It's full of niggers," my Uncle Luke said. "Let's get out of here."

This was February of 1944, and you could hardly walk through any street in New York without stumbling upon a place offering live jazz. I had asked Luke to take me to this particular bar because Biff Anderson was playing here this weekend. There were eight Biff Anderson records in my brother's collection, two of them with him backing the blues singers Viola McCoy and Clara Smith, four of them made when he'd been playing with Lionel Howard's Musical Aces, the remaining two featuring him on solo piano. His early style seemed to be premised on those of James P. Johnson and Fats Waller. Waller, I had already learned, was the man who had most influenced Tatum. And Tatum was where I wanted to be.

I was not surprised that the place was full of black people. I had begun subscribing to *Down Beat* and *Metronome*, which my father read aloud to me, and I knew what color most of the musicians were; not because they were identified by race, but only because there were pictures of them in those jazz journals. My father would say, "This Tatum is a nigger, did you know that?" (He also told me Tatum was blind, which was of far greater interest to me, and which confirmed my belief that I could one day play like him.) Or "Look at this Jimmie Lunceford," he would say. "I *hate* nigger bands. They repeat themselves all the time." I knew Biff Anderson was black, and I expected him to have a large black audience. But my Uncle Luke must have been shaken by it; he immediately asked the bartender for a double gin on the rocks.

"How about your friend here?" the bartender asked. He was white.

"I'll have a beer," I said.

"Let me see your draft card," he said, and then realized I was blind, and silently considered whether or not blind people were supposed to register for the draft, and then decided to skip the whole baffling question, and simply repeated, "Double gin on the rocks, one beer." *We* had to register for the draft same as anyone else, of course, and—at least according to a joke then current—even blind people were being called up, so long as their Seeing Eye dogs had twenty-twenty vision. I didn't have a draft card because I wasn't yet eighteen. I'd have skipped the beer if the bartender had raised the slightest fuss; I was there to hear Biff Anderson play, and that was all.

The bar was a toilet. I've played many of them. It did not occur to me at the time that if someone of Biff's stature was playing a toilet in the Bronx, he must have fallen upon hard times. Nor did I even recognize the place as a toilet. I had never been inside a bar before, and the sounds and the smells were creating the surroundings for me. Biff must have been taking a break when we came in. The jukebox was on, and Bing Crosby was singing "Sunday, Monday, or Always." Behind the bar, the grain of which was raised and then worn smooth again, I could hear the clink of ice and glasses, whiskey being poured, the faint hiss of draft beer being drawn. There was a lot of echoing laughter in the room, mingled with the sound of voices I'd heard for years on "Amos 'n' Andy." The smells were beer and booze and perfume, the occasional whiff of someone who'd forgotten to bathe that month, the overpowering stench of urine from the men's room near the far end of the bar—though that was not what identified this particular dump as a toilet. To jazz musicians, a toilet is a place you play when you're coming up or heading down. I played a lot of them coming up, and I played a few of them on the way down, too. That's America. Easy come, easy go.

"Lots of dinges here tonight," the bartender whispered as he put down our glasses. "What're *you* guys doin' here?"

"My nephew's a piano player," Luke said. "He wants to hear this guy."

"*He's* a dinge, too," the bartender said. "That's why we got so many of them here tonight. I never seen so many dinges in my life. I used to tenn bar in a dump on Lenox Avenue, and even *there* I never seen so many dinges. You hole a spot check right this minute, you gonna find six hundred switchblades here. Don't look crooked at nobody's girl, you lend up with a slit throat. Not you, kid," he said to me. "You're blind, you got nothin' to worry about. You play the piano, huh?"

"Yeah," I said.

"So whattya wanna lissen to *this* guy for? He stinks, you ask my opinion. I requested him last night for 'Deep Inna Hearta Texas,' he tells me he don't know the song. 'Deep Inna Hearta Texas,' huh? *Anybody* knows that song."

"It's not the kind of song he'd play," I said.

"You're tellin' *me*?" the bartender said. "He don't *know* it, how could he play it? I don't recognize half the things he plays, anyway. I think he makes 'em up, whattya think of that?"

"He probably does," I said, and smiled.

"He sings when he plays," the bartender said. "Not the words, you unnerstan' me? He goes like uh-uh-uh under his breath. I think he's got a screw loose, whattya think of that?"

"He's humming the chord chart," I said. "He does that on his records, too."

"He makes records, this bum?"

"He made a lot of them," I said. "He's one of the best jazz pianists in the world."

"Sure, and he don't know 'Deep Inna Hearta Texas,'" the bartender said.

"There's got to be four hundred niggers in this place," Luke said.

"You better lower your voice, pal," the bartender advised. "Less you want all four hunnerd of 'em cuttin' off your balls and hangin' 'em from the chandelier."

"There ain't no chandelier," Luke said.

"Be a wise guy," the bartender said. "I tole the boss why did he hire a dinge to come play here? He said it was good for business. Sure. So next week *this* bum goes back to Harlem and *we're* stuck with a nigger trade. And he can't even play 'Deep Inna Hearta Texas.' Can *you* play 'Deep Inna Hearta Texas'?" he asked me.

"I've never tried it."

The bartender sang a little of the song, and then said, "*That* one. You know it?"

"I've heard the song, but I've never played it."

"You must be as great a piano player as him," the bartender said.

"How about another double?" Luke asked.

"Fuckin' piano players today don't know how to play *nothin'*," the bartender said, and walked off to pour my uncle's drink.

"*I* know 'Deep in the Heart of Texas,'" Luke said.

"Whyn't you go play it for him?" I said.

"Nah," Luke said.

"Go on, he'd get a kick out of it."

"Nah, nah, c'mon," Luke said. "Anyway, here he comes."

"Who?"

"The guy you came to hear. I *guess* it's him. He's sittin' down at the piano."

"What does he look like?"

"He's as black as the ace of spades," Luke whispered.

"Is he fat or skinny or what?"

"Kind of heavy."

"How old is he?"

"Who can tell with a nigger? Forty? Fifty? He's got fat fingers, Igg. You sure he's a good piano player?"

"One of the best, Uncle Luke."

"Here's your gin," the bartender said. "You want to pay me now, or you gonna be drinkin'?"

"I'll be drinking," Luke said.

From the moment Biff began playing, his heritage was completely evident. Johnson had taught Waller, and Biff had learned by imitating both, and when Tatum took Waller a giant step further, Biff again revised his style. He played a five-tune set consisting of "Don't Blame Me," "Body and Soul," "Birth of the Blues," "Sweet Lorraine," and "Star Eyes." This last was a hit recorded by Jimmy Dorsey, with Kitty Kallen doing the vocal. It was, and *is*, a perfect illustration of a great tune for a jazz improvisation. The melody is totally dumb, but the chord chart is unpredictable and exciting, with no less than nine key changes in a thirty-two-bar chorus. I still use it as a check-out tune. Whenever I want to know how well someone plays, I'll say, "Okay, 'Star Eyes.'" If he comes up with some fumbling excuse like "Oh, man, I don't like that tune so much," or "Yeah, yeah, like I haven't played that one in a long time," I've got him pegged immediately. It's a supreme test tune for a jazz musician, and Biff played it beautifully that night.

He played it beautifully because he played it *exactly* like Tatum. A tribute, a copy, call it what you will, but there it was, those sonorous tenths, those pentatonic runs, the whole harmonic edifice played without Tatum's speed or dexterity, of course, but letter perfect stylistically. I was sitting not fifty feet from a man who could play piano like Tatum, and I had been breaking my balls *and* my chops for the past seven months trying to learn Tatum by listening to his records.

"Let me have another one of these, huh?" Luke said.

"Hey, Uncle Luke," I said. "Go easy, huh?"

"Huh? Go easy?"

"On the gin."

"Oh. Sure, Iggie, don't worry."

The music had stopped; I could hear laughter and voices from the bandstand.

"What's he doing up there?" I asked Luke.

"He's standing near the piano, talking to a girl."

"Can you take me up there?"

"Sure, Iggie. What're you gonna do? Play a little?"

"I just want to meet him. Hurry up. *Please.* Before he leaves."

"He's lookin' down her dress, he ain't about to leave," Luke said, and he offered me his elbow, and I took it and got off the bar stool, and followed him across the room, moving through a rolling crest of conversation and then onto a slippery, smooth surface I assumed was the dance floor, and heard just beyond earshot a deep Negro voice muttering something unintelligible, and then caught the tail end of a sentence.

". . . around two in the mornin', you care to hang aroun' that long," and the voice stopped as we approached, and my Uncle Luke said, "Mr. Anderson?"

"Yeah?" Biff said.

"This is my nephew," Luke said. "He plays piano."

"Cool," Biff said.

"He wanted to meet you."

"How you doin', man?" Biff said, and he must have extended his hand in greeting because there was a brief expectant silence, and then Luke quickly said, "Shake the man's hand, Iggie."

I extended my hand. Biff's hand was thick and fleshy and sweating. On my right, there was the overpowering, almost nauseating smell of something that was definitely not *Je Reviens.*

"You play piano, huh?" Biff said.

"Yes."

"How long you been playin'?"

"Twelve years."

"Yeah? Cool. Hey, Poots, where you *goin'*?" he said, his voice turning away from me. There was no answer. I heard the click of high-heeled shoes in rapid tattoo on the hardwood floor, disappearing into the larger sound of voices and laughter. Somewhere behind me, the jukebox went on again—David Rose's "Holiday for Strings."

"Dumb *cunt*," Biff said, and turned back to me again. "So you been playin' twelve years," he said without interest.

"I've been trying to learn jazz," I said.

"Mmm," he said, his voice turning away. I heard the sound of ice against the sides of a glass. He had picked up a drink from the piano top.

"He's real good," Luke said. "He studied classical a long time."

"Yeah, mmm," Biff said, and drank and put down the glass again with a small final click.

"Why'n't you play something for him, Iggie?"

"That's okay, I'll take your word for it," Biff said. "Nice meetin' you both, enjoy yourselves, huh?"

"Hey, *wait* a minute!" Luke said.

"There's somethin' I got to see about," Biff said. "You'll excuse me, huh?"

"The kid came all the way here to listen to you," Luke said, his voice rising. "I went all the way uptown to get him, and then we had to come all the way down here again."

"So what?" Biff said.

"*That's* what!" Luke said. His voice was louder now. "He's been talkin' about nothin' but you ever since he found out you were gonna be playing in this dump."

"Yeah?" Biff said. "That right?"

"*Yeah!*" Luke said, his voice strident and belligerent now. It was the gin talking, I realized. I had never heard my uncle raise his voice except while playing poker, and nobody was playing poker right that minute. Or maybe they were. "So let him play piano for you," Luke said. "It won't kill you."

"You think I got nothin' better to do than . . .?"

"What the hell *else* you got to do?" Luke asked.

"That's okay, Uncle Luke," I said.

"No, it *ain't* okay. Why the hell can't he listen to you?"

"I just wanted to meet him, that's all," I said. "Come on."

"Just a minute, you," Biff said.

"Me?"

"You're the piano player, aren't you?"

"Yes."

"Then that's who. What can you play?"

"Lots of things."

"Like what?"

"Tatum's 'Moonglow' and 'St. Louis Blues,' and . . ."

"That's plenty. Just them two, okay? If you're lousy, you get one chorus and out. Now if your uncle here don't mind, I'm goin' to the *pissoir* over there while you start playin', because I got to take a leak, if that's all right with your uncle here. I can listen fine from in there, and soon's I'm finished I'll come right back. If that's all right with your uncle here."

"That's fine," Luke said.

"Show him the piano," Biff said. "I'll cut off the juke on my way." He climbed down from the bandstand and walked ponderously past me toward the men's room.

"Black bastard," Luke muttered under his breath, and then said, "Give me your hand, Iggie," and led me up the steps and to the piano.

I played. I wish I could report that all conversation stopped dead the moment I began, that Biff came running out of the men's room hastily buttoning his fly and peeing all over himself in excitement, that a scout for a record company rushed over and slapped a contract on the piano top. No such thing. I played the two Tatum solos exactly as I'd lifted them from his record, and then I stopped, and conversation was still going on, laughter still shrilled into the smoky room, the bartender's voice said, "Scotch and soda, comin' up," and I put my hands back in my lap.

"Yeah, okay," Biff said. I had not realized he was standing beside the piano, and I did not know how long he'd been there. I waited for him to say more. The silence lengthened.

"Some of the runs were off, I know," I said.

"Yeah, those runs are killers," Biff said.

"They're hard to pick up off the records," I said.

"That where you got this stuff? From Art's records?"

"Yes."

"Well, that's not a bad way. What else do you know?"

"A lot of Wilson, and some Waller and Hines . . ."

"Waller, huh?"

"Yes."

"Takin' off note by note from the records, huh?"

"Yeah."

"Mmm," Biff said. "Well, that's okay. What've you got down of Fats?"

"'Thief in the Night' and 'If This Isn't Love' and . . ."

"Oh, yeah, the sides he cut with Honey Bear and Autrey, ain't they?"

"I don't know who's on them."

"That's all shit, anyway," Biff said. "That stuff he done with 'Fats Waller and his Rhythm.' 'Cept for maybe 'Dinah' and 'Blue Because of You.'"

"I can play those, too."

"Can you do any of his early stuff?"

"Like what?"

"Like the stuff he cut in the twenties. 'Sweet Savannah Sue' and . . . I don't know, man. . . . 'Love Me or Leave Me.' That stuff."

"No, I don't know those."

"Yeah, well," Biff said. "Well, that wasn't half bad, what you played. You dig Tatum, huh?"

"Yes. That's how I want to play."

"Like Tatum, huh?"

"Yes."

"Well, you doin' fine," Biff said. "Jus' keep on goin' the way you are. Fine," he said. "Fine."

"I need help," I said.

"Yeah, man, don't we all?" Biff said, and chuckled.

"A lot of Tatum's chords are hard to take off the records."

"Jus' break 'em up, that's all. Play 'em note by note. That's what I used to do when I was comin' along."

"I've tried that. I still can't get them all."

"Well, kid, what can I tell you? You wanna play Tatum piano, then you gotta listen to him and do what he does, that's all. Why'n't you run on down to the Street; I think he's playing in one of the clubs down there right now. With Slam, I think."

"What street?" I said.

"*What* street? *The* Street."

"I don't know what you mean."

"Well, kid, what can I tell you?" Biff said, and sighed. "While you're down there, you might listen to what Diz is doin'. Dizzy Gillespie. Him an' Bird are shakin' things up, man, you might want to change your mind. Hey, now, looka here," he said.

"Hello, mothah-fugger," someone said cheerfully.

"Get up there an' start blowin'," someone else said. "We heah to help you."

"Don't need no help, man," Biff said, and chuckled.

"Whutchoo doin' in this toilet, anyhow?" the first man said. "*Disgraceful!*"

Biff chuckled again, and then said, "Kid, these're two of the worl's *worse* jazz musicians. . . ."

"*Sheeee-it,*" one of them said, and laughed.

"Been thrown off ever' band in the country, 'cause they shoot dope an' fuck chickens."

All three of them laughed. One of them said, "We brung Dickie with us, he gettin' his drums from the car."

"The shades is he's blind," Biff said, and I realized one of the other men must have been staring at me. "Plays piano."

"Hope he's better'n you," one of them said, and all of them laughed again.

"What's your name, man?" Biff said. "I forget."

"Iggie."

"This's Sam an' Jerry. You sit in with 'em, Iggie, while I go dazzle that chick. I'm afraid she goan git away."

"Hey, come down, man," one of them said. "We here in this shithole to blow with *you,* not some fuckin' F-sharp piano player."

"I'm not an F-sharp piano player," I said.

"Hey, man, gimme a hand with this," somebody said. I figured that was Dickie who'd been getting his drums from the car. "Come on, Jerr, move yo' black ass."

"Any blind piano player I *know*'s a F-sharp piano player," the other man insisted.

"*Tatum's* blind," Biff said, "and he can cut your ass thu Sunday."

"He only *half* blind," Sam said.

"I can play in any key on the board," I said.

"There now, you see? Sit down with Iggie here, an' work out a nice set huh? And lemme go see 'bout my social life. Play nice, Iggie. Maybe you can cover up all they *mis* takes."

"*Sheeee*-it," Sam said, and then laughed.

I listened as the drummer set up his equipment and the trumpet player started running up and down chromatics, warming up. Sam asked me to tune him up, and when I asked him what notes he wanted me to hit, he said, "Jus' an A, man," sounding very surprised. I gave Jerry a B flat when he asked for it, and he tuned his horn, and meanwhile Dickie was warming up on his cymbals, playing fast little brush rolls, and pretty soon we were ready to start the set. I'd never played with a band before, but I wasn't particularly scared. I'd listened to enough jazz records to know what the format was. The piano player or the horn man usually started with the head chorus (I didn't yet know it was called the head), and then the band took solos in turn, and then everybody went into the final chorus and ended the tune. I figured all I had to do was play the way I'd been playing for the past seven months, play all those tunes I'd either lifted from my brother's record collection or figured out on my own. Biff, after all, was a well-known and respected jazz musician, and he had told me that what I'd played wasn't half bad, which I figured meant at *least* half good. Besides, *he* was the one who'd asked for me to sit in.

"You *sure* you ain't a F-sharp piano player?" Sam asked behind me.

"I'm sure," I said.

"'Cause, man, I don't dig them wild stretches in F sharp," he said. "You got some other keys in your head, cool. Otherwise, It's been graaaand knowin' you."

"Well, *start* it, man," Jerry said to me. He was standing to my right. The drummer was diagonally behind me, sitting beside Sam. I took a four-bar intro, and we began playing "Fools Rush In," a nice Johnny Mercer-Rube Bloom ballad, which I'd never heard Tatum do, but which I played in the Tatum style, or what I considered to be the Tatum style. We were moving into the bridge when Sam said, "Chop it off, kid." I didn't know what he meant. I assumed he wanted me to play a bit more staccato, so I began chopping the chords, so to speak, giving a good crisp, clean touch to those full tenths as I walked them with my left hand or used them in a swing bass, pounding out that steady four/four rhythm, and hearing the satisfying (to me) echo of Sam behind me walking the identical chords in arpeggios on his bass fiddle. As I went into the second chorus, I heard Jerry come in behind me on the horn, and I did what I'd heard the piano players doing on the records, I started feeding him chords, keeping that full left hand going in time with what Sam and the drummer were laying down, though to tell the truth I couldn't quite understand *what* the drummer was doing, and wasn't even sure he was actually keeping the beat. It was the drummer who said, "Take it home," and I said, "What?" and he said "Last eight," and the horn man came out of the bridge and into the final eight bars, and we ended the tune. Everybody was quiet.

"Well, you ain't a F-sharp piano player, that's for sure," Sam said. "But you know what you can do with that left hand of yours, don't you?"

"You can chop it off and shove it clean up your ass," the trumpet player said. "Let's get Biff."

They were moving off the bandstand. In a moment, and without another word to me, they were gone. I sat at the piano alone, baffled.

"What's going on here?" a voice asked. "Who the hell are you? Who's that band? Where's my piano player?"

The voice belonged to a fat man. I could tell. I could also tell he was Jewish. I know it's un-American to identify ethnic groups by vocal inflection or intonation, but I can tell if a man's black, Italian, Irish, Jewish, or what*ever* simply by hearing his voice. And so can you. And if you tell me otherwise, I'll call you a liar. (And besides, what the hell's so un-American about it?) I was stunned. Some black bastard horn player had just told me to shove my precious left hand up my ass, and I didn't know why.

"You!" the fat man said. "Get away from that piano. Where's Biff?"

"Cool it, Mr. Gottlieb," Biff's voice said. "I'm right here; the boy's a friend of mine."

"Do you know 'Deep in the Heart of Texas'?" Gottlieb said. "The bartender wants 'Deep in the Heart of Texas.'"

"Beyond my ken," Biff said, in what sounded like an English accent.

"What?" Gottlieb said, startled.

"The tune. Unknown to me," Biff said.

"What?"

"Advise your barkeep to compile a more serious list of requests," Biff said in the same stuffy English cadences, and then immediately and surprisingly fell into an aggravated black dialect, dripping watermelon, pone, and chitlings. "You jes' ast you man to keep de booze comin', an' let *me*—an' mah frens who was kine enough to come see me heah— worry 'bout de music, huh? Kid, you want to git off dat stool so's we kin lay some jazz on dese mothahs?"

"What?" Gottlieb said.

"I'll talk to *you* later," Biff said as I climbed off the stool and off the bandstand.

*

My Uncle Luke had drunk too much. His head was on the table, touching my elbow, and I could hear him snoring loudly as Biff talked to me. On my right, the girl with the five-and-dime perfume sat silent and motionless, her presence detectable only by her scent and the sound of her breathing. The trumpet player had left around midnight. The bass player and the drummer had followed him at about one. We were alone in the place now, except for the bartender, who was washing glasses and lining them up on the shelves, and Gottlieb, who had tallied his register and was putting chairs up on tables, preparatory to sweeping out the joint. As he passed our table, he said, "This ain't a hotel, Mr. Jazz," and then moved on, muttering.

"Cheap sheenie bastard," Biff said. "He's got his bartender watering my drinks. You okay, Poots?" he asked the girl. The girl did not answer. She must have nodded assent, though, the motion of her head and neck unleashing a fresh wave of scent. Biff said, "Fine, that's fine, you jus' stick aroun' a short while longer. Now, you," he said. "You want to know what's wrong with how you play piano?"

"Yes," I said.

"You're lucky Dickie's a gentle soul. The drummer. Otherwise he'da done what Jo Jones done to Bird in Kansas City when he got the band all turned around. He throwed his cymbal on the floor, and that was that, man, end of the whole fuckin' set. 'Scuse me, Poots."

"Well, *they* ended the set, too," I said. I still didn't know that Bird was someone's name. This was the second time Biff had used it tonight, and each time I'd thought he meant bird with a lower-case *b*; the reference was mystifying. For that matter, I didn't know who Jo Jones was, either. But I figured if he'd thrown a cymbal on the floor, he had to be a drummer, whereas all I could think about the use of the word "bird" was that it was a black jazz expression. (Come to think of it, it *was*.) "And I'll tell you something, Mr. Anderson, your bass player pissed me off right from the start. Excuse me, Miss. Making cracks about F-sharp piano players."

"Well, le's say he ain' 'zackly de mos' tac'ful of souls," Biff said in his watermelon accent, and then immediately added in his normal speaking voice, "But he's a damn fine musician, and he knows where jazz *is* today, and *that's* what he was trying to convey to you."

"I'm no damn F-sharp piano player," I said.

"He didn't know that. Anyway, that ain't what got him or the other boys riled."

"Then what?"

"Your left hand."

"I've got a good left hand," I said.

"Sure," Biff said. "If you want to play alone, you've got a good left hand, and I'm speakin' comparative. You still need lots of work, even if all you want to play is solo piano."

"That's what I want to play."

"Then don't go sittin' in with no groups. Because if you play that way with a group, you're lucky they don't throw the *piano* at you, no less the cymbals."

"Mr. Anderson," I said, "I don't know what you're talking about."

"I'm talking about that bass," he said.

"That's a Tatum bass," I said. "That's what you your*self* played. That was Tatum right down the line."

"Correct," Biff said.

"So?"

"Maybe you didn't notice, but I was playin' *alone*. Kid, a rhythm section won't tolerate that bass nowadays. Not after Bird."

"What do you mean, *bird*? What's that?"

"Parker. Charlie Parker. Bird."

"Is he a piano player?"

"He plays alto saxophone."

"Well . . . what *about* him?" I said. "What's *he* got to do with playing piano?"

"He's got everything to do with everything," Biff said. "You tell me you want to play Tatum piano, I tell you Tatum's on the way out, if not already dead and gone. You tell me you want to learn all those Tatum runs, I tell you there's no room for that kind of bullshit in bop. You know why Sam . . ."

"In *what*, did you say?"

"Bop, that's the stuff Parker's laying down. And Fats Navarro. And Bud Powell. Now *there's* the piano player you ought to be listening to, Powell; he's the one you ought to be pickin' up on, *not* Art Tatum. You want to know why the boys shot you down, it's 'cause you put them in prison, man, you put them in that old-style bass prison, and they can't play that way no more. These guys're cuttin' their chops on bop. Even *I'm* too old-fashioned for them, but we're good friends, and they allow me to get by with open tenths and some shells. Sam wants to walk the bass line himself, he don't want to be trapped by no rhythm the *piano* player's layin' down, he don't even want to be trapped by the *drummer* no more. Didn't you hear what Dickie was doing behind you? You didn't hear no four/four on the bass drum, did you? That was on the cymbals; he saved the big drum for klook-mop, dropping them bombs every now and then, but none of that heavy one, two, three, four, no, *man*. Which is why they told you to stick your left hand up your ass, 'scuse me, Poots, to *lose* it, man. They wanted you to play shells in the left hand, that's all, and not that pounding Tatum rhythm, uh-uh. You dig what I'm saying?"

"What's a shell? What do you mean, they wanted me to play shells?"

"Shells, man. You know what a C-minor chord is?"

"C, E flat, G, and B flat," I said.

"Right. But when Powell plays a C-minor, all he hits are the C and the B flat. With his pinkie and his thumb, you dig? He leaves out the insides, he just gives you the shell. He feeds those shells to the horn players, and they blow pure and fast and hard, without that fuckin' pounding rhythm and those ornate chords and runs going on behind them all the time, and lockin' them in, 'scuse me, Poots. Piano players just can't *play* that way no more."

"*Tatum* does," I said. "And so does Wilson."

"A dying breed," Biff said in his English accent, "virtually obsolete. *Look*, man, I was with Marian McPartland the first time she heard Bud play, and she said to me, 'Man that is *some* spooky right hand there,' and she wasn't shittin'. That right hand *is* spooky, the things he does with that right hand. He plays those fuckin' shells with his left—the root and seventh, or the root and third—because he's got tiny hands, you see, he couldn't reach those Tatum tenths if he stood on his fuckin' head, 'scuse me, Poots. Some of the time he augments the shell by pickin' up a ninth with the right hand, but mostly the right is playin' a *horn* solo, you dig? He's doin' Charlie Parker on the piano. There are three voices dig? Two notes in the shell, and the running line in the right hand, and that's it. Tatum runs? Forget 'em, man! They're what a piano player does when he can't think of nothin' new, he just throws in all those rehearsed runs that're already in his fingers. That ain't jazz, man. That's I don't know what it is, but it ain't jazz no more."

"You people going to pay rent on that table?" Gottlieb said.

"What're you thinking, kid?" Biff asked. "I can't tell what you're thinking behind the shades."

"I just don't understand what you're saying."

"You don't, huh? Well, here it is in a nutshell, kid. The rhythm ain't in the left hand no more—it's passed over to the right. The left hand is almost standin' still these days. And if you want to keep on playin' all that frantic shit, then you better play it all by yourself, 'cause there ain't no band gonna tolerate it. That's it in a nutshell."

"I still want to play like Tatum," I said.

"You'll be followin' a coffin up Bourbon Street," Biff said. "Look, what the hell do I care *what* you play? I'm just tryin' to tell you if you're startin' *now*, for Christ's sake, don't start with something, already *dead*. Go to the Street, man, Fifty-second Street, dig what the cats are doin'. If you don't like it, then, man, that's up to you. But I'm tellin' you, sure as this sweet li'l thing is sittin' here beside me, Tatum and Wilson are dead and the Bird is king, and jazz ain't never gonna be the same again." He suddenly burst out laughing. "Man, the cat's goan drum me clear out of the tribe. They got strong hostility, them boppers."

"I want to hear them play," I said.

"Get your uncle to take you down the Street. Diz an' Oscar—Pettiford, Oscar Pettiford—got a fine group at the Onyx, George Wallington on piano. Go listen to them."

"Will *you* take me there, Mr. Anderson?"

"Me? I don't know you from a hole in the wall," Biff said.

"Oh, *take* the fuckin' kid," Poots said.

—Evan Hunter

5. Art Tatum. Photograph by William P. Gottlieb, © 1979.

Chorus: Wing

[An excerpt from *The Horn*]

"Let me look into a human eye . . .
this is the magic glass, man."

—Melville

Wing Redburn was not alarmed when Walden caught up with him and told him that Edgar had probably had enough at last. He had just wedged himself into a slot in the revolving door that interceded between the uncertainties of Forty-sixth Street and the hushed cream-white lobby of the WELL Studios, when he heard somebody call out, "Hey, there, man." He turned around right inside, where the neutral odor of air-conditioning was always the strongest, just as the door ejected Walden and continued to revolve with an autonomous whish-whah, whish-whah. They stood by an ash stand whose bowl of fine white sand had yet to know a butt, and drew together, coat collars confidentially up, and Walden said earnestly, "Yes, he cut out last night from Blanton's, where we were playing, with a look—Oh, man, you know! *That* look! I thought maybe you heard, or had some notion—"

Wing was not alarmed, for nothing alarmed him much any more, but he knew the look all right, for Edgar's face struck everyone who saw it as laboring to produce that look—the face itself contending with the man to shape the expression (ironical, staring, doomed) for which it seemed fated. And so to Wing it was like hearing of the death of a man who had been mortally sick but who continued to abuse himself. For an instant, despite his annoyance at the figure of the young tenor man, hunched down with the furtiveness of musicians cupping cigarettes on Sixth Avenue outside the Union Hall, he felt like smiling sadly and nodding his head.

"I got to find him though, because he took it wrong. I mean, *I* cut him.

You know?" with a wince of pained, earnest modesty. "But you *used* to know him, and I can't even remember where his pad is at. Where could he have gone, you think?"

"Man, I wish I knew," Wing sighed, throwing out his hands, for he had been overcome, not by everything contained in the word "used" (the years, the astonishing inconstancy of time, spent idealism), but only by the fact that Edgar's face had finally produced out of the man the look that everyone knew it would fashion once the man let go. For with that fact had come back to him not only the life he had abandoned when he gave up irregular employment in small jazz groups and took the job in the studio band, but also the puzzling realization that it had gone on without him. He would never think of that world, to which he no longer really belonged, without seeing Edgar's midnight face.

"Man, I wish I knew!" he repeated, this time somewhat defensively, for Walden stood as a reproach to him.

"Well, I got to find him. I mean, I blew just like him for years. I mean, he was the end to me. You know."

"Well, whyn't you try Geordie? Or Junius—Hell, I don't know where the son of a bitch could have got to. I don't *know* him."

"Geordie was there. She saw it. She got one look at him afterwards and— Well, you know, she pretends not to care, but I could see—"

"I can't help you, man. I got to go to work."

And he expected to see the pout that, three years before, had deformed his own lips at the obstacle-raising, the "well-buts," and the mechanical objections of the square: the man who was captive in a world of regular hours, transportation difficulties and lean thoughts. But it did not come.

There was only a crestfallen stare of disappointed awe that reminded him that he was not just another musician to Walden, but Eddie Win(g)field Redburn, the prima alto in modern jazz music, so startling and original that amid the changing fashions and new sounds he already occupied that peculiar obscurity into which only an unassailable fame can wall a man. He knew they said of him on Broadway street corners at three o'clock in the morning, "What ever happened to Wing? Where is he? What is he thinking?" and shook their heads, because where Wing went and what he did could not alter that part of him which already belonged to them; not even his absence from their night, his non-jazz job, his steady hundred-and-five a week.

"Oh, okay, Wing, I dig you. I'll try Junius then. But if you hear—
Maybe I'll call you later. I mean, he may get run down by a car or picked
up, and I feel responsible." Walden's face had already withdrawn from
him with odd respect, and his glance was black and large and madden-
ingly without resentment. "Well, I'll cut out then . . . Later, pops," and
he stepped sideways into the revolving door as it turned, and the words
were sucked away.

Upstairs, amid the tangle of cables, music stands and folding chairs in
Studio Three, the drummer for the house band good-naturedly chased
Wing's warm-up runs with precise rim-shots, while the others smoked
their cigarettes down to the end and tried to wake up. Wing stood, facing
pointedly into a corner, his horn sitting on his belly, held vertical in a
kind of present arms, and blew a little rondo on "How High the Moon."
The others always listened, for (even when warming up) he blew more
reed than horn—a strange parakeet of an alto, with a pure, savage, vibra-
toless tone. He never smiled or suffered or strained when he played; he
just set his horn on his belly, widened his stance a little, took the mouth-
piece between workmanlike jaws, and blew clear.

The other musicians in the nine-piece group (white realists who knew
their trade, and had kept their eyes out for a safe berth from the begin-
ning) admired him because, though he had stood up ten years before
and, with those darting, bravura phrases that wheeled and flashed like
the wings of a frenetic hummingbird (hence his name), had played
things then that few other men could rightly under*stand*, and though
they knew he sometimes listened to Bartok, Hindemith, and "those
cats," and had accomplished (without self-consciousness or pretension)
the feat of hearing all music with the same ear—though all of this hung
about him invisibly, yet palpably, nevertheless he was there on time
every day, and was a good, disciplined sideman, with years of band work
already behind him by the time he began to be talked about in L.A. in
1944, when, in Junius Priest's shuttered apartment, he sat with his hat
down over alert, emotionless eyes and blew strange through the after-
noons. They knew that he had once heard the big, plumed Bird who
sings somewhere in the center of America—a wild, harsh eagle song—
and still sometimes heard it, even in the modest jump of their little band
of lazy cynics; and soloing on some copybook riff, played clear, original
things, and sometimes experienced a thin pleasure in it.

For, though his reasons for being there were much like theirs, Wing was not one of them, and when he blew with them on "I Cover The Waterfront" (the theme of the show), one eye on the engineer's forefinger that magically faded them away for the announcer, he was thinking of Edgar with baffled annoyance.

Something about Edgar had always annoyed Wing. The very name conjured up the specter of a hipness he had renounced: the soft collars and loose suits and wide ties that made the rashest movement languid and tentative; the weary, vaguely insolent language of the jazznight, growing ever more involuted as more and more aspects of reality became square; until what had started as an attitude changed to a neurosis, and what had been an individuality disappeared behind the uniform eccentricity of the dark glasses and berets, the rabbinical beards and arabic names; until a man's very inability to live in the world was a mark of his evolvement, and everyone repeated with awe Edgar's famous remark, delivered with a Promethean sigh: "Man, I got to get high before I can have a *hair*cut. I got to get *lifted* before I can *face* it!"

"He was everybody's evil father," Wing thought, remembering the young musicians during the war who were in ferment all over the country, to whom Edgar's horn and Edgar's pitiless standards had been an omen and a challenge and a promise, and out of whose obsession with his sound the irreverent furor of bop had come. He was everybody's evil, worldly father: the father never seen enough to evoke love, the father you envy and cannot impress, the father who sees through your accomplishments and does not even *need* your admiration. Wing thought of Junius Priest and Curny Finnley and himself and the few others who had taken everything that was latent in Edgar's horn, and brooded upon it through the wartime nights, and finally found a way to blow it out— and all Edgar had ever said to them was: "All right, all right, I'm hip, you all can sure twiddle your fingers . . . But, man, now do me some *blues!*"

Coming from anyone else, they would have sneered at this, because they knew that what they were doing would change everything, and that the grimmest resistance would probably come from the older musicians who could not hear it as they did. But coming from Edgar, from the Horn—whose tone and dress and attack and attitudes and even vices they had studiously or unconsciously aped—it worried them.

For the foundation of their admiration for him above any other jazz-man of his time had always been that Edgar, years before most others, had been a skilled, devoted servant of his horn; an adept in the complexities of harmony and rhythm of which it was capable; able to comprehend, and even transcribe its magic in an abstruse notation that preserved it; willing to risk himself in the tenuous, hairbreadth rapport of improvisation so that the unnameable truth of music (which all can hear and no one can explain) might happen; as faithful to the horn as if it was, itself, the holy vessel of American song—and yet living at a time when most of these things were derided by the traditional, scoreless two-beat bands, and ignored by those who danced to them, and unimportant to the operators who paid the fee, and nonexistent to everybody else. He knew the secrets coveted and striven after and lusted for by Wing's generation, and knew them the only way a man can know such things: having coveted and striven after and lusted for them himself, and what is more, having done all this almost alone, for the most part unaided by the music or musicians of his time, and getting little from them but the scorn and obloquy which seem to be the one reward of those who are the first in any art to see what must come next. And so it seemed inconceivable to them that he would mock what they were doing.

But, still, when he bumped into Wing in the uproar of clubs thereafter, his mouth deceptively ingratiating under the drooping mustache, and the small watery eyes pale with irony, Edgar would always say, "Man, was that 'Night and Day' you just blew, or 'Begin the Beguine,' or what *was* that? . . . Like I was just saying to some stud at the bar, 'Now, man, don't put that boy down. He could blow "St. Louie," or "West End," or "Beale Street," if he *wanted* to,'" the laugh as soft and sly and impenetrable as the most careful innuendo. "You know, that's just what I said."

And this worried Wing, because sometimes when he was alone, running his scales, trying new changes, practicing, he blew nothing, blew just an easy, natural flow of notes around three simple chords, blew blues—and felt each time the inexhaustible welling of song potential in them, a strand of melody that might unfold endlessly in an ever perfecting symmetry toward the final, faultless music that a man could blow. And yet, intent just then upon his newfangled complexities, he had dismissed the feeling. Nevertheless, his annoyance with the hipness Edgar represented had grown in exact proportion to his suspicion that there was truth in what Edgar said, and the collision had eventually occurred.

It had happened just three years before, during a disastrous concert weekend in St. Louis, for which the dickerings of an affluent entrepreneur had regrouped the nucleus of the original bop fraternity, now gone their separate ways—Curny temporarily between bands, Junius lured from home in Harlem, Wing from dreary two-weeks gigs around New York and Boston—with, as an added draw, Edgar Pool.

From the moment they boarded the seven o'clock out of Penn Station, it had all gone wrong, and whatever had once bound them together, no longer held. Separately, they had grown too eminent to be close. Junius was uncommunicative, as if he had finally gotten out of the habit of talk, his dark glasses lowered blindly over a volume on abnormal psychology. Curny rushed up and down the aisles, his face a mask of shrewd glee, deciphering timetables with the help of weary conductors, checking his watch at every stop, renting more and more pillows as the dark came down outside on Pennsylvania. Wing mused out the window on the raw immensity of the American night, disheartened by the stir of old affections that were now somehow inexpressible, unable to revive the excitements of five years before, and unhappily aware that for months now he had been blowing as if he had blown everything before. And in the midst of them all, Edgar slouched with a flask and a cigarette interchangeably lifted to his sullen mouth, studying them with the gloomy exasperation of an old sinner biding his time among seminarians. All night he watched them with his cold eyes and destructive lips and closed heart—an atheist old man maddened by the certainties of youth.

Just two days later Wing was on a bus heading for New Orleans, fleeing forever from the nightmare which had grown out of that look of Edgar's, fleeing from the whining, haughty voice complaining about the rooms in the hotel and the food in the restaurant and the acoustics of the theatre, arguing about the rhythm section with which he was expected to work, and the amount of money he was to receive; fleeing from the carping voice which announced loftily to no one in particular that *he*, the Horn, didn't share a room with anybody "who got between his legs what I got," but, all right, if that was the kind of cheap gig it was going to be, Junius could take the other bed, because "he's the most like no one of any of you cats"—the voice explaining in an insulting drawl that he didn't like his chicken fried in batter but in grease, and when he said a *double* bourbon he didn't mean "no one-and-a-half-ounce shot of pig-water bar whiskey either;" the steady, echoing drone of that voice in the darkened theatre in the afternoon, rejecting one drummer because he was given to press-rolls, and lecturing another on "them bombs you always dropping on the bridge—oh, I heard you do it before;" the stubborn tactlessness of that voice as it said to the promoter who was staging the concert (a brash, eccentric young white man who affected high-button fire-house shoes, box-back suits, double-breasted waistcoats, and who drove a huge burnished 1929 Reo touring car): "Man, you a first-class fool! How can you ever make the nut to pay all these cats? You can't even afford yourself a *car!*"

Two days later Wing was trying to forget that he, too, had laughed unwillingly at this, and other things (because all ironies have truth, and Edgar was their ironical father after all); he was also trying to forget the argument with the white cab driver, and the incident in the elevator with the woman's hat, and what had happened at high noon at the Milles fountain outside the railroad station. He was systematically not thinking about Edgar's sudden two-hour disappearance before show time, and the frantic young promoter, sweating onto the phone dial, trying to locate him and regretting that he had ever gotten into this; and Edgar's equally sudden reappearance at the last minute, openly smoking the thin acrid cigarette (clearly not his first), which the surly young punk in the beard and the camel's hair coat, whom he had found somewhere, kept taking from him for a quick, hissing drag. Wing was trying to forget the image of Edgar peeking through the curtains, counting the house on his fingers and snapping out, "I coulda tol' you you didn't do enough advertising. Man, you got to spend to make. Don't you even know that, with your trashy shoes?;" and the sight of Edgar drifting up to the microphone, beyond which the huge thronged cavern of the theatre opened out, to introduce his first number; and the memory of what he had said into that microphone, while the promoter, standing nearby in the wings, unconsciously tore up a five dollar bill with shocked disbelief.

But he was not trying to forget the contemptuous, hungry glint in Edgar's eyes as the spots caught them while he played, the glint that said that anything but his own paralyzing boredom was absolutely square, the glint that too clearly stated: "There. That's good enough for you. *I'm* blowing it, ain't I? . . . Well, then, what more do you want?"

Indeed, he was attempting to remember forever his own thoughts as Edgar tweetled on an indifferent parody of something he had played a thousand times before, never trying to blow as well as he could, and even refusing to solo at all on one number, so that the pianist went on hopelessly spinning out his chorus, waiting for the relief that never came. He was trying to remember what he had said to himself that had seemed then such a revelation, not only about Edgar, but about them all, and particularly about his own recent feeling of having blown everything there was to blow: "But he ain't good enough any more to justify this kind of hype. He ain't been good enough for a year to make up for the way he comes on. And only the work can justify what a man does . . . But nobody realizes it yet, *he* don't even realize it—But, man, all I know is, *this* ain't it. *This* may be good enough for them"—because respectful waves of applause were, at that moment, rolling across the footlights for the man, if not the horn, even though the man had turned away from them as if he would not even deign to notice what was only his obvious due— "it may be good enough for them to*night*, and next *week*, and maybe even next *year*, but it ain't good enough for me any more . . . Man, there must be something else!"

And sitting on that bus, with only the overnight bag he had brought from New York, and his horn case, he was trying to remember most of all the bitter look of emptiness in Edgar's eyes as he came off the stage, refusing even to consider the encore that the applause so humbly asked for—a look in which there did not seem to be even an inkling any longer that there could be something else, something else; a look that did not flicker or deepen or change at all, as he said, "Man, I don't have to work like this no more. No, no. Not for this cheap kind of money, I don't! Not *me*! . . . And where's that goddamn creep with the pot!" Wing sat on the bus, fleeing from that look, a look which (he felt with a shiver) all the concerts, gigs and jazz clubs of his own life would inexorably fashion on his own face unless he broke away—fleeing toward a girl and a truth, one of which he would have to lose to gain the other.

He fled down the immemorial Big River of his music, wanting to follow moving water because it went somewhere, and all complexities and attitudes and wraths were swept away before it. And so he fled down the Great Brown Snake that made the entire continent one vast watershed to it, and that from deepest, woodsy north at its trickling beginnings over smooth Canadian pebbles, to its final, timeless spending in the Gulf, drained out of the heart of America, smelling Pittsburgh slag from the Monongahela with dust that blew across the faceless Badlands to the Milk, gathering as the rivers, tributary to it, met (the Platte, the Kansas, the Missouri; the Minnesota, the Chippewa, the Illinois; the Little Sandy, the Cumberland, and the Ohio) to flow, terrific, widening and assuageless, ever south, where still others emptied into it (the White, the Big Black, and the Red), until in huge, instinctive death beyond the last bayous, it joined the other waters of the world. Wing went down the river as jazz, just forty years before, had beaten its way back up after the Great Dispersal, going down it as if to listen to the source again, to hear the secrets of the river's mouth that in cane field, board church, sod levee or cheap crib had aroused some inexpungeable longing once that only jazz could ease.

He never got to New Orleans (perhaps it was fortunate), because one night in Louisiana, drifting down a shanty street on the edge of Algiers, he heard the crude guttural of a cornet, poked his head through a paintless door, and found a Saturdaynightfull of dockworkers, drinking sour mash and whooping as they danced. Through the wild candor of all those hot faces, the faded print dresses snatched above the pumping knees of the girls, and the outlandish gusto that rocked the worn floor boards, his eye fell on one girl across the room.

Her dark face shone with that lip-parted, calm-eyed expression of anticipated tenderness, that tensionless acceptance of the world and its dealings which is a rebuke to all who look upon it. Her dewy gaze, eager for an object on which to lavish itself, was so utterly simple, so without sin, that had she suddenly impelled herself forward right into the throng of bent-kneed, flung-footed dancers, into the thresh of peg pants and French stockings, shaking her wide shoulders until her small hard breasts lifted, and raising her skirt, the action would have seemed too natural to the onlooker to be unchaste. For the whole reality of that night (so wild and rich and powerful-with-life after what he had just left)—the dusty pavements, the sweet odor of parched oleanders, the proximity of giddy flesh—seemed poised around her seventeen-year-old face, to which time had yet to add that something that denoted she must perish. She had more life ahead than death beyond, and she was as slender, fresh and inwardly shy as young girls have always been who made aging men stop dead and gasp with loss.

Her name was Fay Lee, and Wing never got to New Orleans, but found himself a room in a crumbling house by the river, and saw her whenever he could. He had no reason, and that was why.

He never even unpacked his horn, and the afternoon she first came there, noting the dirty shirts and trays of butts with a grave eye of respect for such masculine disorder, and let him touch her young untouched body, she stood, after it was over, looking at his sax (which he got out to show her) that was the color of new pennies in the shaft of blind sunlight falling through the arras, and suddenly exclaimed, "Oh, isn't it blessed! Isn't it just holy golden!" But he only seized her hand and drew her down again and lay, shifting and perplexed, through the heavy afternoon, robbed (as grown men sometimes feel robbed) of those furious male obsessions that always prove too brittle and unreal for mating with the simple nakedness of a girl. He wanted to lie upon the rugless floor with her and catch her moan in his mouth, and afterward feel the coolness of her fingers, fond, dear, and comforting. But she only blushed with an incomprehensible joy that somehow infuriated him.

He was near the river, and they loitered there in the long, opaque shadows of the motionless evenings, when silence seemed to swim out of the bayous upriver, huge, ominous and profound. And then night, which wakes a half-savage possibility in the American heart, brought the tart slice of whiskey, the shuttered laments of conflicting radios, and the lights swinging in the river like submerged lanterns. He sweated in his shirts till the backs were rotted through, and drank his whiskey neat, and the uncrushed, calm oval of her face always aroused him, as if it was a strange face, fleetingly glimpsed in a crowd, on which such inner recognition glowed that the intimacy of that one glimpse choked him with an unsuspected loneliness. She was simple, pellucid, and she learned his complex city ways with quiet joy in the learning itself; but still she undressed as if he were not there, folding her slip carefully in a square and placing her shoes side by side. Afterward, bathing his face from the chipped crockery bowl on the washstand, not daring to look back to the bed lest the very languor he had sought to create in her fine, agile limbs should infuriate him with a last desire now that it was achieved, he took to talking aloud, speaking as if he were alone, unconnected, unfinished sentences, a jumble of images from a hip, disordered world that she had never known. He ranted, he mused, he boasted and complained, he talked of Edgar almost obsessively. She listened with a steady, patient gaze, and did not hear or care about the words, and could not be impressed by fame or art; and then he watched her dress again, always with the same annoyed pinch of regret, and they went out and had a drink; and then he took her home to the kitchen that maddened him because, even with the new refrigerator set proudly so that it could be seen from the front room, there was an air of earnest humility about it; home to her waddling, bandannaed mother who treated him like a white man because he had come downriver, and her brothers who lounged around, splay-legged, listening to the radio.

His money started to run out, and he thought furiously, destructively, of marrying her, and forcing that simple, living look out of her eyes with awareness of him, *him*. He bought her fancy underwear, all white-girl-silk, all scalloped edges, all hip and jaded and indecent; and talked aloud while she tried it on in the heat of his room, cursing, mocking her, wheedling. But she only giggled to catch sight of herself in his shard of mirror, and said, "Ain't I cute though! Look at that!" He stopped seeing her for a week and got out his horn for the first time and sat in his drawers on the bed edge and played absently, hoping for accident to seize him, but playing nothing that he had not played before. He slept in long, sweating binges in which he did not even dream. He wanted her blackly, and prolonged the wanting of her, until he realized that it was not her he wanted, but something else, that something else: the calm of her eyes at which he imagined Edgar drawling sarcastically, "She just a little Topsy, now isn't she? She's a rag doll!"

Then one twilight he wandered down to the river and saw her sitting on the pier, dangling her legs, a small, rapt silhouette watching the lights come on in perfect solitude. He drew nearer, thinking to reach around her unawares, cup her breasts, and frighten her into his life. But then, as he crept closer, he heard her singing an absent line of blues without words, a line too simple, too isolated from all other music by its spontaneity to be remembered, so that the moment it dried on her moist lips he could not recall it. He stood not four feet behind her, paralyzed by the perishability and the keenness of that moment, as by an immense truth. And everything there became real to him, at last.

The dusk, the small outline of the girl, beyond which the river swept wide and murky moving heedlessly, deeply, gathering speed before it gave itself up in broad, doomed immolation in the Gulf: its tragic swiftness in the huge hush, and the small awkward silhouette against all that impermanence, and the heavy delta smells, and, at the last, the inconsolable reality of that reality came up into his heart like a sob; and his illusions and his rages left him in an instant, and he was alone there in the way of human beings one with the other, with only a song between. He sat down and held her hand and used her no more. . . .

Now, in the studio, he stared at the crooner who was reading his ad libs from a cue sheet—that hard, unblinking stare that is so unnerving because there is no attention behind it—and he was wondering distractedly where she had gotten to. Moved to another street, married someone's brother, had gleeful children, given in to fat. Loss! He could not even remember her face, just the huddled outline against the evening river. And for a moment life amazed him again, because human routine, the flawless achievement of ambitions, and even the neatest of men were all part of its great, disordered confluence with time; and the truths and certainties a man shored against that fact changed it not at all. Loss—he had lost it all! He had squandered the calm he might have had with her; he had thrown away the simplicities of contact in his discovery of that song; he *would* have his music at any cost. Yes, yes.

He had used her no more after that, and felt the hungry, Edgar-like ironies in him die, and had known then that everything was simpler than irony, and even thought for a minute that he might show her that he knew, but then had seen in her eyes that utter innocence to which no river could ever be tragic, no dead irony real. So he had taken a bus for New York three days later, with his meager truth, while she wept on a bench in the bus station, weeping easily as women do, and then walked away, her sources of renewal undamaged. He had been unaccountably separated from the men he worked with ever since, playing a pure line; and finally he had separated himself from them by taking the studio job. And just then he realized in a flash that men have only this sad knowledge with which to heal themselves: when you lose life, you grow wise. But that is better than maiming life to hold it.

"'Blue moon,'" the crooner was warbling, "'you saw me standing alone'"—rubbing his neck—"'without a dream in my heart.'" Wing stared at him fixedly over the curve of his horn—the high-waisted trousers, the $25 shoes, the handsome empty face: a nice enough fellow, quick, sharp, friendly, in his own broil. But everything that Wing knew counted for nothing to that boy, the years, the losses, what he had *seen* with his eyes. So what was it worth? he thought, just as they came to the release where sixteen bars had been left open for him. What was the moment on the river worth when he had realized that he had had that dark, sour look of Edgar's in his own heart all the time, and in the exact instant of the realizing felt it thaw and disappear? "All right, man, but now blow me some *blues!*" Edgar had said with an oily sneer, mocking not Wing but the truth; mocking it *because* it was the truth, and mockery was all the tribute he had left. What was learning that sad fact worth?

He started to blow, taking up the particular chords into his horn and forgetting them, his mind clear (as it was when he played) except for the feeling (that he had had since coming North again) that at the bottom somewhere there was song, the same song, the one song—to know which, suddenly, was worth to him whatever life might take away. He blew a long line, a tumbling zigzag in which he barely toed the chords as he passed, like an ecstatic base runner so fleet that he veers off the infield lines and cuts back to touch second, and then sprints, whooping, toward the farther stands, but wheels and comes home at the last, leaving everyone gaping and dumbstruck. He could not play any other way now, or forget what he knew, even though Edgar Pool had blown his poor head against his ingrown life for which that dark look was only a twisted image to repel the world.

He finished his chorus, and the crooner raised his small, pleasant voice again, in which there was no shred of knowledge that Edgar had been a doomed hero for a whole generation of rebellious musicians, a hero who had persisted beyond his drama to become absurd. But one thing does not change the other, and all men fall from drama into melodrama; and as Wing took his horn back into his mouth for the ensemble, he realized that Edgar was still out in the world while that night moved off the Atlantic over them all; and though he knew things as dark as Edgar now, and knew beyond them too, still a man's work, his blind pursuit of the single truth, cannot be destroyed, even by himself. And Edgar, no matter what had happened since, had chased it selflessly once. For the first time in three years, Wing thought of another man as a man should: "What's happened to him? Where is he now? What is he thinking?"

And knew that after this number, which was the last, he would get a taxi and head uptown, and find Walden somehow, somewhere in that night. And, free of Edgar now, look for him, able to care.

—John Clellon Holmes

The Day Lady Died

It is 12:20 in New York a Friday
three days after Bastille Day, yes
it is 1959 and I go get a shoeshine
because I will get off the 4:19 in Easthampton
at 7:15 and then go straight to dinner
and I don't know the people who will feed me

I walk up the muggy street beginning to sun
and have a hamburger and a malted and buy
an ugly NEW WORLD WRITING to see what the poets
in Ghana are doing these days
                              I go on to the bank
and Miss Stillwagon (first name Linda I once heard)
doesn't even look up my balance for once in her life
and in the GOLDEN GRIFFIN I get a little Verlaine
for Patsy with drawings by Bonnard although I do
think of Hesiod, trans. Richmond Lattimore or
Brendan Behan's new play or *Le Balcon* or *Les Negrès*
of Genet, but I don't, I stick with Verlaine
after practically going to sleep with quandariness

and for Mike I just stroll into the PARK LANE
Liquor Store and ask for a bottle of Strega and
then I go back where I came from to 6th Avenue
and the tobacconist in the Ziegfeld Theatre and
casually ask for a carton of Gauloises and a carton
of Picayunes, and a NEW YORK POST with her face on it

and I am sweating a lot by now and thinking of
leaning on the john door in the FIVE SPOT
while she whispered a song along the keyboard
to Mal Waldron and everyone and I stopped breathing

Garden

Can you dig the recognition performance
preparation organism energies of fusion
the placing experiences metamorphosized
human exchange toward complete submission
to the spirits conscious digestive response
the resulting process many level'd hitting
in various constructs:
                    Group sound
                    speech transported
muscles are taut
                    relax'd talons
                    deifying purpose
a wait above all functioning, building
                    Joy to
                    exhalted elevation
                          ascending life . . .
Rhythm   every where
          in every place
                is
          every thing
                    not think that
                    writing this
                          read it
                          what
                    then never over
                          start
          birth coming
          act an from to
              much
              less
          hear after

                    to & fro
                    S. Murray
                        wind

Days after in rain mostly
but sometimes not, blue certainties,
clouds strung like whatever best recalls
appurtenances remind blood having flowed
closely by stricture/
              grey nights sawed enclosures
              numerous remain ...
a was her not replaced
steady verisimilitude never moon
    placated drip, plastic pressure
              borne ready for next ones ...
And now after throw away
a blaming on those all around
followers as it were
not that in your less than state
function would identify proper style
for cradled inside is a strange undying/
could be malfunction substitution
a readiness to please memories
long finished echoing dropped shadows
hallucinatory whispers currently
wip'd off trapped behind blank stare
unconscionable see what it is
                    feel dry chapping
                      white mud
                    bumps in the wall
                      a reason
                        for ...
                    craze being
a distant mule ridden like moth joint coming yule
a tide slowly engaged in the sorting from differing view
a seizure oozes at its own distinctive bidding.
The head rotates on an axis sweet with the come dip

forward glass to size, semicircled, and back, closing
on time, one action, um———, square to sphere.

The legs are about bending, at casual speed, a time of their own
well found. 2 knees as eyes in flight, margins eclipsed
                                                even squash
fated fallen froth foams and course . . .

Thighs elevated appendages sutured angles spreading
    she rush, at blood speed agape
holder farthest coin at fathom's end, vessel clings . . .
hebetude luxuriant smell salted glow rippling image
slight insouciance paroxysm relieved religiosity
delivered from excess to tumescent billow clasping
fingers too adjacent plains of mist descent wept
swept affably recant laity's soft upon blanketed
sonnet gone, risen, mellow having . . .
The Arse poked out the chest seemingly leans backward
awry all one arch, arc'd romance, as the right then left
hump end of undulating hip, squats, retrieves, pulling
chords gently up . . . circuitously ribbons can't
winde, imagined hill moss topp'd maroon sparrow.
Singer's womb, and arse again momentum sprung
about an outside swing crossin' frontal pelvis in
quiet shroud, heaves pushing so many leaves envelop
iris gage tranquil nectar pulsates spleen splendor
fed shoulders as division nestles, anon nascent un-
born yet wither spool unwinde under a natural kin'
like cork churning unwound rope out of
stream evenness uninterrupted leaves
    too a good tone about . . .
There are many lines, harvest landscape,
reservoirs of wheat, kernals bob in there here
                                        gleaming
Sun's bounty transposing language,
an open field holds *Dibia's* face poised,
happening upright, receiving, mobile.

Menu-open'd pores is discovery reveling
action, applauding life, lines here
have an echo in distant valleys, roots
winding from fertile vegetation
curled sheep's mane crowning broad
wide forehead, sweating toil, beating
beaming, a roar . . .
Feet stalks growing flat stamping
heredity to new definition, lock'd embrace
a child from earth genesis
unformed action, balanc'd pedals pushing ever fire
meeting part, divergent commencement precipitant
toward the other each limb, silent communes
falling to the one river exchanging monolog, each
to the other crystal resolution benign oftener
reign, comely touch sigh—oooh on silences registered
others on fire push'd ever away stages more, stand
rearranging easy body pose natural posture regard
a'gin territories colliding, happenstance in se-
quential ratios unknown call
                shade, color, tone, shapes eaten
                    at world   eyes
                                          ears
                sights sound verities-apart-taken
                to bridge viewing vibration new
                digest sonic trance
Shouting Rings/busts swarming bees, mastodon
genuflect celebrate same mass serving
them bells foot gone toe opposites spott'd air
not by every cell readied steam thru Ring
hands and other to in be something doing special
paint silence rearranging placement altering weights
reason come knowledge from what is feel that
hold whole sense begun babble picture why
later fingers stretch to know not more strain
grass one one tongue 2 natures 1
hierarchy; stroke ending with just all that was (seule)

going, there, without before overstress order lay
gratitude altar offering tides Shouting Rings
coy sublime knowing human need give enriching
character time; space colored; tires purpose
sculpture walk, arrive meaning architecture
To live majestically one faces inevitable woman
destiny fac'd decipherable thru streets knowing
held in hides ceremonies beaten skins preserve
communication body organs speak of selves, others
thorough watch foretelling deed ancillary
guardianship. Tones of Bronze muscle light
aural cavities tapping erogenous canals
in climatic thrusts, *Ol-orun* owner of the sky
hot above waste even toed lightly dap & fea-
ther'd (Bessie, too, best figure finger'd rounded
spine grazing burnished felt oven womb
over pine scent roar transpire brightest
sound connection gazes languidly seeming
indifference daring slant even teeth
burnish'd velvet strutting *Ol-orun*
lives, she, too—in, among selves heaven
across head over body wide appearance
Ilé-Ifé most sacred citizenship there
encompassed more of then, which was, all ever was—
solid ground play'd hunting *Orishanla* big
daddy with dipper, an agent divine, purpose
pure, received the snail, brimm'd with waiting
soil, pigeon and hen. The Bird scatter'd seed
ground buds evening boned till Earth formed.
First sanctity was link, original hookup,
had then width, simply of all following
to come being—Ifé—house of life, centre
of the world (Yoruba) *Ilé-Ifé*
ceremonies fountain finding protection
long ancient stream echo's as sticks
consecrated libation healed certain
chambers. Sheer granite heights guarded

by cylindrical vessels turning into con-
vex lens great distances narrow exits
wind takes a gentle hand spiraling gust
thru stretching fingers inside weights
tombs reverberate the noon attends
Queen's arch heaven frame breath blue-s
arc'd density a bowed raft men walk
from to beginnings camel's nose
pointing direction, dune secret springs
in red, sandals glide tramplin' mounds
falling ease, eve, palm feathers stay
swelling tides glad the pockets of Sahara.
Flap the greatest bat cluster'd in
branch Baobab wings milk wean
approach depart—past waving African
oak to later emerge silk or cotton
Baobab barking leaf rooted angle
high travellin' tall Night, straight
tough then cleansing.
Maroon fez tuft twills husbanding
arcade lain upwards round naked
till, Baobab approaches, mirage
all may have its parts one only the seed(s)
touch'd: Ashanti Adae every 3 or so

mashed plantains	water
sometimes meat	water
blood and alcohol	
offered at stools	
	water

closets, vine, liquids led to overflow murine
edge past Tingle's old one's dread fission red
the eye counting stores alloy shrunken
reminder has gotten blood culled to keep
it is petrol, and dyed ash vibrating warts
on Man's inconstant hand, edge past
startling matters—dread—
    Great Native God King

        Orishanla
        agent of creation form
        Obatala
        Powerful King owner
        the sacred thing
Oriki laid, pick participles each push
plays 'portant part livening separate
starts tribunal way there recognition
        must true gold exchange be found
Juices unencumber'd embrace
        fruit happy to the water know
pleasant prick of tongues identities
forage gather'd dentures elastic
response call juices
                    Oriki
        Seeds in some roots in all
ahead toward divinity necessity protects
the line is many-knowing-why-on way
brave silences, beyond expectation of an
oppressive confusion, coy piteous, yet
privileged vulgarity plurality, choice
fielded in theft hull dimension dam'd
bow of Middle Passage, plural choice
depth grist incarnate slime theft ravaged
men arranging murder on rock bed
slinking oil, dropping elevators for gold
crushing, mutilating—fine, fine than is
the 'art' produced a vision old crook'd tooth
of eternal witch, broom hard in open puss,
mother killing sons, daughters, fathers
blinded by greed, mother or both, brothers
doin' in brothers—yeh yeh—dig that
vision—its continuance—a contrast . . .
Brazen bodies burnished ebonized bullion crescent
gold, are fleeting vessels, tongues attack
saliva as internal spring effulgent efficacious
power to the Stroke from labyrinths inside

co-ordinate gummed correlate tooth opening
hardest textures, those chompers to lap
fruit as repository kinolin future nests—
speech flows at tides grown nappy; aware
of times, places, ago, when sacrifice was
principally gift, propitiation . . .

Skinny Skelton, Pucci Gucci accoutrement
—is what they slink about in   rapping, drinking
                                                    etc etc etc etc
—is what they sink   laughing
            be in   don't stop
                                                don't
                                    agony ain't got time
                                                to hear

Why Not Why Dah
Daah ha ing
Wha na hah Wha
Wha Dah Dah wing
                                    Remember T. Dameron
                                    know tender things un-
                                    tamper'd by populous
                                    ne-be hebetude, tides
                                    overwhelm, ultimatum
                                    perched there a tree
                                    atop includes whole
                                    solids chunks moulds
                                    easily manoeuver'd to
                                    sweet bottoms thru
                                    opening wisest lest
                                    in tune time secretes
                                    all vestiture
                                    tawny nephew tall
                                    rememberin' fast
                                    corners couch
                                    different tastes
                        over   divide

                                    square full bottom.
                                    Remember
                                        Tadd Dameron
                                            (walking starch
                                                laugh!)
Why spot then, are there, vision
among, things immobile to touch
(now debronchily, twardlrack)
acts small rock care places
readyin' your all insulated
mark for due posits ripening

                You there them too others
                she in red big marble'd dark
                sky spent spooning altering
                coke, frank then, now, otherness's
                        care, seemingly—why are you there
                must not self wrought—yeah-ay-pain
                        been overdrawn one face more
                o' when how not do every line impulse
                        a memory gives lie lyin' still now
                for here is it 3 later found nowhere
                        beside or under rollickless frieze
                supporting you not even there
but you have amount full too
ranges dark in your being oil may
a kindle dee granite save
begone knee hopp'd over
    bangli bobbled Indian tree
                                What did I not do then
                                maybe lakes tide awakenings
                                buried summer some
                                lost seeking more
                                softest fleece antler tred
                                and all, dear, silencer
                                    abodes   above
                                        rounded heels

                         'tis spooky/
                    not what
                         a/
                    Why dah
                    ahhhhh
                    wheezin' by—
                    Whoo dah
                    (whar (ropewhilly, oh)
                    pen dar

Me thinks of every day woven baskets holdin' bone
of Geysers deliverance Palm Nuts at *Wine'n Time*
Powers found feeling round chants back breeding
up the winding wind sail imperative Black
to thine rhyme fields alone makin' self echo
Yeah ayheah: call & response environment
Oriki mesmerizes, establishing face,
porous fact, fed, recharged from nature
swollen speech waft'd o'er contact—hummin'
whatever was felt inquiry aft' bow
loosen'd attaining vibes after Core
touch'd twice coming back home all
readied external smile outer dexterity
pointing game not knowing yes found here
differing 'cause the weights now here
close to interest inner elasticity
articulation limb dialogues blood
movement aggregate mobility of space
in time push consecutives accumulated
ascension graduates consuming aware-
ness propelling; ground swell by heat ro-
tating going pervading atmospheres
horizon an only breath one time at
once taken
Monkey skin to the *Auro*
         magic for the protection
                    Zuna

a *Gbau* in knowing cancellation
excessives vengeance without
                    enduring
     Saved by one in many *Bingiya*
Speeds onward as of medicines
          A binza
Scandalized, carrion came crow
western distaste wing'd whip
less grew grew, self—out off out—
split wither'd
separate stances
               confused
red rainbow destiny
               eulogies
other than holders matching sleeveless
buts balancing char w'bitten reeds
gut in poke, at weights edge some water waits

ABORO ATORO   equal pushing
                    mount uplevel
                    stepp'd tippin'
               to a point, perhaps
     Relevance lives meeting
     breath area at least
     2, meeting (yeah-ah)
                    Joy
sunning ground links cups
both rainbows drink
solids hot bring in down
one crystal

Mine motor motioning
                    You I would too
                    s'teared of just walkin'
                    let straps have reckon-

<pre>
                         ing count unknown as
                         grist pass'd if ray's flop
                         or on receiv'd nowhere not
                         straps reckon'd count a dues
churn 3 yrs back
        instead   Training Stuttgart to Paree
                         many cases men boxes uneven hill
                         door opening, light, and thinness there
                         sliver'd strand hide "team" injun
                         good, then
                                 of what part
                         each in it was

Yearn
                         Dark 20 yr old wood
                         iron staples rusted
                         crusts of tile sky
                         snow'd wetted what
                         ever 'dain'd taken.
                         Lot hard to find.

                         Yes now among
                         these cobbled truncheon
                         baying whales fractured
                         corpulence flattening
                         spirit whence lifted
                         floating a bee stutters.
                         Dark to you
                         1 3 years later came
                         wheel under Seine hot
                         as tended crutch leg stiff
                         held out over wheels spinning under

    Right on, Right on
    how stances continue
    defy exterior commerce
    deaths, to mountain exhalt
</pre>

Right, then, initiative going
 on, Right, Right, Right on
Thru knowing essential presence, it is not
contestable possessing unlimited
growing comprehension. A being found
at this seat is embraced, unanimous call
resplendent annoints robes one retires
in solitude to wait upon acceptance
known forthcoming coming forth
patience, wisdom, the growing sword
                    of
                  Kings
Drink the then weight of these barrels now
as time fast mutilates young flash the
'morrow disproportionately wills olden
keeps chatter in stalls slain slaying
merchandise fitting doggerel for kings
who know nothing better than no life for
how comfortable their money be there
tired bones skidattled seeking gout
constipated wretch ring eviscerating
elongated entropisms spasms spinning
time again wearin' lower choices
as medallion hung withering from stump
groin meatless sweat aetherized pristine
platter chatted about ever so drily, delirium
is excusable, it is rich, divorced, usually 1-2 kids
laughs a lot, skin pull'd tight surrounding
brave bodies then buried logic growing in balance
to main with reason—new records then as
now, oblivious, immovable—black rights
cradling impossible flight . . .

Witness, witness across field heritage spoke
alliances conquer'd. Respect Respect
          there is the ritual witness respect
     all seeking augmentation force living

Respect the field witness the plow augment
        principle purpose of sacrifice, propitiation
        gift, presence, at water its flat face
        mirror polarize seeking will oracle's
        possession
                        Respect Respect
                        Aretha aires
                        absolute absolum
                        Aretha absolute
                        Witness sweet inspiration
                            Witness
                        absolute gentleness
                            Aretha
Possess'd
lil' Stevie
by Holy Rock
remains
stand   standing
Wonder
        (too)!
heritage-echos—silence—moving—Universe
manners hip food gatherin a be seen gregarious
slip'en slidin' getting entities hallowed
        thy will be done
foraging among crabs long tongued ancient snapp'd
but regard is weight hipness lighten'd
        Ray Robinson steer, fandancin'
        out orbiting (no game) sludge
knowing out, in, sideways tall, possibility axis & fall
        Muhammad Ali
        like Amma, arboreal
        corpuscle twine harmonium
them 2 legs (Dinosaurs) that's got
        each (fine graining) his
natural (from Jack Johnson portent
        know, see, the
        Barring—

                —apart from—
                over-reigning
                head, scalp, forehead
                Domed)
of color'd goings doings love our Way
his own
                Johnson then Robinson War
                Clay now ('them-thar lookin'
                            fidgetin' wonderin'
                            how—admiratin'
                            to—ball breakin')
        Johnson—Robinson—Armstrong—Louis—Ali
inscription held fertile glories passed
magnificence back & forth on & on —
in grain tones ring a certain way
sprung seeing scene own'd, full dress
panoply you sing to as want bees announced
any how any way shadows living inside
media happens, harvest—high voltage, links
clouds. Evening cleansed then a distant
forehead plain, unseason'd rain expec-
tant Luyia away banish keep hum
maroon bows before Rosewinds by dusk.
Esoteric rocks, ivory lilting, formation—
acolytes above been hand'd mission
that quiet known Baobab changing
spring:
        to touch key becomes grace twine tawny
        both moon annoints pyramid storm peril'd
        together an axe jettisoned or thrown
        over & once dropped board from
        Baobab curving, rub'd cup dipping
                di di di di ah hah hahing ah
                whum whum um———tah
                twi twa ta ju——— ba ———
                dee-haw ob du du wa
                um ah humahah doo betah

chambers touch'd in one being anchors
part
leaving Mother thought whatever
is irreversible, unanswer'd
intra sectionalizing, nevertheless
planes way is certain the anchor
plants. Mutual wills mesh
mesmerized whistle prone
moving masters.
Drink the weight fast upon barrels
oak like tiger's mane carved glyphic
ensembled thy script edges, still
fluid, shaping moves flat faced
flower might geld, crystal
leopard filling gently as gadfly
made ready with unsteady wa-onts
would not weigh whether patience
outshines, virtue young'uns guard
flame brings even those who can't
see. Easy odor uncomforting memo-
ry, convenient antidote dolts
languidly relieve them—out house
selves.
Parades in homage toward the figure one
must be watched thru blinds not sensing close
to a binding be. Shortest fly ecstacy
when in stings retrieve but faint woe
circumference here is more than quic-
kest draw: augers pointedly facts
studd'd ivory sapling sprung neat tingles
a mode, tangled layers invisibly starch
quicksand of emotion has been slow'd
centuries dominant death wore
vengeance lip upturn'd then, mu-
tilated thin now giving off its own
taste remnant shred bitter gaul
invisible wheels turn tide lighten gaits

free the waters
to make Oriki
        a
labyrinth open'd
unto mariner's
spring
lineage, in beats total thrust size seizing
moulding terracotta face & body framed
Noh civilization 2000 yrs being now then
before our fingers touch, shades shape
passage voices heal kneel shudder
resonance carries—unformed
transmission—unending cataclysm
prayer. Petition and praise conjugal
union existence 2 rainbows
culminate in same search
are then an augmentation force
invoking powers of supreme being
(shadows juice apart lips left planting)
music maintained controlled is
        —stroke—
For imperial West it is the darkest side
of fear, never seen, unable to face or
leave, attrition modal gait, calcimined
grin, catatonic moral gauge, to no-thing
evaporation driven without entrail
can color exist or its white matter be
        —strokin'—
Taste the ebony flavor resin'd ivory hued
mechanics forgettin' there ripplin' strides
lacerating unmoving cinderblock —
J. Owens J. Borican W. McKinley, at 1-200 mtrs.
6-3-1000, 4-600, (Jackal gazelle antelope)
brazen bodies bursting presumptuous pain.
Winde as smoking lanterns silhouetted flies
hearths still'd talk yet over a gone moment
lak' twas thin, nothin' all so quick again

they each at an end thar way too in spread
out gone shape walled fires calling stitch
stick of lantern shade a shudder amongst
herbic foliage flung as it were filing nights
lost doing.
Yeah, an ARSE 'protrudes' as if in shitting its only g
wore lace 'surprises', wind late expression role
separate, fertile justice at an even footed
webbing, balanced weight harmoniously flies
out over somewhere in more over down some-
where begin; separate matings shadows devour
meanings inherent operation alone—yeah apart
wire coddling blood of so ancient pole facing run-
ning minuets disquieted seas, dripping lilacs
for want of something rain and mattering
there we can behold ancient gold man
belly lidded rupture reptile writhing arms
circle pass exteriors angel home atop soil
leaving smoke grey whisper'd leapt thru reason
rope entwine then the here when after logic
dry irrelevant disappears stems have
become as arms were never anchor'd
face o'topped sprout often leaf taken oral
green to mouth and frontal grain petal cumu-
lous mountain opening cortex wide forest
forever to seed warmth waver bowels co-
vered in oil, a portion being of not dwelt on
but there and when feeling its completion.
Youth took off eyes behind see grey cones
strands jiving pumpkin not big between
straggled upshot indivisible right
hardon smoking scent saturnine gait
maker lend some palm etched giddily
a gadfly romancing Juba before
Jubilation dark all once again
in get some out them going natchurel
sculpted heads enduring

                              more in least
Not pin'ed, regretting never fully,
me egg in century Indian nose an axe
fulsome cropped nodds breakage rivers
cushioning murmur new falls nature
                              the get away! —
                              advance age
Somnolent figures in glass brittle to
placate immanent   breaking
skirts (frill) edge of uncontrolled mayhem
                              act of several roles
                              none (perchance?)
                                          too specific
                              just a gathering
                              (perhaps)
                                          loose leaves
                              unsheathed 2 empty pots
                              random
                              nerve end twitch
Seeds others jacks
around not nowhere urgent touch
were sound inside fury
    an immense tomb trembles —
                              blinks/
rhythm is mounting consecutives finite
                              endings
transplanting the Universes eternal movement
specific acts define role limiting area
                              breath
put down hiply (procreation)
                              breathe
winds occur thru sound exhuming —
expulsion feeds, exudation secretes
    explosion drives
then quickly retires retrieving
that which got away
    the sleeve emptying —

As it goes
Marcellus
of the bells
            upon this weight there is one ty
                            what not
                        in the ever
                            matter
                        ever what source
                        were found
            there, may clover by 'middey' bottl'd
(Don.) Tin
thin pleasant
hearing next
of kin spoke
vines curliquing
green bands
jinglin' early
up 'pone wide
brown earth
rope neath
    plow'd
    dawn
    shaft
between hearing
        and
    knowing
mountain tops
    (Cherry)
                    an open window
                    faded muslin drawn
                    to square's upping
                    border
                            slit
                        brown crook
                        waved 2 lines
                        single arm
                    dull was why cups

upon, on lined, in rows
seem'd to sit
moving
open in angle
thru wise iris without
blinking glide along
Hokusai's brim
Window over
open

it stays on
upon this weight
2 buttons
orange night
the stage moved
suit.
trumpet   sailor cap
it takes
off laughing
at
made weight
impulse more pausin'
to growing *too* know
maybe it stays —
passages
impulse weight
Decomposition changed
balance
ebb so flow
spreading weight
rolling
then on now
rolling
time
spaced water
spread
repossessing
next

```
        tune
ingredient
            time
        spreading
line change rolling
    necessary
red suit
(a link there!)
E. G.'s
hookage!
```
upon this weight
more is one tie—

—Cecil Taylor

For Miles

Your sound is faultless
   pure & round
      holy
   almost profound

Your sound is your sound
   true & from within
   a confession
   soulful & lovely

Poet whose sound is played
   lost or recorded
   but heard
   can you recall that 54 night at the Open Door
   when you & bird
   wailed five in the morning some wondrous
   yet unimaginable score?

6. Miles Davis. Photograph used with permission from Prestige Records.

The Planets

In the spring of 1953, three young men, good friends, walked from East 10th Street to West 52nd Street, to hear some music at a nightclub called Le Downbeat.

As they went in the front door they saw Stan Getz and Bobby Brookmeyer playing to an empty house, but they played like the joint was jammed, with such conviction if one closed one's eyes, the place *was* jammed. But both eyes open there was nobody there save the bartender who served the young men beer. Having paid, they sipped, tapped their feet to the swift, neat melodic interplay of tenor saxophone and trombone, maybe a little too sweet, but a trademark anyway, to the three young men, unthinkable, these days, that no one else was there.

One of the young men said,

"That's Tommy Potter on bass, Roy Haynes on drums and Al Haig on piano."

Oh *man! Wow! Dig* it!

The bar was about twenty feet long, to the left of the front door. At the far end, up some five steps, a small bandstand.

The place itself was like a long, rather wide, hallway, the restaurant section at the far end, rear wall, under a high ceiling. Tables in rows. Neat white tablecloths, napkins, glasses and silverware sparkled. Chairs snug, looked upholstered. It had a silver-draped, polished-mirror, upholstered-blue luxury liner effect, heightened in the far left corner, way in the back, where a flight of carpeted steps led up to a shadowed balcony with a white railing, beyond which, against its rear wall, a long white sofa was flanked by upholstered chairs and chrome cigarette stands.

People came in, had a drink, listened a while, and left.

Al Haig's head was down, face averted, right ear almost on the keyboard. His hands moved left and right, fingers dancing on the keys: seized a rung of music, climbed up and down a ladder of sound.

The young men were impressed, sipped beer, snapped their fingers, tapped their feet, nodding their heads to the beat, fixing on Al Haig, and his hard, fast bop piano on the very edge of percussion.

The front door opened. A couple of guys came in.

The three young men turned. Not prepared for what they saw or, for that matter, what would follow, in Le Downbeat.

A very large, plump white man in a worn gray suit over a clean white t-shirt, leather shoes, who looked like an M.D. has been, speaking in soft, pleading tones to the small, slender, young black man at his side, dressed in threadbare dark suit, frayed white shirt open at the collar, scuffed leather shoes. He seemed not to have slept in a week, and each day was a trial. His head was up, as on a shelf, eyes wide, lips parted in a way like a puzzled infant, not quite seeing the world, but as a man, young as he was, he'd seen too much, was a down and out wreck, a little stooped, and bitter, sad, angry, disgusted, bugged, and very very stoned.

"Miles," the white guy said, frowning, "will you take care of yourself? Please?"

Miles growled, "Yeah."

"I mean it. Will you be okay?"

Harsh whisper. "Yeah."

"Promise?"

"Unh huh." Laryngitis. "I promise. You can go."

So the big guy, with a worried look, watched Miles walk to the bar, and sit on a barstool next to the third young man, at whom the big guy looked, in an expectant way, and the young man, baffled, didn't know what to do, think of it—he knew who Miles was, he had the records— and there Miles was, sitting beside him, and he missed the message the big guy was giving him: would *he* take care of Miles?

Complete confusion.

The big guy left.

The young guys looked at each other, in particular at the third young man who was gazing down at Miles, seated—slumped, on the barstool beside him. Stan Getz, Bobby Brookmeyer, Roy Haynes, Tommy Potter and Al Haig slamming away, Miles raised his head, and as he looked up at the young man, gestured with his right thumb at the bandstand, to keep the young man laughing for the rest of his life, in that grating, gruff whisper, Miles asked:

"Who's that?"

The three young men, about to laugh, checked it, not altogether sure if they should, for the glance from Miles held such deep wickedness it was difficult to interpret, it had come in a flicker and gone in a wink: he had seen them about to laugh, and stop, so he turned away and looked across, up at the roaring bandstand, then down at the bar.

The set came to an end.

It was not known how Miles made it up and onto the bandstand, but there he was, and things got going, except he couldn't find the mouthpiece. It was on the trumpet, right where it should be, but his lips couldn't find it, everybody behind him blasting away, yet how strange! Tommy Potter, Roy Haynes and Al Haig had stayed on the stand, to back up Miles or so it appeared—there they were! As Miles found it, breathing light and easy, his fantastic lyric character, uneven, a little lost, that night, but tart, and pure: "The Way You Look Tonight."

It couldn't last.

But for a while.

Next thing they knew, he was walking down the steps, off the stand, and listen to this. He turned left, walked the length of the whole joint, the place deserted, clear back, up the steps onto the rear balcony, and sat on the long white sofa, slumped to his left, his head landing bam in the lap of a seated, beautiful, she was incredible, Swedish blonde with page-boy bangs, in a long white gown. She put her hand on the back of his head. Getz, Brookmeyer, Tommy Potter, Roy Haynes and Al Haig were blasting away. The blonde stared down the length of the place, over the heads of the young men at the bar and out the front door above 52nd Street, above New York City, beyond the North American Continent and off the edge of the world into endless, galactic space, where planets whirled, and suns burned, yet also seemed to twinkle, to living music, played live, to be heard forever. And ever.

Al Haig died of a heart attack on November 16, 1982. He was 58. He had played everywhere, with everybody. Was influenced by Teddy Wilson, Nat Cole and Bud Powell.

Full Circle

The same night after Miles had spoken with the odd young man in the powdered wig, at the bar in the Café Bohemia, the young poet came in around midnight, and had a bottle of beer, at the bar. Remained standing, listening to Miles, Coltrane, Red Garland, Paul Chambers, and Philly Joe make music he had not just never heard before, but couldn't believe he was hearing. They were getting better and better and better.

He was very poor in those days, often going for two and three days without food. He rolled his own cigarettes and could live for a week on a dollar, as A&P eggs were 49 cents a dozen, margarine 10 cents a stick, a loaf of bread 29 cents and a dime for a sack of Bull Durham tobacco which came with two packets of cigarette papers free. But to hear Miles, he bummed and begged—and worked—for a couple of dollars: there wasn't a cover or minimum at the Bohemia, and a bottle of beer, which cost a dollar, in sips, lasted at least two sets.

Imagine being a poet, sipping from a bottle of beer, while listening to those guys take their solos and come in strong together at the end. To open, Miles began, John next, then Red, Paul and Philly Joe, imagine it, alive, *live music*, the place not crowded on weeknights, music! giving life to love, and liberty to rhythm tapping his feet he closed his eyes, hearing Miles and Coltrane tear the front door off, on Miles' farewell to Charlie Parker: "Bye Bye Blackbird," with those three great aces backing them up.

He stood about a third of the way down the bar. Didn't sit. He knew how to listen to music, and he was listening to this music in that way of hearing new work that the opening outward of the inner ear does something to balance. In suspense hearing nothing but music, there was nothing but music, anywhere, he was up in a world and the world was music.

The beginning of this tune went by so fast he didn't recognize it, not that they played it so fast, no, it was so familiar he missed what it was, and being smart enough not to listen back to get it, and miss what was going on, he followed, and that's why what happened had such an impact, because he was altogether inside the music—to anticipate Miles was impossible and he had tried—while smoking dope and listening to records with his pal John Chamberlain—so, on this song, once again the elusive Miles Davis got away by keeping in front, and as everybody knew, as everyone knows, hearing it live and on record—well. That night this song went on forever, on and on, the tables, glassware, chairs, barstools seemed to dance, leaving the crowd stunned, and before the young man knew it, Miles was doing what he always did: walked over to stand beside each of the other four as each took their solo, so in a wink, Miles was standing, facing Philly Joe Jones, Miles snapping his fingers, holding his trumpet at his side, would the ceiling collapse? Philly Joe! Before his eyes, perhaps the poet had had a lapse, Miles was center stage between the overhead red spotlights, beside Coltrane, raised his trumpet to his lips, Coltrane's tenor raised—they all five hit together, in 16ths, for about ten seconds, in the perfect, very funny, even zany, melody, of "Billy Boy," and Aunty Mary laughed . . .

Miles

The way it had all begun was he heard that Miles Davis had a quintet that was playing in the Village, at the Café Bohemia.

So one evening he went over, heard two sets and came out ears ringing, starry-eyed and weak in the knees.

He had never, but never, heard anything like that, ever, *any*where, and it didn't take him a few days to recover, no, because he never did recover, for there was no recovery, this was permanent.

A college pal had gone into publishing pamphlets, very esoteric stuff, classy formats, limited editions in a series, one of which, in the fall of 1955, had been a booklet of eight of his poems. An edition of 150 copies from which he received 25 copies as payment, and after the four seasons had passed by twice, he had only two copies left. There were no more. That, was that.

In the area below 14th Street where he lived, in those days, he often encountered older artists who lived in the neighborhood. They would stop and talk, or go into The Colony, have coffee or beer, and talk or, more like it, he would listen, to them. He wanted to see, and be seen looking. The painter he most wanted to see him was Philip Guston, who was himself difficult to see, so often distracted or depressed the young man knew not what to say. Against his youthful, and demanding will, seeing Philip Guston on the street, Philip passed him by, not seeing him, which disappointed, depressed, hurt and pissed the young poet off. Although he knew that Philip, having painted all day, took afternoon breaks. Went to the movies. What he saw while watching the screen is not known, but images appeared in his later work that suggest possibilities. He emerged from the movie house so distracted and dazed anybody who knew him knew enough to avoid him: he had a house of cards inside a circle of dominoes in his head, to at last clear up the meaning of the initials PG on movie ads and billboards: *You will see strange figures and objects involving indiscretion and violence.*

One morning, around noon, the young poet awoke and realized the person who would see him and most understand his poetry was Philip Guston, and after breakfast, in a kind of fervor, he dressed, took in hand the next to last copy of his booklet, left his building and walked down to 10th Street. Found the address. Walked up the steps, you could do that then, didn't have to phone first. Knocked on the studio door. No answer. Guston wasn't there. Maybe he's at a movie. Poet disappointed.

Sat on the stairs and thought, and having a pencil with him, wrote a brief note on the flyleaf and signed his name, nickname, rather—Philip knew him. He put the booklet on the floor, and leaned it against the bottom of the studio door.

Walking home it was okay and good, but it wasn't complete. He wanted to give it to Philip.

"Here. This is for you. I hope you like it."

The next to last copy!

Panic!

No!

An about face, ran back praying Philip was still at the movie. Ran up the stoop, in the door, up the steps and there it was where he'd left it. Picked it up, went down the stairs, out the door, down the stoop to the sidewalk bang met a pal. They went to The Colony, had a few beers.

That evening, in another bar, still with his next to last copy, while talking with friends he fell into reverie, realizing the Miles Davis Quintet was right across town, and in a little while, why not go over, hear some music, and give Miles the booklet? The pencil in his pocket had an eraser, so erase the note to Philip (he'll be sorry) and write in a new note to Miles? Swell! Erase the nickname, sign his proper name! No sooner thought than done.

Standing at the bar in the Bohemia, having erased as best he could, he wrote a note to Miles Davis and signed his name. But he was nervous and self-conscious. Scared. Things were tough enough on Miles, the place was so racist. The Italian gangsters talked—if they talked—with their tongues glued behind their teeth. Skin drained gray, eyes dead: they saw you, they saw you dead. Their bodies were full, and lumpy, stuffed with meat, bread and blood. One stood near the men's room, a living human-oid of mutilation with heavy-lidded rattlesnake eyes, thick, gray slabs of cheeks, gray suit, green shirt, brown tie, so that as the set ended, the five black musicians had to pass him, to go outside for a smoke.

The way that guy looked at them almost made the young man ill, yet his anger at the injustice—the rape of their creative intelligence in a racist killer's sneer—kept him alert. Plus, in the poet's hunger for life, he knew the musicians knew who that gangster was, oh yes, that was part of the music! Who else ran the clubs?

Sure enough, the set was over. The five men came down off the stage to applause, and made their way to the front door.

The area along the bar was wide enough—beyond the barstools—to walk in twos, passing both restrooms, heading toward the hat/coat checkroom by the front door. In the space between, the thug leaned against the wall, on an angle away from the young poet, standing at the bar nervous as he was, without that goon being there, and as the mu-sicians approached, the gangster regarded them with the contempt he held for obvious victims. Each of the five men set his face in mask: one peek behind, into the volcano.

"Excuse—excuse me, Miles?" the young poet stammered, as the mob-ster drifted away, back toward the service end of the bar. The poet held out the booklet. "I'd like—I'd like to give this to you."

The five men stopped.

"What is it?" Miles asked. His great voice.

"A book, a booklet, of poems, a-a-eight poems I wrote."

"Are you a writer?"

Pause. "A poet."

Miles said to the others, they could go outside, he'd be out in a minute.

As they went, Miles accepted the gift, thanking the young man, not much younger than himself, and opening the cover to the flyleaf, read the inscription.

"Thank you," Miles said again, holding up a hand. "I'll give it to the bartender, to keep for me." His expression was complex because he was accepting something while on his way outside, where they waited, and he would have to go back before he could go out, which the poet understood, and watched, as Miles went back down the bar and gave it to the bartender, speaking in a low voice, the bartender nodded. Miles returned, seeing the other eager to say something more. Eager, and agitated.

"May I—Miles! May I say one more thing? I know you're on break, and—"

"Sure," Miles said. "It's okay."

"Oh—oh, *man*, I studied trumpet in college, I didn't get very far, I was drafted, but I I mean I listened to your records and, I mean, I hear what you're doing, and you're great, Miles, you're *great!*"

Miles looked at him.

"And I know this is crazy, my asking you this, but the poet Robert Creeley, in his new book, in the introduction, he says his poetic line follows your melodic line, on "But Not for Me." His line—his poetic line—"

Gruff. Yeah! "I get it. Sounds good!"

"Could I ask you, to, and of course this is im-impossible but, is there a chance, wu-would you, play it for me?"

Miles smiled, but shook his head.

"The numbers are decided beforehand." Seeing deep embarrassment added, "I'm sorry." And walked outside.

Well, the poet sighed, embarrassed, self-conscious, dismayed, and angry at himself, yet understanding the professional situation, arrived at peace of mind in the happy thought that he had given Miles the booklet, and! in a pre-Egyptian, sculpted burnished blackened bronze, how handsome Miles was, to deepen the image, and add to the already profound.

Sipping beer be realized he was far ahead of himself without knowing it, because those five guys had walked by him going out, and they would walk by again coming in, and in the way of his awareness of FIVE GREAT MUSICIANS, his spirit took off, sure enough, there they were, walking right by him on the way to the stage, next they were on the stage, next with instruments in hand: Miles's trumpet. Coltrane's tenor. Philly Joe's sticks. Red's hands above the keys and Paul poised above catgut, but not yet, no, because Miles said something to John, crossed stage to Paul, spoke with him. Next with Philly Joe, back to Red, a murmured message. Miles, standing between the two red cones of light, having put his dark glasses on, he raised his muted trumpet, as Red with both hands, Paul cool on bass and Philly Joe set the beat, they came in together with Miles, as never before, and never again, played the soft, poetic, no vibrato, ever dancing melody on a muted horn: "But Not for Me."

Followed by Coltrane

Wow.

Not an easy tale to tell at a party or a bar. In fact forbidden, except to the most perceptive friends, in no less than the perfect setting, as he discovered the hard way. Ever mistaken for a story about Miles Davis being a nice guy after those other stories, or, for one of a young poet who gave a great trumpet player a booklet, and the musician played the song requested.

Somewhere along the line, no doubt early on, Miles had his variation of Aunty Mary. So, beyond his knowledge, through her (or him—an uncle!), he shared a kinship with the poet.

His lyric went around his rage and gave him a foundation for expression—beauty, wit, tenderness, and fear, and helplessness—which included the Aunty Mary figures by paying homage to her, while feeling the exact opposite.

His gift, that of the classic lyric, no matter how he felt, *for any reason*, was thus a curse, and the reason why, in the doll jokes of the day, he was described as the Miles Doll. Wind him up and he turns his back on you, before a full house in London. Yes! Turned his back on the audience, began to play, and continued to play, and the English were oh well very very. This was on his European tours late that fall, and the following spring. His star was becoming a comet.

7. John Coltrane. Photograph courtesy of the Institute of Jazz Studies, Newark
New Jersey.

Late that next spring, almost summer, the Quintet returned, and opened at the Bohemia. The happy evenings of just a few people at the bar, and scattered couples at tables, where you heard every note, were gone. The house wasn't packed, but it was full, and the ugly days of down and out Miles, were also gone. He looked great. Stovepipe pants and raglan sleeves. The group was red hot, they played patterns of music as complex as Schoenberg. Coltrane followed Miles in grand, rising howls and outcries peaked with a scream, dropped three octaves to the melody, Red, Paul and Philly Joe spread out a background galaxy, Coltrane had all the space he wanted, and Miles stood beside him, trumpet in left hand, snapping the fingers on his right, head a little down, as he listened.

It kept going, and going, and going. Better and better. Polished to an enamel surface against blue electricity, which Miles kept rough on the edges: never before, music like that. Never again. The night they played "Billy Boy," and Aunty Mary had laughed, the audience applauded. The young poet was speechless, his whole body tingling, felt himself begin to crumble, and the set was over. The five masters came off the stage, and in a bit of a crush accepted compliments from fans, and made their way outside.

"Miles, *Miles!*" cried the poet. "BILLY BOY! *The best yet!* Man, I have *never*, EVER HEARD *ANYTHING*—LIKE IT!"

Clapped his hand over his mouth, and turned away. Good God—in this crowd Miles had his hands full, *leave him alone!* Yet Miles had seen him, and in fact was pleased, but the poet, filled with self-loathing, would he *never* learn to shut up? Couldn't he have said, Excuse me, before he spoke or just said, Great, Miles. Great. Why all the blah blah BLAH BLAH BLAH BLAH! but felt someone touch him, he turned, and there was Miles, smiling, his hand on the poet's shoulder, Miles' eyes direct, understanding, and warm, as he said, It's okay,

"I've still got the book."

—FIELDING DAWSON

Battle Report

One thousand saxophones infiltrate the city,
Each with a man inside,
Hidden in ordinary cases,
Labeled FRAGILE.

A fleet of trumpets drops their hooks,
Inside at the outside.

Ten waves of trombones approach the city
Under blue cover
Of late autumn's neoclassical clouds.

Five hundred bassmen, all string feet tall,
Beating it back to the bass.

One hundred drummers, each a stick in each hand,
The delicate rumble of pianos, moving in.

The secret agent, an innocent bystander,
Drops a note in the wail box.

Five generals, gathered in the gallery,
Blowing plans.

At last, the secret code is flashed:
Now is the time, now is the time.

Attack: The sound of jazz.

The city falls.

Walking Parker Home

Sweet beats of jazz impaled on slivers of wind
Kansas Black Morning/ First Horn Eyes/
Historical sound pictures on New Bird wings
People shouts/ boy alto dreams/ Tomorrow's
Gold belled pipe of stops and future Blues Times
Lurking Hawkins/ shadows of Lester/ realization
Bronze fingers—brain extensions seeking trapped sounds
Ghetto thoughts/ bandstand courage/ solo flight
Nerve-wracked suspicions of newer songs and doubts
New York altar city/ black tears/ secret disciples
Hammer horn pounding soul marks on unswinging gates
Culture gods/ mob sounds/ visions of spikes
Panic excursions to tribal Jazz wombs and transfusions
Heroin nights of birth/ and soaring/ over boppy new ground.
Smothered rage covering pyramids of notes spontaneously
    exploding
Cool revelations/ shrill hopes/ beauty speared into
    greedy ears
Birdland nights on bop mountains, windy saxophone
    revolutions
Dayrooms of junk/ and melting walls and circling vultures/
Money cancer/ remembered pain/ terror flights/
Death and indestructible existence

In that Jazz corner of life
Wrapped in a mist of sound
His legacy, our Jazz-tinted dawn
Wailing his triumphs of oddly begotten dreams
Inviting the nerveless to feel once more
That fierce dying of humans consumed
In raging fires of Love.

O-JAZZ-O War Memoir: Jazz, Don't Listen To It AtYour Own Risk

In the beginning, in the wet
Warm dark place,
Straining to break out, clawing at strange cables
Hearing her screams, laughing
"Later we forgave ourselves, we didn't know"
Some secret jazz
Shouted, *wait, don't go.*
Impatient, we came running, innocent
Laughing blobs of blood & faith.
To this mother, father world
Where laughter seems out of place
Se we learned to cry, pleased
They pronounce human.
The secret Jazz blew a sigh
Some familiar sound shouted *wait*
Some are evil, some will hate.
"Just Jazz, blowing its top again"
So we rushed & laughed.
As we pushed & grabbed
While jazz blew in the night
Suddenly they were too busy to hear a simple sound
They were busy shoving mud in men's mouths.
Who were busy dying on the living ground
Busy earning medals, for killing children on deserted street corners
Occupying their fathers, raping their mothers, busy humans we
Busy burning Japanese in atomicolorcinemascope
With stereophonic screams,
What one hundred per cent red blooded savage, would waste precious
    time
Listening to jazz, with so many important things going on
But even the fittest murderers must rest
So they sat down in our blood soaked garments,

and listened to jazz
    lost, steeped in all our death dreams
They were shocked at the sound of life, long gone from our own
They were indignant at the whistling, thinking, singing, beating,
    swinging.
They wept for it, hugged, kissed it, loved it, joined it, we drank it,
Smoked it, ate with it, slept with it
They made our girls wear it for lovemaking
Instead of silly lace gowns,
Now in those terrible moments, when the dark memories come
The secret moments to which we admit no one
When guiltily we crawl back in time, reaching away from ourselves
They hear a familiar sound,
Jazz, scratching, digging, blueing, swinging jazz,
And listen,
And feel, & die.

—BOB KAUFMAN

The Rare Birds

for Ted Berrigan

brook no obscurity, merely plunging deeper
for light. Hear them, watch the blurred windows tail
the woman alone turning and listening to another time
when music brushed against her ankles and held a low light
near the table's edge. These birds, like Yard and
Bean, or Langston grinning at you. Can't remember the shadow
pulled tight around the door, music about to enter. We hum
to anticipate, more history, every day. These birds, angular
like sculpture. Brancusian, and yet more tangible like Jake's
colored colorful colorado colormore colorcolor, ahhh, it's about
these birds and their grimaces. Jake's colors, and lines. You
remember the eyes of that guy Pablo, and his perfect trace of
life's austere overflowings.

Williams writes to us
of the smallness of this American century, that it splinters into worlds it
cannot live in. And having given birth to the mystery
splits unfolds like gold shattered in daylight's beautiful hurricane.
(praying Sambos blown apart) out of which a rainbow of anything you need.
I heard these guys. These lovely ladies, on the road to Timbuctoo
waiting for Tu Fu to register on the Richter scale. It was called
Impressions, and it was a message, from like a very rare bird.

In the Tradition

(Not a White Shadow but Black People Will Be Victorious)
for Black Arthur Blythe

Blues walk weeps ragtime
Painting slavery
Women laid around
working feverishly for slavemaster romeos
as if in ragtime they spill
their origins like chillers (lost chillen
in the streets to be
telephoned to by Huggie
Bear from Channel 7, for the White Shadow
gives advice on how to hold our homes
together, tu también, Chicano Hermano

> genious bennygoodman headmaster
> philanthropist
> romeos—
> but must coach
> cannot shoot—
>
> hey coah-ch
> hey coah-ch
> trembling fate wrapped in flags
> hey coah-ch
> you can hug this
> while you at it
> coah-ch

Women become
goils gals grinning in the face of his
no light
Men become
boys & slimy roosters crowing necros
in love with dressed up pimp stupidity death

hey coah-ch
wanna outlaw the dunk, cannot deal with skyman darrell
or double dippin hip doctors deadly in flight
cannot deal with Magic or Kareem . . . hey coah-ch coah-ch
bench yrself in the garbagecan of history o new imperial dog
denying with lying images
our strength & African
Funky Beauty

        nomatter the three networks idiot chatter
        Arthur Blythe
        Says
        it!
        in the
        tradition

         2
        Tradition
        of Douglass
        of David Walker
        Garnett
        Turner
        Tubman
        of ragers yeh
           ragers

                    (of Kings, & Counts, & Dukes
                    of Satchelmouths & SunRa's
                    of Bessies & Billies & Sassys
                    & Ma's

        Musical Screaming
        Niggers
        yeh
    tradition
        of Brown Wells
        & Brown Clifford
        of H Rap & H Box
Black baltimore sisters blues antislavery singers
        countless funky blind folks

8. Sun Ra. Photograph by W. Patrick Hinely, © 1989.

      & oneleg country beboppers
      bottleneck in the guitarneck dudes
      whispering thrashing cakewalking raging
      ladies
      & gents
      getdown folks, elegant as
      skywriting
   tradition
   yeh
   tradition
   of Brown Wells
   & Brown Clifford
   of H Rap & H Box
Black baltimore sisters blues antislavery singers
     countless funky blind folks
     & oneleg country beboppers
     bottleneck in the guitarneck dudes
     whispering thrashing cakewalking raging
     ladies

& gents
getdown folks, elegant as
skywriting
tradition
of DuBois
Baby Dodds & Lovie
Austin, Sojourner
I thought I heard Buddy Bolden
  say, you're terrible
  you're awful, Lester
  why do you want to be
  the president of all this
of the blues and slow sideways
horn, tradition of blue presidents
locked up in the brig for wearing zoot suit
of marylous and notes hung vibrating blue just beyond just after
just before just faster just slowly twilight crazier than europe or its
racist children
  bee-doo dee doo bee-doo dee dooo doo (Arthur
  tradition
  of shooters
  & silver fast dribblers
  of real fancy motherfuckers
  fancy as birds flight, sunward/high
    highhigh
    sunward
    arcs/swoops/spirals
  in the tradition
$\frac{1}{4}$ notes
eighth notes
16th notes
32nds, 64ths, 128ths, silver blue
presidents
  of Langston & Langston Manifestos
  Tell us again about the negro artist
  & the racial mountain so we willnot
  be negro artists, McKay Banjos and

Homes In Harlem, Blue Black boys &
Little Richard Wrights. Tradition of
For My People Margaret Walker & David Walker & Jr Walker
& Walker Smith Sweet Ray Leonard Rockin In Rhythm w/Musical Dukes
What is this tradition Basied on, we Blue Black Wards strugglin
against a Big White Fog, Africa people, our fingerprints are everywhere
on you america, our fingerprints are everywhere. Césaire told you
that, our family strewn around the world has made more parts of that world
blue and funky, cooler, flashier, hotter, afro-cuban james brownier
                    a wide panafrican
                    world
Tho we are afro-americans, african americans
let the geographic history of our flaming hatchet motion
                            hot ax motion
                            hammer & hatchet
                our cotton history
                our rum & indigo
                        sugar cane
                        history

Yet, in a casual gesture, if its talk you want, we can say
Césaire, Damas, Depestre, Romain, Guillén
You want us to say Dumas, Pushkin, Browning, Beethoven
You want Shaka, Askia, (& Roland Snellings too)
            Mandingo, Nzinga, you want us to drop
            Cleopatra on you or Hannibal
                what are you masochists
                paper iron chemistry
                    & smelting
                    I aint even mentioned
                        Toussaint or Dessalines
                        or Robeson or Ngugi

Hay, you bloody & dazed, screaming at me to stop yet,
No, hah, you think it's over, tradition song, tradition
poem, poem for us together, poem for arthur blythe
who told us again, in the tradition

                    in the
                  tradition of
                  life & dying
            in the tradition of those klanned & chained
            & lynched and shockleyed and naacped and ralph bunched

hah, you rise a little I mention we also the tradition of amos and andy
hypnotized selling us out vernons and hooks and other nigger crooks of
gibsons and crouchs and other assorted louses of niggers that turn from
gold to shit proving dialectics muhammad ali style

But just as you rise up to gloat, I scream COLTRANE! STEVIE WONDER!
                        MALCOLM X!
                    ALBERT AYLER!
                  THE BLACK ARTS!
Shit & whistling out of my nkrumah, cabral, fanon, sweep—I cry Fletcher
Henderson, Cane, What Did I Do To Be So Black & Blue, the most perfect
couplet in the language I scream Mood Indigo, Black Bolshevik, Koko,
Now's The Time, Ark of Bones, Lonely Woman, Ghosts, A Love Supreme,
Walkin, Straight No Chaser, In The Tradition
                        of life
                        & dying
                  centuries of beautiful
                        women
                        crying
                  in the tradition
                        of screamed
                        ape music
                        coon hollers
                        shouts
                        even more profound
                        than its gorgeous
                        sound
                  in the tradition of
all of us, in an unending everywhere at the same time
line
in motion forever

like the hip chicago poet Amus Mor
like the Art Ensemble
like Miles' Venus DeMilo
       & Horace Silver reminding us
       & Art Blakey sending us messages
       Black Brown & Beige people
       & Pharoah old and new, Blood Brotherhoods
       all over the planet, land songs land poems
       land sculptures and paintings, land niggers want still want
       will get, land
in the tradition of all of us in the positive aspect
all of our positive selves, cut zora neale & me & a buncha other
folks in half. My brothers and sisters in the tradition. Vincent
Smith & Biggers. Color mad dudes. Catlett & White Chas & Wm. BT. .
Overstreet
& the Sixties muralists. Jake Lawrence & Aaron Douglass & Ademola.
Babatunde building More Stately Mansions
We are the composers, racists & gunbearers
We are the artists
Dont tell me shit about a tradition of deadness & capitulation
of slavemasters sipping tea in the parlor
while we bleed to death in fields
tradition of cc rider
see what you done done
dont tell me shit about the tradition of slavemasters
& henry james I know about it up to my asshole in it
dont tell me shit about bach mozart or even 1/2 nigger
beethoven
get out of europe
come out of europe if you can
cancel on the english depts this is america
north, this is america
where's yr american music
gwashington won the war
where's yr american culture southernagrarians
          academic aryans
          penwarrens & wilburs

          say something american if you dare
                if you
                        can
                              where's yr american
                              music
                                      Nigger music?
(Like englishmen talking about *great* britain stop with tongues lapped on their
cravats you put the irish on em. Say shit
man, you mean irish irish literature . . . when they say about they
you say nay you mean irish irish literature you mean, for the
last century you mean, when you scream say nay, you mean yeats,
synge, shaw, wilde, joyce, ocasey, beckett, them is, nay, them is
irish, they's irish, irish as the ira

you mean nigger music? dont hide in europe—"oh thats classical!"
        come to this country
                  nigger music?

you better go up in appalachia and get some mountain some coal mining
songs, you better go down south in our land & talk to the angloamerican national
minority
they can fetch up a song or two, country & western
could save you from looking like saps before the world
otherwise
        Palante!
        Latino, Native American
        Bomba, Plena, Salsa, Rain dance War dance
        Magical invective
        The Latin Tinge
        Cherokee, Sonny Rollins w/Clifford Brown
        Diz & Machito, or Mongo Santamaria

        Comin Comin World Saxophone Quartet you cannot stand up
against, Hell No I Aint goin To Afghanistan, Leon Thomas million year
old pygmies you cannot stand up against, nor Black Arthur tellin you
like Blue Turhan Bey, Odessa, Romance can Bloom even here in White Racist
Land It can Bloom as Beautiful, though flawed by our oppression it can
bloom bloom, in the tradition

of revolution
                    Renaissance
                    Negritude
                    Blackness
                    Negrissimo
                    Indigisme
            sounding niggers
            swahili speaking niggers niggers in turbans
        rn & app & aprp & cap black blacks
    & assembly line, turpentine, mighty fine female
        blacks, and cooks, truck drivers, coal miners
            small farmers, iron steel and hospital workers
                in the tradition of us
                the reality not us the narrow fantasy
        in the tradition of african american black people/america
nigger music's almost all
you got, and you find it
much too hot
            in the tradition thank you arthur for playing & saying
            reminding us how deep how old how black how sweet how
we is and bees
when we remember
when we are our memory as the projection
of what it is evolving
in struggle
in passion and pain
we become our sweet black
selves
once again.
            in the tradition
                    in the african american
                    tradition
            open us
            yet bind us
            let all that is positive
            find
            us

we go into the future
carrying a world
    of blackness
    yet we have been in the world
    and we have gained all of what there
    is and was, since the highest expression
    of the world, is its total

& the universal
is the entire collection
of particulars

ours is one particular
one tradition
of love and suffering truth over lies
and now we find ourselves in chains
the tradition says plainly to us fight plainly to us
fight, thats in it, clearly, we are not meant to be slaves
it is a detour we have gone through and about to come out
in the tradition of gorgeous africa blackness
says to us fight, it's all right, you beautiful
as night, the tradition
thank you langston/arthur
says sing
says fight
in the tradition, always clarifying, always new and centuries old
says
    Sing!
    Fight!
        Sing!
        Fight!
            Sing!
        Fight! &c. &c.
                Boosheee dooooo dee dooo dee dooo
                dooooooooo!

                DEATH TO THE KLAN!

Now and Then

This musician and his brother always talked about spirits. They were good musicians, talking about spirits, and they had them, the spirits, and soared with them, when they played. The music would climb, and bombard everything, destroying whole civilizations, it seemed. And then I suppose, while they played, whole civilizations, actually *were* destroyed. Leveled. The nuns whimpered with church spears through their heads. Blind blond babies bled and bled. Dogs ate their mothers and television was extinct except the image burned in it forever, in the future soft museums of our surviving civilization. A black way. A black life. From the ways and roads of the black man living, surviving, being strong.

But when they stopped, the brothers, they were not that strong. Like any of us, the music, their perfection, was their perfect projection of themselves, past any bullshit walking around tied up unspiritual shit. They could be caught with white girls, and talk unintelligibly, or sometimes around one's glasses a little sliver of white fear would idle, and he'd laugh it away, and talk about his music, shadowboxing, practicing his survival and perfection.

Mostly their peters slammed them, and brought them lower than themselves, or the need to live, like to have money, and be whole in the tincan halfassed sense the white man's way, which he put on us, and is still so much a part of all our lives. (A man on the radio explaining black-power.)

I mean they could only talk when they were not playing. As I can only talk, or feel the frustration of needing too. Of not sitting in the circle of circumscribed light. Reeling. Passing. (Like my dead lovely girl, passed, passed, passed, gone.) Getting into the next level of vision. Seeing and being. I want to go. I want to fly. Lift me spirit. Help me. Just talk. That's all. With the tongue in the roof of my mouth. Just spirit. Nothing but. I hurt. I want. I need. All these endless flesh frustration categories. Which are only that. This is a saint. No place. This is a god. No where. This is a feeling. Me. I am all feeling. Here by the wet window burned in its tone. I am all the not being that my limit has set, not knowing yet my whole. Yet I do and cannot speak with my entire spirit. Cannot fly. Though I understand the need. The way. I do not cannot be do are. Walls. Walls. Lie in the death of the almighty. Wishing.

Like I write to keep from talking, and try by that to see clear to where I must go. Chakra. Enlightenment. The seven lives. The many planetary adventures. Air fire water. Scale. Hung in the balance to see the deaths. Tell them horns. Tell them words. Tell them example of a man little man with big eyes went away came back grew loved made things died without point, in the history of no world and the world passed, the continent sank, and nothing but nothing was ever accomplished since everything was already done, and what more could be done.

The brothers cast shadows in the world, and tales were told about them. They told tales about themselves. One was short and one was tall. They scared a lot of people because they were new. They *were* spiritual. But not like Norman. Black Norman short brother brought to my house one afternoon, he was looking like the passer, like he knew more, than any of us. "You think it's about personalities." He said that. "About personalities," and the door swung open sunlight, no, nothing, came in, to the force of, to the heart of, my self. I cdn't speak. You think it's about personalities. You think it's about your self. Whew. was in the air. I see him years later standing in a doorway on 125th street, the ways of men. Further out, gone, than any of us. Even now, with the wind of God blows through me. "Come on faggot," his face turned on 130th street in that stance of hard ashy elbows, and read the deep cowardice of a wd be killer. All of the would be killers, cowards, and dancers with high fists, killing the village white killers. And the killer, JM, the soldier, subsided. To darkness of more fears, and another road he had to find, having seen the fire in Black Norman rage into heavens we know nothing of.

Black Norman, was not always Black Norman either. He was weaker too. He was not always in the rain on the street in the doorway communing with God. He wanted money. He wanted his flesh. He *thought* he was strong sometimes (though in his weakest moments). God of Norman of God of where I touch. Feel this, and pass. All you dudes. Feel this, and pass.

But they, the brothers were pals of mine. Good friends, in a world of alligators and shitheads, lunatics, happy liars, cowards, white people. There was warmth. There was something done, in our inch. But God knows. God chooses whom he will. (Your prerogative, ol man, to call such, knowing the blue eyes of the will, of the days, of the number passing, all, such, and me, and the. . . . heart stopped, girl, please, I want to know, where's the door I came in yestiddy, where??? I cdn't, don't, and they look at me, I want, ... stop it, stoooopidt!)

My pals and me, against everything. It seemed. They made music like heaven's bowels. I loved them in the sound. They loved women tho. Like Amos and Andy in the Harem of the Butchers. It was a conquest they thought about winning shit. Like boys. The tall one was all boy, a kid, really. Raw, like they say, of new kinda gunfighters type. The other rooted in a cleaner rhythm than the world around him, though he created the things that could weaken him. Responded. There are invisible allegiances in our bones. Things we must look at. Why? The smoke of smells. The web of things we've touched or seen. Womb-earth.

People can be corny at the same time they're not. Can reach that? (Children line up against the wall and select your failure machine. He's going down, wind, scarf badarf waves, hello clancey jackson sits on the steps looking at the girl, can grow, the G clef vibrates hairs pussies, conglomerates of afternoon triumphs, evening walks across the floor, as beautiful. They want to be Gods. We must desire god and his ism.

(I can describe one guy tall with a large adam's apple. With wirerim glasses and sneaky smile. Sneaky high up there, pardner? Har to breaf???

The other more flash gordon without the popsicle. Maybe a joint sometime. Whenever. And a white tuft of sparks thrust out his lower jaw.

This is the scandal of a small town that all the stupid people are the same as in a big town, so they seem, stupider. Dig?? So the lovers, seem, s-o-m-e-h-o-w, loveier (is that a category of human espresso??)

Sometimes they looked like Batgroup unemployed. No place, like, to hover. (In all honesty, this is a one-way street, come back, the shit's changed. Evolver, which is different from revolver, which has long hair and kills. Even in song.)

"Black People We Must Take Over This Planet As The Prime Possessors Of Natural Energies." Red Hook always wanted them to write a song with that as the title, but they didn't when I was "knowin'dem" (a description of batstreet, in back of the sixteenth dead president, in bronze and the key to the city in the future brain of the tall basketball players dodging father divine's hustlers on the street. You cannot ask for more than immaculation????? (I cdn't wish no worse on you.) Except we need each other. Red Hook would lecture like Sun Ra sometimes, when Ra is talking to certain corny niggers about selling out black people. Batgroup would leave for the Midwest at night, zooming, and blowing, and come back hooked up, literate, in dey shit, fresh.

Or trailing chicks around, they'd go get the energy to do that. Here. One's wife was somewhere and somewhere else. One was a pole. Like wood. Wresting a killer humility. An egogod, telling the shadow of what you claim you never had. Or left, the older ones claim to have gained knowledge through error. And how much of that is really true. Guess?? And they'd follow, or one would, Red Hook, or the source. Maybe rubbed on Hook's coat or African shirt. A dazzle, a stink glow of the source, the possibility of being kings and loved men of a strong people.

They wanted a show. A place. It was good and bad. There too was too much slack for bad wind. They schemed, and darted. Made shit, and you think, didn't realize it? Think about yrself. You do the same shit. People watch. They watch from across the street through the window with their linoleums drying in late afternoons. They chart your life. They know you walk on glass splinters running shit, like on the radio. Murray the K type shit. "We've all seen what you can do, man." JB talking.

So they'd make both scenes like on a bridge, going to Europe with the Snowmen, then coming back with the key to the invasion of the warm countries by barbarians, the coldbeasts. And snuggled up with one, a lady, MY GOD WHAT WOULD THEY TELL THEM BITCHES LOCKED UP IN COPEN-HAGEN? WITH ICE BLOWING AGAINST THE WINDOWS. AND SOME SHIT HAPPEN-ING IN NEW YORK OR CLEVELAND DIDN'T INVOLVE YOU? YOU DIDN'T KNOW??? WHAT??? and come back to Atomic Bomb shit.

"You shure yo' shit strong enough, my man??"

Ornette in a hindu Edwardian sack of jewish bass stealers.

But it is in an age of The Miracles. Which must be put to work for us. All our energy. Even the brothers must finally be used for the lot. To raise u. To fly us all into the grace we seek. Which is, without light what they mean then by, Power. Amen.

The night I want to talk about they had gone to this girl's house I know. (She was sort of an unofficial city limit hostess in them parts. And she had a sickness then, covered people, turn them into different parts of a whole. You want I should characterize that whole? You want I shd patch my wings or retreat to the cellar to brood? I was spread so clean and cool tight got mucho everything-o actually, everybody had some of the shit inem. People stood around. Music was playing. Slick thin insect pee pees were uncovered. Screens full of air. And the aspirations of all the neighbors, in that particular part of the earth, they had rent to pay, get up next day for hip jobs, meet head on with the white unicorn unfortunately being ignorant and blowing bugles on top of the baptist churches (UNCONSCIOUSLY, MOTHERFUCKER, ALRIGHT!!!???) to warn Cary Grant's boys that eastboots were about to slay them.

Is this the scene yr *avant-garde* shit degravitates? Inhabitates?? Jawohl, marches out the plank splashes into the little rich lady section of universal attention. A vibration in the yellow pages. Pussy for sale!

Aww crisscross shit. Crisscross shiiiiiit, yeh. Reall crisscross shit. People opening and closing doors. Telephones. Creep business being done. Yeh. Singing chicks. Chick wd stand there like some mediocre white lady with one-strap gown and janis paige button and lion eatin her ass, really swingingk.)

The husband was calling for the muslim woman. She was devout and weird to the poorer americans. "ALLAH WAS VERY HIP." That's a photomontage of success. "Yesh I was righteous before Bud or Elijah." Meanwhile, there is a trumpet player fuggingkher. He's hip. He's a spiritual beingk. He's spooky. He knows about ghoses. He's a strongbean like John Carradine of duh good guise. He's fuggingkher, riley, really. You goddamn catholic pay attention to the meter!

"You mean. . . . What . . . naw . . . really no kidding. Really?"

Yeh it's the tall brother . . . yeh, goes in the room with the broad, then she gets a call from whatsaname, the hostess, that this muslim dude is comin. Like her husbain. Yeh.

Was he playing earlier that evening . . . tall brother? (Nobody here to ask, children playing in the streets. Gentle movement of the earth.) But anyway around that same time he walked water legends with his sound and grew into something he'd never be except in that thrust of his own invisible energy.

Chick hears this and panics. Everybody in the joint did. Hostess. Lil brother. Lil bro's woman, who's really pinhead priest's chick, stopped making it with funkybutt the organist for a minute, took up with higher math cats. Maybe bealbelly the mystic ex-photographer saxophone player who has speakers inserted in the stones. They blah. They blah. They blah.

Cat comes in finally, the muslim. Tall brother splits to the bedroom lays on the bed under the cover, stiff as wood pole. (Remember I described him befoe??) Hostess pins him almost faints. Muslim chick, Opuretwat the black beauty, pulls it all off, except for a second she fades into the bedroom for a suck off a burning joint. Frozen for a second, in tableau,

the shit is run successfully

muslim chick and her husband

leave

another frozen moment (EXCEPT THE RUSH OF ALL THINGS IS THE RUSH OF ALL THINGS AND ON IS STILL EVER WAS AND IS NOW OMMMMMMMMMMMMMMMMMMMMMMMMMMMMMMM THE ENDLESS)

Then everybody unfreezes and a loud cackle of success in America rises up from this not really humble abode. Lil brother is happy, and puts on his newest record. Hostess titters walks around touching her guests on the arm. Tall brother finally comes out of the bedroom sez, "Shit, that cat cdn't seen me anyway, even if he'd come in there. I was really a ghost."

Exactly before the laughter

9. Art Blakey. Photograph by W. Patrick Hinely, ©.

Answers in Progress

Can you die in airraid jiggle
torn arms flung through candystores
Touch the edge of answer. The waves of nausea
as change sweeps the frame of breath and meat.

"Stick a knife through his throat,"
he slid
in the blood
got up running toward
the blind newsdealer. He screamed
about "Cassius Clay," and slain there in the
street, the whipped figure of jesus, head opened
eyes flailing against his nose. They beat him to
pulpy answers. We wrote Muhammad Ali across his
face and chest, like a newspaper of bleeding meat.

The next day the spaceships landed. Art Blakey records was what they were looking for. We gave them Buttercorn Lady and they threw it back at us. They wanted to know what happened to The Jazz Messengers. And right in the middle, playing the Sun Ra tape, the blanks staggered out of the department store. Omar had missed finishing the job, and they staggered out, falling in the snow, red all over the face chest, the stab wounds in one in the top of a Adam hat.

The space men thought that's what was really happening. One beeped (Ali mentioned this in the newspapers) that this was evolution. Could we dig it? Shit, yeh. We were laughing. Some blanks rounded one corner, Yaa and Dodua were behind them, to take them to the Center. Nationalized on the spot.

The space men could dig everything. They wanted to take one of us to a spot and lay for a minute, to dig what they were in to. Their culture and shit. Whistles Newark was broke up in one section. The dead mayor and other wops carried by in black trucks. Wingo, Rodney and them waving at us. They stopped the first truck and Cyril wanted to know about them thin cats hopping around us. He's always very fast finger.

Space men wanted to know what happened after Blakey. They'd watched but couldn't get close enough to dig exactly what was happening. Albert Ayler they dug immediately from Russell's mouth imitation. That's later. Red spam cans in their throats with the voices, and one of them started to scat. It wigged me. Bamberger's burning down, dead blancos all over and a cat from Sigma Veda, and his brothers, hopping up and down asking us what was happening.

We left Rachel and Lefty there to keep explaining. Me and Pinball had to go back to headquarters, and report Market Street Broad Street rundown. But we told them we'd talk to them. I swear one of those cats had a hip walk. Even thought they was hoppin and bopadoppin up and down, like they had to pee. Still this one cat had a stiff tentacle, when he walked. Yeh; long blue winggly cats, with soft liquid sounds out of their throats for voices. Like, "You know where Art Blakey, Buhainia, is working?" We fell out.

* * *

Walk through life
beautiful more than anything
stand in the sunlight
walk through life
love all the things
that make you strong, be lovers, be anything
for all the people of
earth.

You have brothers
you love each other, change up
and look at the world
now, it's
ours, take it slow
we've long time, a long way
to go,

we have
each other, and the

world,
dont be sorry
walk on out through sunlight life, and know
we're on the go
for love
to open
our lives
to walk
tasting the sunshine
of life.

    Boulevards played songs like that and we rounded up blanks where we had to. Space men were on the south side laying in some of the open houses. Some brothers came in from the west, Chicago, they had a bad thing going out there. Fires were still high as the buildings, but Ram sent a couple of them out to us, to dig what was happening. One of them we sent to the blue cats, to take that message, back. Could W dig what was happening with them? We sent our own evaluation back, and when I finished the report me and Pinball started weaving through the dead cars and furniture. Waving at the brothers, listening to the sounds, we had piped through the streets.
    Smokey Robinson was on now. But straight up fast and winging. No more unrequited love. Damn Smokey got his thing together too. No more tracks or mirages. Just the beauty of the whole. I hope they play Sun Ra for them blue cats, so they can dig where we at.
    Magic City played later. By time we got to the courthouse. The whole top of that was out. Like you could look inside from fourth or fifth floor of the Hall of Records. Cats were all over that joint. Ogun wanted the records intact.
    Past the playgrounds and all them blanks in the cold standing out there or laying on the ground crying. The rich ones really were funny. This ol cat me an Pinball recognized still had a fag thing going for him. In a fur coat, he was some kind of magistrate. Bobby and Moosie were questioning him about some silver he was supposed to have stashed. He was a silver freak. The dude was actually weeping. Crying big sobs; the women crowded away from him. I guess they really couldn't feel sorry for him because he was crying about money.

By the time we got to Weequahic Avenue where the space men and out-of-town brothers were laying I was tired as a dog. We went in there and wanted to smoke some bush, but these blue dudes had something better. Taste like carrots. It was a cool that took you. You thought something was mildly amusing and everything seemed interesting.

I talked with Pinball and the blue leader about Ben Caldwell's paintings ... the one where the guy is smoking the reefer. We thought about the changing reference, of our new world. As it stood already in the old ruins. And we all felt like Bird. The old altosaxophonist ... but the limits opened out into the pure lyric tone of powerful beings. But when the Sun Ra tape came on this blue dude really opened up. He dug the hell out of it. Perfect harmony these cats had too. Booooooo-Iiiiiiiiioooooooooooooo ... daaaaa ahhhhhhh aaaaahhhhhh ... booooo oooooooooooooo ooooooooooaaaaaaaaoooaaaaa

Claude McKay I started quoting. Four o'clock in the morning to a blue dude gettin cooled out on carrots. We didn't have no duty until ten o'clock the next day, and me and Lorenzo and Ish had to question a bunch of prisoners and stuff for the TV news. Chazee had a play to put on that next afternoon about the Chicago stuff. Ray talked to him. And the name of the play was Big Fat Fire.

Man I was tired. We had taped the Sigma. They were already infested with Buddhas there, and we spoke very quietly about how we knew it was our turn. I had burned my hand somewhere and this blue cat looked at it hard and cooled it out. White came in with the design for a flag he'd been working on. Black heads, black hearts, and blue fiery space in the background. Love was heavy in the atmosphere. Ball wanted to know what the blue chicks looked like. But I didn't. Cause I knew after tomorrow's duty, I had a day off, and I knew somebody waitin for me at my house, and some kids, and some fried fish, and those carrots, and wow.

That's the way the fifth day ended.

—AMIRI BARAKA

String of Pearls

Lester Young! why are you playing that clarinet
you know you are Horn in my head? the middle page is
missing god damn it now how will I ever understand Nature
And New Painting? doo doot doo Where is Dick Gallup
his room is horrible it has books in it and paint peeling
a 1934 icebox living on the fifth floor it's
ridiculous

        yes and it's ridiculous to be sitting here
in New York City 28 years old wife sleeping and
Lester playing the wrong sound in 1936 in Kansas City (of
all places) sounding like Benny Goodman (of all people) but
a good sound, not a surprise, a voice, & where was Billie, he
hadn't met her yet, I guess Gallup wasn't born yet neither was
my wife Just me & that icebox I hadn't read HORN by John
Clellon Holmes yet, either

What is rhythm I wonder? Which was George & which Ira
    Gershwin? Why
don't I do more? wanting only to be walking in the New
    York Autumn
warm from coffee I still can feel gurgling under my ribs
climbing the steps of the only major statement in New York City
(Louis Sullivan) thinking the poem I am going to write seeing
the fountains come on wishing I were he

Will the Circle Be Unbroken?

At the edge of the spiral of musicians Probe sat cross-legged on a blue cloth, his soprano sax resting against his inner knee, his afro-horn linking his ankles like a bridge. The afro-horn was the newest axe to cut the deadwood of the world. But Probe, since his return from exile, had chosen only special times to reveal the new sound. There were more rumors about it than there were ears and souls that had heard the horn speak. Probe's dark full head tilted toward the vibrations of the music as if the ring of sound from the six wailing pieces was tightening, creating a spiraling circle.

The black audience, unaware at first of its collectiveness, had begun to move in a soundless rhythm as if it were the tiny twitchings of an embryo. The waiters in the club fell against the wall, shadows, dark pillars holding up the building and letting the free air purify the mind of the club.

The drums took an oblique. Magwa's hands, like the forked tongue of a dark snake, probed the skins, probed the whole belly of the coming circle. Beginning to close the circle, Haig's alto arc, rapid piano incisions, Billy's thin green flute arcs and tangents, Stace's examinations of his own trumpet discoveries, all fell separately, yet together, into a blanket which Mojohn had begun weaving on bass when the set began. The audience breathed, and Probe moved into the inner ranges of the sax.

Outside the Sound Barrier Club three white people were opening the door. Jan, tenor sax case in his hand, had his game all planned. He had blown with Probe six years ago on the West Coast. He did not believe that there was anything to this new philosophy the musicians were talking about. He would talk to Probe personally. He had known many Negro musicians and theirs was no different from any other artist's struggles to be himself, including his own.

Things were happening so fast that there was no one who knew all directions at once. He did not mind Ron and Tasha coming along. They were two of the hippest ofays in town, and if anybody could break the circle of the Sound Club, it would be friends and old friends of friends.

Ron was bearded and scholarly. Thickset, shabbily dressed, but clean. He had tried to visit the Club before. But all of his attempts had been futile. He almost carried the result of one attempt to court. He could not understand why the cats would want to bury themselves in Harlem and close the doors to the outside world. Ron's articles and reviews had helped many black musicians, but of all of them, Probe Adams had benefited the most. Since his graduation from Yale, Ron had knocked around the music world; once he thought he wanted to sing blues. He had tried, but that was in college. The best compliment he ever got was from Mississippi John or Muddy Waters, one of the two, during a civil rights rally in Alabama. He had spontaneously leaped up during the rally and played from his soul. Muddy was in the audience, and later told Ron: "Boy, you keep that up, you gwine put me back on the plantation."

Ron was not fully satisfied that he had found the depth of the black man's psyche. In his book he had said this. Yet he knew that if he believed strongly enough, some of the old cats would break down. His sincerity was written all over his face. Holding Tasha's hand, he saw the door opening. . . .

Tasha was a shapely blonde who had dyed her hair black. It now matched her eyes. She was a Vassar girl and had once begun a biography of Oliver Fullerton. Excerpts had been published in *Down Beat* and she became noted as a critic and authority on the Fullerton movement. Fullerton's development as an important jazz trombonist had been interrupted soon after Tasha's article. No one knew why. Sometimes Tasha was afraid to think about it. If they had married, she knew that Oliver would have been able to continue making it. But he had gotten strung out on H. Sometimes she believed her friends who said Oliver was psychopathic. At least when he stopped beating her, she forgave him. And she did not believe it when he was really hooked. She still loved him. It was her own love, protected deep inside her, encased, her little black secret and her passport to the inner world that Oliver had died trying to enter. It would be only a matter of time. She would translate love into an honest appraisal of black music.

"I am sorry," the tall brown doorman said. "Sessions for Brothers and Sisters only."

"What's the matter, baby?" Jan leaned his head in and looked around as if wondering what the man was talking about.

"I said . . ."

"Man, if you can't recognize a Brother, you better let me have your job." He held up his case. "We're friends of Probe."

The man called for assistance. Quickly two men stepped out of the shadows. "What's the trouble, Brother?"

"These people say they're friends of the Probe."

"What people?" asked one of the men. He was neatly dressed, a clean shaven head, with large darting eyes. He looked past the three newcomers. There was a silence.

Finally, as if it were some supreme effort, he looked at the three. "I'm sorry, but for your own safety we cannot allow you."

"Man, what you talkin bout?" asked Jan, smiling quizzically. "Are you blockin Brothers now? I told him I am blood. We friends of the Probe."

The three men at the door went into a huddle. Carl, the doorman, was skeptical, but he had seen some bloods that were pretty light. He looked at this cat again, and as Kent and Rafael were debating whether or not to go get Probe's wife in the audience, he decided against the whole thing. He left the huddle and returned with a sign which said: "We cannot allow non-Brothers because of the danger involved with extensions."

Jan looked at the sign, and a smile crept across his face. In the street a cop was passing and leaned in. Carl motioned the cop in. He wanted a witness to this. He knew what might happen but he had never seen it.

Jan shook his head at the sign, turning to Ron and Tasha. He was about to explain that he had seen the same sign on the West Coast. It was incredible that all the spades believed this thing about the lethal vibrations from the new sound.

Carl was shoving the sign in their faces as the cop, a big, pimpled Irishman, moved through the group. "All right, break it up, break it up. You got people outside want to come in . . ."

Kent and Rafael, seeing Carl's decision and the potential belligerence of the whites, folded their hands, buddha-like. Carl stood with his back to the door now.

"Listen, officer if these people go in, the responsibility is yours."

The Irish cop, not knowing whether he should get angry over what he figured was reverse discrimination, smirked and made a path for the three. He would not go far inside because he didn't think the sounds were worth listening to. If it wasn't Harlem he could see why these people would want to go in, but he had never seen anything worthwhile from niggers in Harlem.

"Don't worry. You got a license, don't you?"

"Let them go through," said Rafael suddenly. A peace seemed to gather over the faces of the three club members now. They folded their arms and went into the dark cavern which led to the music. In front of them walked the invaders. "See," said Jan, "if you press these cats, they'll cop out." They moved toward the music in an alien silence.

Probe was deep into a rear-action sax monologue. The whole circle now, like a bracelet of many colored lights, gyrated under Probe's wisdom. Probe was a thoughtful, full-headed black man with narrow eyes and a large nose. His lips swelled over the reed and each note fell into the circle like an acrobat on a tight rope stretched radially across the center of the universe.

He heard the whistle of the wind. Three ghosts, like chaff blown from a wasteland, clung to the wall. . . . He tightened the circle. Movement began from within it, shaking without breaking balance. He had to prepare the womb for the afro-horn. Its vibrations were beyond his mental frequencies unless he got deeper into motives. He sent out his call for motives. . . .

The blanket of the bass rippled and the fierce wind in all their minds blew the blanket back, and there sat the city of Samson. The white pillars imposing . . . but how easy it is to tear the building down with motives. Here they come. Probe, healed of his blindness, born anew of spirit, sealed his reed with pure air. *He moved to the edge of the circle, rested his sax, and lifted his axe.* . . .

There are only three afro-horns in the world. They were forged from a rare metal found only in Africa and South America. No one knows who forged the horns, but the general opinion among musicologists is that it was the Egyptians. One European museum guards an afro-horn. The other is supposed to be somewhere on the West Coast of Mexico, among a tribe of Indians. Probe grew into his from a black peddler who claimed to have traveled a thousand miles just to give it to his son. From that day on, Probe's sax handled like a child, a child waiting for itself to grow out of itself.

Inside the center of the gyrations is an atom stripped of time, black. The gathering of the hunters, deeper. Coming, laced in the energy of the sun. He is blowing. Magwa's hands. Reverence of skin. Under the single voices is the child of a woman, black. They are building back the wall, crumbling under the disturbance.

In the rear of the room, Jan did not hear the volt, nor did he see the mystery behind Probe's first statement on the afro-horn. He had closed his eyes, trying to capture or elude the panthers of the music, but he had no eyes. He did not feel Ron slump against him. Strands of Tasha's hair were matted on a button of Ron's jacket, but she did not move when he slumped. Something was hitting them like waves, like shock waves. . . .

Before his mind went black, Jan recalled the feeling when his father had beat him for playing "with a nigger!" and later he allowed the feeling to merge with his dislike of white people. When he fell, his case hit the floor and opened, revealing a shiny tenor saxophone that gleamed and vibrated in the freedom of freedom.

Ron's sleep had been quick, like the rush of post-hypnotic suggestions. He dropped her hand, slumped, felt the wall give (no, it was the air), and he fell face forward across a table, his heart silent in respect for truer vibrations.

The musicians stood. The horn and Probe drew up the shadows now from the audience. A child climbed upon the chords of sound, growing out of the circle of the womb, searching with fingers and then with motive, and as the volume of the music increased—penetrating the thick callousness of the Irishman twirling his stick outside of black flesh—the musicians walked off, one by one, linked to Probe's respectful nod at each and his quiet pronouncement of their names. He mopped his face with a blue cloth.

"What's the matter here?"

"Step aside, folks!"

"These people are unconscious!"

"Look at their faces!"

"They're dead."

"Dead?"

"What happened?"

"Dead?"

"It's true then. It's true . . ."

—Henry Dumas

Foo to the Infinite

"Play vanilla," Lester Young is said
to have said to a piano player
comping too elaborately behind his solo . . .
but I like your noise
in here with my own,
but how much? How much
anything in here with my
own? How is that true? My "own"
is only the hue of ruddy purple
on the otherwise black
massed segments of a fly's eye—
which may be more
sun accompaniment than
what I generate. What do I generate?
A swath through front walk snow,
at least a place for me to walk, and
you too, if you come out
before the god of snow,
neither hostile nor loving,
dumps again. A place for your feet,
a kind of box to walk in,
a kind of end that goes on
50 feet before turning to lice—
I propped an l against ice,
so as to not come to conclusion here,
Ira Clayton Eshleman,
but the play has started up, I mean
the play called Foo To The Infinite—
until now, I realize, I had been offstage
glittering with the thought of thinking I was on.
That was because the other side could not be seen.

10. LESTER YOUNG. PHOTOGRAPH BY WILLIAM P. GOTTLIEB, ©.

But now it is happening, and the audience
—I think there is one out there—has brought its lunch
—yes, there he is—my father
eating the skeleton of a hamburger
motions "You want some too?"
Play vanilla, I say to him, and he to me: "play dead."

1977

Bud Powell, 1925-1966

The notice, dead at 41, Kings County Hospital, reached me at 20 when, for 3 years I attempted to play jazz. I'd studied piano 12 years, learned exercises, rigid, couldn't swing & wanted to make a manhood, make my own 21 years. I always thought he was older, perhaps 40 and was astonished in Los Angeles later to learn he was 17 or 18 in the first Norman Granz cuts, when I first heard him. He was the first man I heard swing.

It was very awkward at times, especially in the sides where he used no rhythm & in the *Moods*, in *Hallelujah*, seemed to start over & over again, losing time, screwing up the beat, a mess of a recording session for me who thought all jazz was perfect. That is, jazz swung man; I wanted to swing and could never make time, let go, feel into the rhythm of another, say a bassman or horn. I held to the metronome of my 20 years Northside Indianapolis home, which is to say not just white and middle-class, but the idea of whiteness, the lack of any values of the body, without vibration or motility, not jazz.

It is amazing to me how much of him came through to me then, and after a year of off & on listening to 5 longplay albums (I remember *My Devotion* seemed to me the best) I tried for a whole semester in a Poetry Writing Class to write an Ode to Bud Powell to take care of a two-week assignment (the poem to be twice as long as a weekly assignment). Professor Yellen hoped something would happen—the sheets turned out to be Wasteland imitation worksheets with all sorts of veiled references to the Black Orchid, a colored Indiana Avenue Bar in Indianapolis where occasionally in late teens we, with dates, would go to hear jazz rock &

roll—not bad—but not Powell. Tho he was there as I sense it then, that is, he was why, beyond black or white, I went there, for there was where the jazz was & that is what turned me on, tho what I got was ass or not-ass. But how much can one expect, given the circumstances?

Bud Powell important, and beautiful, to jazz in somewhat the same way Soutine is central to art, Crane (Hart) to poetry: wild flowing spirit, a fire-thief, possessed, beyond questionable technique; that his left hand was discordant, off, a kind of paw chomping, no matter—both hands *were* for someone who had heard Powell. He fucked his mother when he played, his sisters, his brothers and he fucked me, all the way up thru my anus thru my eyes; how can you not praise & praise a person who began to unthaw you, to restore some of what you know is your humanity, a teacher in the truest sense, a motherfucker.

Bud Powell was snapped beyond the contraries I was prey to so as to not be able to make jazz. He paid, probably since he was born, and without respite, in a way that no matter what happens to me I never will. A man does not swing who has not suffered, but to suffer is not to swing. I mean Powell knew joy, he was off into Niagaras & brooks of intuitive visions to which the left hand, like a cripple circumambulating a stupa, when it was needed, shoveled in earth.

4 August 1966

—CLAYTON ESHLEMAN

Newark

John Coltrane died this morning, LeRoi's in jail.

Whatever you say of the daytime
it gives you a taste
for the obvious

the places where
night is
filled with a different wisdom

but on deck, both feet firm
in the sunshine
Coltrane died this morning
& had nothing to say about this
       But at star-rise (she said)

the rifles
firing into the sky behind the movie house
shooting up the airport
24 (to pick a number
out of the air) dead in Newark,
      Coltrane dead & all

our flights cancelled
out of the air
   but Roi, where is the night, where is the dark
brooding hot snake-mother gives us birth
where no sun comes to distinguish our skins?
        at star-rise
(she said) we shot together,
light of Unukalhai, Snake-Neck,

light of the seven weepers
                        weeping bullshit
                        all over the Jersey lawns

(no rain . suspension of thick sweet New York air,
where had he been, where did he get the .38s
anyhow?
            Do you propose to shoot me down? up?
at star-fall (she said) the smog so thick.
can't tell one mother from another, what
.38s?
            she said at star-fall the light began,
people moved out of their houses, the man died,
                                    a man is his meat

no meat in the night
if we get to the night together
we'll be somewhere
                        (action from star-rise,
cool it, the troops pulled out,
a work accomplished
some black men dead, a poet in jail,

check the famous empty
dawn rising over the meadows
                        (she said "I'm sorry I was ever
for them, I say take out machine guns & shoot them down")

cool dawn   .   cool
                        cell they work somebody over in
(she said he asked for it) (did you see any guns?)

                                    Trane
rode out on a bad rime, bad shit
they shoot us to live on
                    The words
break down,
                    he made it
say itself inside our heads.

19

(CLIO — KHU)

In my Biṅu shrine, the sogo altars pull me home.
The stone I lay upon on Teo found itself
in a dance of stones,
four sisters turning near a brown pond,
each a promise of the sea within me.
For years now, Bamako has been dry.
Millstones,
        which held Nommo's
              and the rain gods' gifts,
fade into the bilious doors.
Nevertheless,
the bilu still whisper in spirit ears,
and my father seeds my spirit
           with the first fruits of autumn,
pots that address the dead in me.
Yet I know myself an "intangible ethereal casing,"
lucent intelligence,
heavenbound by being bound to the emblems
                of my person.
Clio call me,
scroll of the brave,
with one foot in the bush,
        one foot in the city,
a human tongue fit for taunting
the pretensions of pure love,
and an ear for the wind sound of a woman
riding a seashell into this desert desolation.
Though I have second sight,
my creations wither and die.
The balance I found easy escapes from my gardens.

I continue to weave my checkerboard,
cloth of the Word,
healing music of the head,
my soul's improvisation.
(*Art Tatum*)

When I sit at the piano,
I don't count the keys.
I see you looking at my eyes;
you wonder what I see.
What I see is in my touch,
and in the assurance
that the sound will be right there.
Some cats always carp.
They say the music isn't mine,
keep asking me for "an original."
So I lay two notes in the bar ahead,
diminish a major,
tunnel through the dark
of the brightest minor,
and come out on the right side of the song.
I pick the composer's pocket,
and lay the hidden jewels out there.
This wired, hammering woman
wants her fortune told.
Hammer and anvil guide the music of my house,
smithy of the ear's anticipation, forge
of the mind in what it denies
                and what it fulfills.
On the terrace,
altars resonate with the water sound
of goatskin over hollow wood,
and the frog pitch of the mudbanks
within the house
                answer.
I dream of the smith music within me,
and hear its cithara voice in the dyēli's craft.

The End of an Ethnic Dream

Cigarettes in my mouth
to puncture blisters in my brain.
My bass a fine piece of furniture.
My fingers soft, too soft to rattle
rafters in second-rate halls.
The harmonies I could never learn
stick in Ayler's screams.
An African chant chokes us. My image shot.

If you look off over the Hudson,
the dark cooperatives spit at the dinghies
floating up the night.

      A young boy pisses
on lovers rolling against each other
under a trackless el.

   This could have been my town,
with light strings that could stand a tempo.

     Now,
     it's the end
     of an ethnic dream.

I've grown intellectual,
go on accumulating furniture and books,
damning literature, writing "for myself,"
calculating the possibilities that someone
will love me, or sleep with me.
Eighteen-year-old girls come back from the Southern
leers and make me cry.

     Here, there are
     coffee shops, bars,

natural tonsorial parlors,
plays, streets,
pamphlets, days, sun,
heat, love, anger,
politics, days, and sun.

Here, we shoot off
every day to new horizons,
coffee shops, bars,
natural tonsorial parlors,
plays, streets,
pamphlets, days, sun,
heat, love, anger,
politics, days, and sun.

It is the end of an ethnic dream.
My bass is a fine piece of furniture.
My brain blistered.

—Jay Wright

Rose Solitude

for Duke Ellington

I am essence of Rose Solitude
my cheeks are laced with cognac
my hips sealed with five satin nails
i carry dreams and romance of new fools and old
flames
between the musk of fat
and the side pocket of my mink tongue

Listen to champagne bubble from this solo

Essence of Rose Solitude
veteran from texas   tiger from chicago   that's me
i cover the shrine of Duke
who like Satchmo   like Nat (King) Cole
will never die because love they say
never dies

I tell you from stair steps of these navy blue nights
these metallic snakes
these flashing fish skins
and the melodious cry of Shango
surrounded by sorrow
by purple velvet tears
by cockhounds limping from crosses
from turtle skin shoes
from diamond shaped skulls and canes
made from dead gazelles
wearing a face of wilting potato plants

11. Duke Ellington. Photograph by William P. Gottlieb, © 1979.

of grey and black scissors
of bee bee shots and fifty red boils
yes the whole world loved him

I tell you from suspenders of two-timing dog odors
from inca frosted lips
nonchalant legs
i tell you from howling chant of sister Erzulie
and the exaggerated hearts of a hundred pretty
women
they loved him
this world sliding from a single flower
into a caravan of heads made into ten thousand
flowers

Ask me
Essence of Rose Solitude
chickadee from arkansas that's me
i sleep on cotton bones
cotton tails
and mellow myself in empty ballrooms
i'm no fly by night
look at my resume
i walk through the eyes of staring lizards
i throw my neck back to floorshow on bumping goat
skins
in front of my stage fright
i cover the hands of Duke who like Satchmo
like Nat (King) Cole will never die
because love they say
never dies

Solo Finger Solo

When evening goes down into its jelly jelly jelly
into drain pipe cuts and stitches and vaccinations
protruding from arms

And spirit of the five by five man pushes
his sweet potatoes in the air
feather daddy leaps into a falcon of tropical bird squats
rubber legs swing into offbeat onijos onijos
then into your solo finger solo
the blues chantress jumps up and
repeats her nasal volcanic chant calling

Count Basie   Count Basie   Count Basie

And Count Basie
you burn through this timbale of gooseflesh rhythms
a drop of iodine on your starfish lips
the intonation of your kiss of melodica trilling
into a labyrinth of one o'clock jumps
into corpuscle flashes of the blues torpedo
the erupting volcano of the blues shouters chanting your name

Count Basie   Count Basie   take em to Chicago Count Basie

And Count Basie
you punctuate this strong bourbon mist of gamma globulin breath
a mixture of chords like serpentariums coiling
from the deep everglades of your body
and when the luscious screams of three headed root doctors split
Kansas City reeds in unison with this triple tapping
double stopping   slow grinding   loosey butt night swinging
with the blues chantress
erupting volcano of the blues torpedoes chanting your name

Count Basie
you reach through the bottom of the music
way down beneath cross rhythm vamps
below air stream of the lowest octave
into depths of a sacred drum
and Count Basie   Count Basie   Count Basie
how powerful and dignified and exquisite and direct and sharp
your solo finger solo is

I See Chano Pozo

A very fine conga of sweat
a very fine stomp of the right foot
a very fine platform of sticks
a very fine tube of frictional groans
a very fine can of belligerent growls
a very fine hoop of cubano yells
very fine   very fine

Is there anyone finer today   ole   okay
Oye   I say
I see Chano Pozo
Chano Pozo from Havana Cuba
                          You're the one
You're the one who made Atamo into
a tattooed motivator of revolutionary spirits

You're the one who made Mpebi into
an activated slasher of lies

You're the one who made Donno into
an armpit of inflammable explosives

You're the one who made Obonu into
a circle of signifying snakes

You're the one who made Atumpan's head strike
against
the head of a bird   everynight   everyday
in your crisscrossing chant
in your cross river mouth
                              You're the one
Oye   I say
Chano
what made you roar like a big brazos flood
what made you yodel like a migrating frog
what made you shake like atomic heat
what made you jell into a ritual pose
Chano   Chano   Chano
what made your technology of thumps so new so
mean
I say
is there anyone meaner than Chano Pozo
                              from Havana Cuba

Oye
I'm in the presence of ancestor
                              Chano Pozo
Chano connector of two worlds
You go and celebrate again with
the *compañeros* in Santiago
      and tell us about it
You go to the spirit house of Antonio Maceo
and tell us about it
You go to Angola
and tell us about it
You go to Calabar
and tell us about it
You go see the slave castles
you go see the massacres
you go see the afflictions
you go see the battlefields
you go see the warriors

you go as a healer
you go conjurate
you go mediate
you go to the cemetery of drums
return and tell us about it

Lucumi   Abakẃa   Lucumi   Abakẃa

Olé   okay
Is there anyone finer today
Oye   I say
did you hear
Mpintintoa smoking in the palm of his hands
did you hear
Ilya Ilu booming through the cup of his clap
did you hear
Ntenga sanding on the rim of his rasp
did you hear
Siky Akkua stuttering like a goat sucking hawk
did you hear
Bata crying in a nago tongue
did you hear
Fontomfrom speaking through the skull of a dog
did you hear it   did you hear it   did you hear it

A very fine tree stump of drones
a very fine shuffle of shrines
a very fine turn of the head
a very fine tissue of skin
a very smack of the lips
a very fine pulse
a very fine *encuentro*
very fine   very fine   very fine
Is there anyone finer than
Chano Pozo from Havana Cuba
Oye   I say
I see Chano Pozo

Tapping

for Baby Laurence, and other tap dancers

When i pat this floor
   with my tap

when i slide on air
   and fill this horn intimate with
the rhythm of my two drums

   when i cross   kick
scissor   locomotive

   take four for nothing
four we're gone

when the solidarity of my yoruba turns
join these vibrato feet
   in a Johnny Hodges lick
a chorus of insistent Charlie Parker riffs

   when i stretch out for a chromatic split
together with my double X
   converging in a quartet of circles

when i dance my spine in a slouch
   slur my lyrics with a heel slide
arch these insteps in free time

   when i drop my knees
when i fold my hands
   when i decorate this atmosphere
with a Lester Young leap and

enclose my hiplike snake repetitions
in a chanting proverb
    of the freeze

I'm gonna spotlite my boogie
    in a Coltrane yelp

echo my push in a Coleman Hawkins whine

i'm gonna frog my hunch in a Duke Ellington strut

quarter stroke my rattle
    like an Albert Ayler cry

i'm gonna accent my march in a Satchmo pitch

    triple my grind in a Ma Rainey blues

i'm gonna steal no steps

    i'm gonna pay my dues

i'm gonna   1   2   3

    and let the people in the apple
go hmmmp   hmmmmp   hmmmmmp

—JAYNE CORTEZ

17:ll:82

Thelonious Monk dies
today my 45th birth
day
years ago
a Seattle dj
told me this story:

    Thelonious was playing here
with the Giants of Jazz group
dodged all requests for interviews
but I got through somehow & found him
in his hotelroom laying down
w/ a pacemaker on his chest
his silence unhinged me
but I kept talking
& after a while
he'd say something
nothing really
a grunt
& I asked him
what it was that he did
I mean
what he thought when he played
some dumb thing like that
like what he thought his music did
Monk didn't answer
he kept looking at a second-hand
circle the electric clockface
on the dresser
then looked at me & said
"I put it down.
You got to pick it up."

18:VI:82

for Art Pepper

Paul's *niemandsrose*
I place in Art's brass bell
alto Selmer on its stand

despite
encyclopedic light
held & shattered
by its curves
the horn's silent

& the rose
white like paper

—DAVID MELTZER

Don't Say Goodbye to the Porkpie Hat

Mingus, Bird, Prez, Langston, and them

Don't say goodbye to the Porkpie Hat that rolled
along on nodded shoulders
> that swang bebop phrases
> in Minton's jelly roll dreams
Don't say goodbye to hip hats tilted in the style of a soulful era;
the Porkpie Hat that Lester dug
swirling in the sound of sax blown suns
> phrase on phrase, repeating bluely
> tripping in and under crashing
> hi-hat cymbals, a fickle girl
> getting sassy on the rhythms.
Musicians heavy with memories
move in and out of this gloom;
the Porkpie Hat reigns supreme
smell of collard greens
and cotton madness
commingled in the nigger elegance of the style.
> The Porkpie Hat sees tonal memories
> of salt peanuts and hot house birds
> the Porkpie Hat sees . . .
Cross riffing square kingdoms, riding midnight Scottsboro
trains. We are haunted by the lynched limbs.
On the road:
It would be some hoodoo town
It would be some cracker place
you might meet redneck lynchers

face to face
but mostly you meet mean horn blowers
running obscene riffs
Jelly Roll spoke of such places:
the man with the mojo hand
the dyke with the .38
the yaller girls
and the knifings.

Stop-time Buddy and Creole Sydney
wailed in here. Stop time.
chorus repeats, stop and shuffle.
stop and stomp.
listen to the horns, ain't they mean?
now   ain't they mean
in blue
in blue
in blue streaks of mellow wisdom
blue notes
coiling around
the Porkpie Hat
and ghosts of dead musicians drifting through
here on riffs that smack
on one-leg trumpet players
and daddy glory piano ticklers
who
twisted arpeggios
with diamond-flashed fingers.
There was Jelly Roll Morton, the sweet mackdaddy,
hollering Waller, and Willie The Lion Smith—
some mean showstoppers.

Ghosts of dead holy rollers ricocheted in the air funky
with white lightnin' and sweat.
Emerald bitches shot shit in a kitchen smelling
of funerals and fried chicken.
Each city had a different sound:

there was Mambo, Rheba, Jeanne;
holy the voice of these righteous sisters.
Shape to shape, horn to horn
the Porkpie Hat resurrected himself
night to night, from note to note
skimming the horizons, flashing bluegreenyellow lights
and blowing black stars
and weird looneymoon changes; chords coiled about him
and he was flying
fast
zipping
past
sound
into cosmic silences.

And yes
and caresses flowed from the voice in the horn in the blue
of the yellow whiskey room where bad hustlers with big
coats moved, digging the fly sister, fingerpopping while
tearing at chicken and waffles.

The Porkpie Hat loomed specter like, a vision for the world;
shiny, the knob toe shoes,
sporting hip camel coats
and righteous pinstripes—
pants pressed razor shape;
and caressing his horn, baby like.

So we pick up our axes and prepare
to blast the white dream;
we pick up our axes
re-create ourselves and the universe,
sounds splintering the deepest regions
of spiritual space
crisp and moaning voices
leaping in the horns of destruction,
blowing death and doom to all who have no use for the spirit.

So we cook out of sight
into cascading motions of joy delight
shooflies the Bird lolligagging
and laughing for days,
and the rhythms way up in there
wailing, sending scarlet rays, luminescent,
spattering bone and lie.
we go on cool lords
wailing on into star nights,
rocking whole worlds, unfurling song on song
into long stretches of green spectral shimmerings,
blasting on, fucking the moon with the blunt edge
of a lover's tune, out there now, joy riffing
for days and do
railriding and do
talking some lovely shit and do
to the Blues God who blesses us.

No, don't say goodbye to the Porkpie Hat—
he lives, oh yes.

Lester lives and leaps
Delancey's dilemma is over
Bird lives
Lady lives
Eric stands next to me
while I finger the Afro-horn
Bird lives
Lady lives
Lester leaps in every night
Tad's delight
is mine now
Dinah knows
Richie knows
that Bud is Buddha
that Jelly Roll dug juju
and Lester lives

in Ornette's leapings
the Blues God lives
we live
live
spirit lives
and sound lives
bluebird lives
lives and leaps
dig the mellow voices
dig the Porkpie Hat
dig the spirit in Sun Ra's sound
dig the cosmic Trane
dig be
dig be
dig be
spirit lives in sound
dig be
sound lives in spirit
dig be
yeah!!!
spirit lives
spirit lives
spirit lives
SPIRIT!!!
SWHEEEEEEEEEEEEEEEETTT!!!

take it again
this time from the top

Harlem Gallery: From the Inside

for Melvin Tolson

The bars on Eighth Avenue in Harlem
glow real yellow, hard against formica
tables. They speak of wandering ghosts
and Harlem saints; the words lay slick
on greasy floors: rain-wet butt in the junkie's
mouth, damp notebook in the number runner's hand.
No heads turn as the deal goes down—we wait.

Harlem rain explodes, flooding the avenues
rats float up out of the sewers.
Do we need the Miracles or a miracle?

Listen baby, to the mean scar-faced sister,
between you and her and me and you there are no
distances, short reach of the .38, a sudden
migraine hammering where your brains used to be;
then it's over, no distance between the needle
and the rope, instant time, my man, history as
one quick fuck.

Uptight against these sounds, but everything ain't
all right, the would-be
warriors of the nitty-gritty snap fingers,
ghosts boogaloo against this haze
Malcolm eyes in the yellow glow;
blood on black hands,
compacted rooms of gloom;
Garvey's flesh in the rat's teeth
Lady Day at 100 Centre Street
Charlie Parker dead in the penthouse
of an aristocratic bitch.

Carlos Cook
Ras
Shine and Langston
the Barefoot Prophet
Ira Kemp
the Signifying Monkey
Bud Powell
Trane
Prez
Chano Pozo
Eloise Moore—all
falling faces in the Harlem rain
asphalt memory of blood and pain.

—Larry Neal

MICHAEL S. HARPER

A Narrative of the Life and Times of John Coltrane: Played by Himself

Hamlet, North Carolina

I don't remember train whistles,
or corroding trestles of ice
seeping from the hangband,
vaulting northward in shining triplets,
but the feel of the reed on my tongue
haunts me even now, my incisors
pulled so the pain wouldn't lurk
on "Cousin Mary;"

In High Point I stared
at the bus which took us to band
practice on Memorial Day;
I could hardly make out, in the mud,
placemarks, separations of skin
sketched in plates above the rear bumper.

Mama asked, "what's the difference
'tween North and South Carolina,"
a cappella notes of our church choir
doping me into arpeggios,
into *sheets of sound* labeling me
into dissonance.

I never liked the photo taken with
Bird, Miles without sunglasses,
me in profile almost out of exposure;

these were my images of movement;
when I hear the sacred songs,
auras of my mother at the stove,
I play the blues:

what good does it do to complain:
one night I was playing with Bostic,
blacking out, coming alive only to melodies
where I could play my parts:
And then, on a train to Philly,
I sang "Naima" locking the door
without exit no matter what song
I sang; with remonstrations of the ceiling
of that same room I practice in
on my back when too tired to stand,
I broke loose from crystalline habits
I thought would bring me that sound.

For Bud

Could it be, Bud
that in slow galvanized
fingers beauty seeped
into *bop* like Bird
weed and Diz clowned—
Sugar waltzing
back into dynamite.
sweetest left hook you
ever dug, baby;
could it violate violence
Bud, like Leadbelly's
chaingang chuckle,

the candied yam
twelve string clutch
of all blues:
there's no rain
anywhere, soft
enough for you.

for Bud Powell

Peace on Earth

Tunes come to me at morning
prayer, after flax sunflower
seeds jammed in a coffee can;

when we went to Japan
I prayed at the shrine
for the war dead broken
at Nagasaki;

the tears on the lip of my soprano
glistened in the sun.

In interviews
I talked about my music's
voice of praise to our oneness,

them getting caught up in techniques
of the electronic school

lifting us into assault;

12. Elvin Jones. Photograph by W. Patrick Hinely, ©.

in live sessions, without an audience
I see faces on the flues of the piano,

cymbals driving me into ecstasies on my knees,

the demonic angel, Elvin,
answering my prayers on African drum,

on *Spiritual*

and on *Reverend King*

we chanted his words
on the mountain, where the golden chalice
came in our darkness.

I pursued the songless sound
of embouchures on Parisian thoroughfares,

the coins spilling across the arched
balustrade against my feet;

no high as intense as possessions
given up in practice

where the scales came to my fingers

without deliverance,
the light always coming at 4 A.M.

Syeeda's "Song Flute" charts
my playing for the ancestors;

how could I do otherwise,

passing so quickly in this galaxy

there is no time for being
to be paid in acknowledgement;
all praise to the phrase brought to me:
salaams of becoming:
A LOVE SUPREME:

Driving the Big Chrysler
across the Country of My Birth

I would wait for the tunnels
to glide into overdrive,
the shanked curves glittering with
truck tires, the last four bars
of Clifford's solo on "'Round Midnight"
somehow embossed on my memo stand.

Coming up the hill from Harrisburg,
I heard Elvin's magical voice
on the tines of a bus going to Lexington;
McCoy my *spiritual anchor*—
his tonics bristling in solemn
gyrations of the left hand.

At a bus terminal waiting to be taken
to the cemetery, I thought of Lester
Young's Chinese face on a Christmas
card mailed to my house in Queens: Prez!
I saw him cry in joy as the recordings
Bird memorized in Missouri breaks
floated on Bessie's floodless hill:
Backwater Blues; I could never play
such sweetness again: Lady said Prez
was the closest she ever got to real
escort, him worrying who was behind
him in arcades memorizing his tunes.

Driving into this Wyoming sunset,
rehearsing my perfect foursome,
ordering our lives on off-days,
it's reported I'd gone out like Bird
recovering at Camarillo,
in an offstage concert in L.A.

I never hear playbacks of that chorus
of plaints, Dolphy's love-filled echoings,
perhaps my mother's hands
calling me to breakfast, the Heath
Brothers, in triplicate, asking me to stand
in; when Miles smacked me for being *smacked*
out on "Woodn't You," I thought how many
tunes I'd forgotten in my suspension
on the pentatonic scale; my solos
shortened, when I joined Monk he drilled
black keys into registers of pain, joy
rekindled in McCoy's solo of "The Promise."

What does Detroit have to give my music
as elk-miles distance into shoal-lights,
dashes at sunrise over Oakland:
Elvin from Pontiac, McCoy from Philly,
Chambers from Detroit waltzing his bass.
I can never write a bar of this music
in this life chanting toward paradise
in this sunship from Motown.

—MICHAEL S. HARPER

13. Chet Baker. Photograph by W. Patrick Hinely, ©.

Finding a Chet Baker Album in the Dimestore 2-for-$1 Pile

I
His face not much older than mine
in the class of '56 photo

when I gave in
borrowed my buddy's tie

split the back of his one-button roll
& said "Aw righty, jack,

take your picture, I'm beautiful."
Never bought a yearbook.

So finding him
in this stack of losers, flush

against a JFK memorium
& a *Cleopatra* soundtrack,

looking innocent of smack—
young-man-with-a-horn hair,

blue eyes wiped blank
like the "most creative" boy's

whose photo doesn't show he hides
fuckbooks under a railroad bridge

& jacks off like crazy, never going home,
as freight-cars couple overhead

blackening his clench-eyed scream
of pre-poetry—

finding his blurred face, called
Polkadots and Moonbeams,

is a shock of looking back
into a mirror of lips that moaned

to suck on big strong poems
and blow the long

tough sweet tone
of that genius horn.

II
I was just too young,
17, to *do* it, to flee

across the Bay to beat cellars
where the wine, weed, jazz & poetry

were free! & too dumb & scared,
couldn't even grow a beard.

Years pass. Alone
as Adam: no choice

but get cool on my own:
chose, finally, women

& words: folksingers with long
brown hair, strong

on racial justice,
dialogue, meaningful relationships

(I always had to piss—
snuck 6-packs into the coffeehouse).

III
Years pass, delusions
of happiness, bliss,

as the Nation awoke
to suicide slowly, because

there was always *we*
& the bed would rush like Mingus

flow like Adderley
& curl & drift away

like the last lost breath
of Miss Anita O'Day, and she

would hold me preciously
until I couldn't hear

the bombs or smell the flesh
& words returned like high white geese

their honking falling lightly
a pure snow of sound

around our bed, around
my head, and

I thought it would never end.
But she found out, inevitably,

that it was true
what Grandma told me

what my father confirmed
& mother declined to deny,

that I was the Devil's child
cursed with a wild need

to find him, my real Pap,
the Devil—and to see a sign,

any clue, I'd rip
my bones apart & drink my brain.

Yes, she knew it was true:
I was crazy. So, so long, poet.

IV
But now, fuck it, I'd do it—
Go be a beatnik!

"Big Daddy Dave"
twining my lines

up the stems of his music
while graybeard angels

& devils nod in the smoke,
eyes shut forever, murmuring

cool   cool   cool   heavenly
as if junk & Europe

never happened to him
nor her America to me.

—DAVID HILTON

LAWSON FUSAO INADA

Filling the Gap

When Bird died, I didn't mind:
I had things to do—

polish some shoes, practice
a high school cha-cha-cha.

I didn't even know
Clifford was dead:

I must have been
lobbing an oblong ball
beside the gymnasium.

I saw the Lady
right before she died—

dried, brittle
as last year's gardenia.

I let her scratch an autograph.

But not Prez.

Too bugged to boo, I left
as Basie's brass
booted him off the stand
in a sick reunion—

tottering, saxophone
dragging him like a stage-hook.

When I read Dr. Williams'
poem, "Stormy,"
I wrote a letter of love and praise

and didn't mail it.

After he died, it burned my desk
like a delinquent prescription . . .

I don't like to mourn the dead:
what didn't, never will.

And I sometimes feel foolish
staying up late,
trying to squeeze some life
out of books and records,
filling the gaps
between words and notes.

That is why
I rush into our room to find you
mumbling and moaning
in your incoherent performance.

That is why
I rub and squeeze you
and love to hear your
live, alterable cry against my breast.

Blue Gene

Put another nickel in
Gene Ammons, down
at his heels, in the bottom
of his day. See him sway,
the juice come
sluicing out from
last year's lean, flux
of flab and splintered reeds.

Blow it, Gene.

Tell it, Gene. Tell me
what the owner told me—
gestures of the dazed
connections, sleepless,
planing in from Chi.

Tell me, Gene. Tell me
what you couldn't tell me
in that freezing room, fly
down, vomit on the bowl,
drops around your eyes
like stuff from wounds.

Blue Gene and those
blue-green mallards
in the river ice outside—

singing and singing in the night.

Wintersong

for Bill Evans

Suspended from the eaves
the feeder swings, cold
plastic pagoda brimmed
with seeds the wind flings
scattering in the snow.
Beyond those low
eaves, the frozen teeth,
are juncos in the trees.
Trees too thin for snow
and three birds weaving
wintersong among them—
music on a sheet.
Music eased by one
alone, from a piano,
brooding over the keys,
holding each note
for all its worth,
alone and whole . . .

When the flourish goes,
emptiness comes, space
of fields simplified
by snow, that between
note and other note,
unreckoned with before.
That which differentiates
lasting deed from forage,
the mindless bickerings . . .

Noon on the kitchen clock.
The mail truck stops

and skitters in the road.
Coming from the box,
I consider the irony
of the house—modern,
spare as any feeder,
the owner somewhere
in Florida—and, caught
once more in the snow,
with stuff disposed of
by the postman—notes
and cancelings from
San Francisco—I know
whatever juncos know.

Blues for Dan Morin

[An excerpt]

"Una Muy Bonita"
—Ornette Coleman

Might as well
sing something
softly to myself, some
Bird thing tripped
quickly off the tongue,
percolator bass,
typewriter
drum like the flicker
gone to my head now, deep
in the attic,
tapping and humming . . .

Might as well
sing something
on the phonograph, blowing
rings around a Spanish tune,
melodious
smoke like lace
pervasiveness of fog
lifting now,
above the Cascades . . .

Might as well
sing and type, thinking
of two now gone:
one anonymous as fog,
the other in some
impossible exile,
drifting through Europe
with a self-tuned violin . . .

Might as well
sing and watch the sun rise—
smoke, fog, music
dispersing
over the heater's shiver,
the field frost's grip and snap . . .

Might as well.
Might as well.

Mist hymn.
The hissing shingle.

Might as well.
Might as well.

Creek crack.
The ringing ripple.

Might as well.
Might as well.

Weed chant.
The clinking field.

Might as well.
Might as well.

Beak clack.
The tinking wheel.

Might as well.
Might as well.

Sun hum muscle
strum mountain
drum roaring
orbit Ornette Morin

BELLS!

Might as well might as well might as well!

—LAWSON FUSAO INADA

Poetry Makes Rhythm in Philosophy

Maybe it was the Bichot
Beaujolais, 1970
But in an a.m. upstairs on
Crescent Ave. I had a conversation
with K.C. Bird

We were discussing
rhythm and I said
"Rhythm makes everything move
the seasons swing
it backs up the elements
Like walking Paul Chambers' fingers"

"My worthy constituent"
Bird said. "The Universe is a
spiralling Big Band in a
polka-dotted speakeasy,
effusively generating new light
every one-night stand"

We agreed that nature can't
do without rhythm but rhythm can
get along without nature

This rhythm, a stylized Spring
conducted by a blue-collared man
in Keds and denims
(His Williamsville swimming pool
shaped like a bass clef)
in Baird Hall

on Sunday afternoons
Admission Free!

All *harrumphs!* must be
checked in at
the door

I wanted to spin
Bennie Moten's
"It's Hard to Laugh or Smile"
but the reject wouldn't automate
and the changer refused to drop
"Progress," you know

Just as well
because Bird vanished

A steel band had
entered the room

14. Bud Powell. Photograph courtesy of the Institute of Jazz Studies, Newark, New Jersey.

Lake Bud

Lake Merritt is Bud Powell's piano
The sun tingles its waters
Snuff-jawed pelicans descend
tumbling over each other like
Bud's hands playing Tea For Two
or Two For Tea

Big Mac Containers, tortilla chip, Baby Ruth
wrappers, bloated dead cats, milkshake
cups, and automobile tires
float on its surface
Seeing Lake Merritt this way is
like being unable to hear
Bud Powell at Birdland
Because people are talking
Clinking glasses of whiskey and
shouting
"Hey, waiter"

—Ishmael Reed

Rhymes with Monk

Dimly seen but off-center. Wood irons in the box.
Reflection in terms of rapture's granitic. Clench
plant an air. The picture is of, overhead chimneys,
slant, then from above. Ring till extents are sound.
No time in the practice of rooms. Stairs that not
repeat. Any window, that's dust. Park car by means
of meter. History coined as bridges that abut.
And there be more holes than. Equippage rhymes.
A vest of interest. And a member close to any closet
darkens. Rings that oppose what one's wall might.
Beeps on the button. Fend might to its original.
Duckings that rhyme. Fingering a plenty article.
Traps that settle and are bridges. And to the side
it said, and in time. The paper on the window
scrape of speakage. That tugs are ever down.
This won't change it winters. A cap that place
it so, it stays. Wood, so untoward, metals. An egg
to a city. The rafters, whistled by. A book's center.
Says one, to someone, find me zero. Sun, and the flat
keeps pace. He would laugh at the dock. Stroll by
means the having words. Gleams mean the brittle
instrument. And he goes, green the rest. Space
to light lets to equal. Mishquamaquoddy. The pin to
all weights. Not forgetting it won't and then but
does come. All, but counter. Have to move to move it.
Shifts by no lonesome. Music a matter of walls.
Breathing in the place of record. And a make that
ring. All beside sound are views. Goes in the channel
of retraces. Just here just there. And it's handed
down that bridges be barred. Chimneys, says the eyer.
A staircase at any event. Place by help of, say,

that ton. Helps to make to have made, and being sound,
helps to see to the seeing it through. A brick,
and it sides with its corner. A family solo farther on.
Procession to the nailings. A cap to pop and he seats.
How work is lodged. Rhyme the chimneys with what plays.
A tip of dawn, no books are on. Clips the parade
in time to stripes of coat. The holding world, my
pocket top. And woke clear of the bop. Went work in
slants. Shades, to spot the sun on hand. Or tunnel,
to hail from. Right as rain, the rights of coincidence.
Lightbulb as hat, piano as light. A thread of wood
styles the thoroughfare. As an hour is only a face.
Face it, room enough for the doing thing. Fly takes air,
and has weight. Come look to the sides of which are his,
the broughtens.

As the room is quiet for the one who listens.

15. Ornette Coleman. Photograph by W. Patrick Hinely, ©.

Of What The Music to Me

How can I say about the music, how can I
deal with all the musics, after they've lasted?
The linch pin is on the snare. And is When
the point?

Sessions in rooms, cardboard jackets, the imprint
tell of the wordless beam. Music loses you aim,
or the target's becoming a surrounding charm. But I
come to my feet as a tenor's blowing at me.
Black discs breeze in my dreams . . .

How could I have come to the deck in my life
where the music goes on even especially when I'm not
listening to it? Listening's maybe only
a matter of the time you think you're listening?

Once, on a demerol pill, I couldn't stop
a Coltrane solo inside my brain. Hours
while I strained to talk. Others in the room,
sun slant from autumn roof, Little Old Lady
and only I could hear. That's when I lost my
grip? and music told me it would be going
on, board sides bent with fog, no matter
my lean and time.

Lee Konitz is unframed. As if he went on
stooping in a litter lot while the notches appeared
on everybody else's weapons. By the arm of his
turn the unconcerned rest is kept. Bottles
go by on bicycles. And the head of the snare
is gleaming. Violet bars rise in the club
to a slotted sign of next week. Sessions.
Plans for overcomings. Horns unpacked and launched
in straddle. Lester winds his head on the beam
of his horn. And later will the cutters sigh.
No more time for tenor, the shrill purses in.

Location of boxcars one foot from your coat.
You go out to Hudson cement in the Half Note rain.
The changes are locked and Lennie's parallel to
no one's glasses. Horns steam had ranged high,
impeccable, if that word hadn't clicks
in it like key-pad goofs impossible to erase
from close-mike disc. All of me is the
stored-up world, astrain askim. We'll shake after that.
Even the ashtrays are collected by migrant botherers
at the shutting of sets. Mirrors that tell you
nothing but the back of the head. A tune of
such device it could collect all the chords.
Variation of crown a ring of the ultimate changes.
Evolution's logical and that's a tune too.
Nobody thought of it done, always to think of as
just begun. Nothing torpid 'bout N'Orleans pepper

rhymes. Sour sunday Chicago in the sun. Even sessions
on bridges (dropped my keys into the drink).
Nobody bothered on the turnaround. To think in
keys. Ornette thinks in all the keys at his kneehigh
window. It's like writing on a shelf, the full time of bop.

Sorry, shrugging listener, did I leave you out?
You'll have your time, a guide to bins you'll
wake up and not find. Impossible dates
with Kneecap on piano, or featuring guys
who never met in life. Maybe Twardzik
won't skip the next time you put him on.

And elbowing-aside Russ Freemans, imperturbable
in outskirt casuals repleat with sharkskin mantles.
Chet and Jeru with venetian blind lines across
their shadows stoop in jam with the outside L.A. sun
lawns stuck with hoses. Their first album session,
or anybody still hip's first date with open machine,
cigarette burns Rudy VanGelder's piano ledge as he shouts
to fire them. Wide as early cuffs, the man is tipping,
How Deep Is the Ocean when Max is Making Wax?
A mere glance at the bar lines to turn around and
swear by. He's off on his Cherokee, he's
observant and sheer. Short the plating off his
axe and one change too near.

Damn, what haven't they played!
Is he as positive as I never heard that.
The music all over the land as it is in hand?
Pausing length of poem on a moment with
Bird, prayer and stroll. Not a
gesture too old.

Not admonish, but to rear back to whole time heights.
Is the snare then near enough to the tom?

Has that jerk on box sapped the time?
Who would know easier than a tent roller?
Or the Baron of Cigarette? Who would hold
a nod for thoughtfulness? Walk up then and
deal! Got to the channel and the apartment
was missing. Cherry slept on his collarbone on stand.
Monk broke through the hum-away standard frame.
And they timed him the blame. Still he'll
arch his back at the reverse of noodling.
Stocks my thrill. Moon over Arbogast.
Pass that salt till the chicken flies.

I made it all up again, let's scribe down
the ointment. Follicle as Bud's Bubble (hallucination
with tuba). The man had ready hands. His time
inertial. And they raided his table to wrest
the gum blot Bird blew at. Unconscionable cog,
the brain of Bud. Dark as piano in a closed
deck. Humans learn at, if you take the time of day,
hum on the pass. Burst by in kilter leaps, clot caught
at the ankle. Play the bead game, mother, and you'll
lean behind. (Bud's double hurried his brother
to rubble of the pike) But I feel the glare
in his notes and scuffle.

How you could go on for liquid pages!
Fruitcake as hiring yourself a blues. A set-up
range of sessions shearing off a cake (not George).
The last one I heard was a Japanese session,
the piano buried in the mix. New bassmen
wire too many solos. The drummers amused.
No longer monikered "Stix" or "Kid Shots."
They raise their rims and fire the whole team (rhymes
with tire). The room is empty and the kid pads home.

I have the imagination of a briar. Where is
Frank Isola? (Ron Crotty? ears askance)

My whole lounge is gathering sidemen. Clear them
a gig! Tear them up those bum checks, they
never got anyway, hear them tell. So long, Unfair List!
Drop that hook, George Wein!

Come back, Joe Dodge, from the use of your car lot,
and drop kick your bassdrum down everybody's new hall.
Yeah, leave the bandages on. A Train's lonesome for you.
Bru's astray. The melody cap's lost. And Desmond
passed praying for your time. Even I want to make
my own disasters. Could you even
my horizon?

Bop never fell out of anybody's mind.
Once they faced up and trod those unfastened banisters.
And "the rooftop of the beatup, tenement, on 3rd & Harrison,
had Belfast painted." (a Kerouac that Williams couldn't hear?)
But creak the hinge and pall of opinion time
foolish as understandings penciled in at the bottom.
No sink to wait. Fervency strolls. And
we quake in the light of Good Bait, stripe and
perfect gate for a tenor. He's mumbling, but
Bird's attire chevrons his lines (squeak reed).
He ribs Bud for foolscap and the crisis is on.
Time's brawn limb bends horn, if not acicular
coughings in the stub of club. Bird's arrayed for
us to pass this point (if not all fell points)
as Lady leans back, curls lip with her weed.
Till even rocks in the street whisper Lester.

I haven't got the time, what's your name (at the least)?
Time for stock shortnesses, if not orients of the
on-go. He hitched up threads, one wife short of
his life and blew. Brew.
Meanwhile I sat back in a canvasback chair
on a Malibu deck and contemplated a map of
Greater L.A. I was looking for aberrances.

The clubs didn't show up. But a few cues did.
Soon I entered a Long Beach hotel to watch
Manne and Hawes move through time.
(Manne looked smaller) They seemed far from
Pacific jazz (or contemporary or fantasy or anything
familiar). They looped toward New York,
sounded as if they were far as Winnemucca
(this was '58). Shelly's crewcut blurted
against the seawalls in the watchcap night.
Hawaiian scenes might have buzzed in his drums.
But fascination faltered not, I wanted to grab
his wrists. Nowadays his swing seems hitched
to a nob, as if he foresaw less space within his beats.
Maybe it's his horses (?)

Which brings me to a widening of the arteries
(the artifice strengthens).
Free particle jazz. Hazy mist mid lot, hang the bars.
And they twin themselves in reverse benefaction.
How to style the stop of hands. The moon moves
down from the trunk. Ornette muse over rivalries
and railleries in sway. No kind of dollar beeps.
He keeps his young ones aBlakey. The old man
up there wide but pressed right. More cymbals,
more dangles, and a room man to set them up
before the stroll. Ornette the curiouser and
came around. But the scribes had cackled over
more rimless buddies. Ornette and Chet
in their clickless reach.

But in Ascension the bits come therming down.
Even Elvin's teeth can't smile. The laces
in the runners are outer. The throng tends to tend to
its time. Plus two takes came without say so
you never knew which you might attach. Was this
the great big stand up leavening with nothing?
How many pennies in the head? At the john door

of the Five Spot the skimmers throttled. In which
end out which lighting human? Cold blows
everybody's nose, even the sifter's. Trane came in
blocked up the door with curious points. Ornette fiddled,
seemed of glee, but wasn't. Night thrown
very large then.

But what is this becoming, an excuse for inroads?
(possible definition of the music) When the pen
runs dry you sing. Then comes the trance, the
other life, the remainder. Nobody's mind is reissued.
It stands then slides past the roadpost marked
Striver's Row. Passing strange this elimination
of known parts. Once the preliminaries to set key,
tempo, and order of entrance, then the red light
and the curving of surfaces. From the top where your
name grants purchase. Summit Ridge Drive.
Grandpa's Spells. Bird Food.

Radio taken up and out? Tell it to Donna Lee.
Tell it on piano as is never in the background.
Music, bending different. Abrasions of amazing
pockets. Time to sit out in the ceiling. Meaning,
a parcel left for Parker at the Icehouse. Marvels
of the thermous oak, and sendings of the told back sound.
He's up there, I heard it through the service door.
Last bars, frantic postcards. Linings of the road.

—Clark Coolidge

Africa, Music and Show Business

I   GEOGRAPHY

so many theories of east and west abound
one thing is certain though
this earth
is round

II   SLAVE BELL

slave
master your bell
your master
like the cat
was belled
with time
no clocks
no clime
stipulate
late afternoon
nor early mourning for the dead
sombre tolls the very same bell that rings for joy
bell
slave
time is your master

III   SPIRITUAL

when i get to heaven gonna play on my harp
gonna play all over god's heaven
but only with the cats who can make the changes

IV WESTERN INFLUENCE

my baybee eesah cryink baa baa
    forra me
i geef her de mango
i geef her de banana
but she's stillah cryink baa baa
    forra me

V RHYTHM AFRIQUE

joey had the biggest feet
so he played tenor

VI BLUES FOR DISTRICT SIX

early one new year's morning
when the emerald bay waved its clear waters against the noisy
    dockyard
a restless south easter skipped over slumbering lion's head
danced up hanover street
tenored a bawdy banjo
strung an ancient cello
bridged a host of guitars
tambourined through a dingy alley
into a scented cobwebbed room
and crackled the sixth sensed district
into a blazing swamp fire of satin sound

early one new year's morning
when the moaning bay mourned its murky waters against the
    deserted dockyard
a bloodthirsty south easter roared over hungry lion's head
and ghosted its way up over hanover street
empty
forlorn
and cobwebbed with gloom

VII

where loneliness' still waters meet nostalgia
and morning breaks the city sun and smoke
and towering grey the buildings murmur
grim subway rumblings in their roots
i scan the vacant faces and sad smiles
and long for home

the night my soul had herringed red
through raucous songs of childhood:
and friends and comic stories long forgotten
were whiskied out of memories dim
to function as narcotic
and silence cruel reality as it screamed
it's neither here nor there

i'm hemisphered
but three
the southern cross and libran scale
and god knows
he knows
where

VIII   BALLET FOR TIRED SONS AND LOVERS

figure belt—is the tragedy of the illustrious son of a suburban african
chief who, disillusioned by the apparent ineffectiveness of his magical
beadwork, discards his girds and elopes with a fast-travelling-north-
bound salesgirl.
After mesmerizing him with her hypnotic, synthetic ornaments, she
locks him up in a fashion magazine and in order to keep him amused,
content and in her power, she clads him with so many figure belts that
he stifles and loses his voice and in final desperation strangles himself and
dies.

IX   WIND UP

the southern spring winds
myself in two
one wintered in cold steel northern city
brittle eyed neon guards my empty stomach
the other
a dimming summer
camera'd in youth
and matinéed each minute of each dreary day

X   DOUBLE CROSS

in the morning came white dressed white men in a big white
    car
they took him away

in the afternoon came black dressed black men in a big black
    car
they took him away

XI

the terrored dusk screams
the land
in the beginning
love was
the fuse igniting all
clay
and green leafed sun dynamoed my buck
which now gallops petrified in the rumbling twilight
through fields of empty stomachs' wide eyed plea
to where the midnight hides
dark robed three armed inevitable
one hand outstretched towards a pair of fleeing balances
one empty hour glassed
and last
a bloodied feather falling from a palsied palm

XII   THE HARMONICA

it has been raining
and in the gutter lies the harmonica
gurgling incoherently

the man stooped
to retrieve the instrument
and it obeyed and played

the people heard and loved him

he dwelt in skyscrapers and blew wind
and soon his feet became unsteady

one morning when he came down to dig his senses
it was too late
the pavement loomed up and cracked him violently in the head
and the children ran away with bits of his brain

and the harmonica rattled back into the gutter where it had
    fallen
with the inauguration of time

FINALE   LIFE IN A NATIONAL PARK/OR—TAKE FIVE

last night two monkeys stumbled onto an
AMAZING
COLOSSAL
FANTASTIC
secret

on the outskirts of an african village
where they had been sleeping off a drunken stupor
they discovered an ancient clock
ticking away in 1979 1/4 / 35 1/2
(they worked it out)
they were jubilant

after much deliberation
as to who the rightful owner was
(they even cast lots)
they finally decided that the whole world should know of this amazing
phenomenon and that by using their usual 'pay-while-you-hear' ritual,
they could ensure themselves a lifetime of happiness and if it came to the
push they would
DISCOVER
EXCAVATE
and even
INVENT
more clocks

this morning for some obscure reason (they thought)
the clock decided to change to 4/4
they were furious

learned gorillas were called in on this appalling example of
    disobedience

the suggestion that the clock's mechanism be studied was
    accepted, halfheartedly

but alas, it was too late
for when they touched the spring, there occurred a terrifying
    explosion
and the whole monkey kingdom was blown to bits

the resultant itch woke up TIME
and she scratched vaguely under her armpit.

—ABDULLAH IBRAHIM

AL YOUNG

Body and Soul

Coleman Hawkins, 1939

My father, who used to bicycle thirty miles one way to court my mother, had this record among his dust-needled 78s. He'd already worn out several copies before I learned to love it from memory, never knowing until much later what a cause it had stirred.

Imagine it's 1939. You talk about a hellraising year, that one had to take the cake with Hitler taking Czechoslovakia, Bohemia, Moravia and Poland; with Stalin taking Finland and Poland (poor Poland); Franco taking Spain; Great Britain and France declaring war on Germany; Mussolini taking Albania; Stalin and Hitler signing their infamous non-aggression pact that would splinter and split all the left-leaning parents of kids I would later meet at college and beyond. My own folks, peasants and proles, knew next to nothing about the left-wing or right-wing of anything but chickens, but they did know right from wrong. Politics to them had something to do with money and power, which in white Mississippi were one and the same.

History and truth are so easily misconstrued. Even dates, names, facts and figures can lie—"Aught's an aught/ Figger's a figger/ All for the white man/ None for the nigger"—depending on who's doing the dating, doing the naming, doing the figuring. The telling of truth is the poet's proper domain and in the head-whipping nations of this darkening, fact-ridden world, people still look to poets and the music they make for light, sweet light illumining everything everywhere.

If it's true that in this alleged 1939 the New York World's Fair "World of Tomorrow" ran for five straight months and that TVA got the Supreme Court go-ahead and that TV in the U.S. was first broadcast publicly from the Empire State Building (covering the opening of that same World's Fair), then it's equally fair to imagine Coleman Hawkins in that crowded year. In October, the Golden Gate Bridge closed down for repairs while on the eleventh day of that same month, Hawkins, just back from a rewarding stay in war-hungry Europe, repaired to the RCA Victor New York studios with some musical friends and cut "Body and Soul"—just like that, in the shadow of the Empire State Building.

You can even picture him slouched in front of one of those weighty old condenser boom mikes, surrounded by smoke, suspendered and hatted, thinking something like: "Well, let's see how what I'm feeling's gonna come out sounding this time, so we can get this session wrapped up and get back to the gig and really do some blowing." After the take he probably remembered how he'd performed this wee hours ballad better a hundred times before. "I'll get it down yet," he told himself, "but this'll have to do for now." And, children, that was that.

When the record came out, saxophonists all over the world, hearing it and sensing that things would never be the same, started woodshedding Hawkins' impassioned licks in their closets and on the stand. Why'd he have to go and do that? Of course, everybody fell in love with it. My father would play it, take it off, play something else, then put it back on. This went on for years. What was he listening for? What were we listening to? What did it mean? What were all those funny, throaty squawks and sighs and cries all about! I knew what a body was, but what was a soul? You kept hearing people say, "Well, bless his soul!" You thought you knew what they meant, but really, you could only imagine as you must now. You knew what they meant when they said "Bless her heart!" because you could put your hand to your heart and feel the beat, and your Aunt Ethel sometimes fried up chicken hearts along with gizzards, livers and feet. But a soul was unseeable. Did animals have souls too? Did birds, dogs, cows, mules, pigs, snakes, bees? And what about other stuff, like corn, okra, creeks, rivers, moonlight, sunshine, trees, the ground, the rain, the sky? Did white folks have souls?

Was a soul something like a breeze: something you couldn't picture or grab but could only feel like you could the wind off the Gulf when the day cooled down, or the way the ground would tremble when the train roared past across the street from where we lived?

Thirty-nine, forty, fifty, a hundred, thousands—who's to say how many rosy chilled Octobers have befallen us, each one engraved in micro-moments of this innocent utterance, electrically notated, but, like light in a photograph, never quite captured in detail, only in essence.

Essence in this instance is private song, is you hearing your secret sorrow and joy blown back through Coleman Hawkins, invisibly connected to you and played back through countless bodies, each one an embodiment of the same soul force.

All poetry is about silent music, invisible art and the clothing of time for the ages.

Moody's Mood for Love

King Pleasure, 1952

What we liked to do at Hutchins Intermediate School in Detroit was get together—a whole gang of us, say, half a dozen to ten kids—and either walk through the halls or hang out by the grocery store over there off Woodrow Wilson, or step through streets singing "Moody's Mood for Love" in loud unison with a vengeance calculated to blow grown people and other squares clean away; keep them right there where we wanted them—at a distance and out of our business.

In the motion picture soundtrack of your mind, you can easily envision and hear us all silly and feisty; arrogant as city mice out to pull the rug out from under our slower, country cousins; that is, anybody who didn't know the words to this tricky vocalese version of an alto saxophone solo James Moody had cut on Prestige Records. From beginning to end, Moody never stated the melody line of the tune whose chordal layout he was bouncing from—Jimmy McHugh's "I'm in the Mood for Love." One wonders why he didn't bother claiming composer credit, for this was how the beboppers had learned to fatten their royalty checks—when they were lucky enough to even get royalties—from record companies and from BMI (Broadcast Music, Inc.), or ASCAP (the American Society of Composers and Publishers). The copyright office said you couldn't copyright a chord progression, only a specific melody. So Moody, living in Europe, had borrowed an alto saxophone from Swedish bopster Lars Gullin and made this three-minute cut, which might have gone the way of many a fine but forgotten jazz solo if it hadn't reached the ears of a mystic and singer named Clarence Beek out in East St. Louis. Clarence Beek changed his name to King Pleasure.

"There I go/There I go/There I go/Therrrrre I go . . ." is what Pleasure had heard Moody whispering as he began to poeticize the urgency of his emotions in a solo that gathered candor the way an object approaching the speed of light accumulates mass, grows tinier and tinier until time stands still. That's all Einstein had been talking about, and there Moody was—like any other outstanding jazz artist—telling such a story in musical notes and tones that Pleasure broke down into language that was far from sounding like the airy sweet nothings we'd been brought up to expect from popular songs: "A. You're adorable,/B. You're so beautiful,/C. You're a cutie full of charm," sung by Perry Como or Doris Day—and, don't get me wrong, Doris Day could sing—but there was something about this invisible collaboration between James Moody and King Pleasure that was irresistible to us adolescents.

There are rumors that the lyrics were really Eddie Jefferson's. But whoever wrote them, these were love lyrics that cut across neat little bar lines and formulas; that were lofty yet earthy—"Pretty baby,/You are the one who/Snaps my control." There was something awfully close to real about them and, because they followed the heated buildup of Moody's soar-and-cruise, the way stories in jazz are traditionally laid out, these were also words that we could taste in our mouths as we sang and said them. By the time we each felt the first climax approaching, the whole gang of us would stop in our tracks and flail our arms toward the sky. All we could do was peep around at one another in anticipatory glee an instant before the beat told us it was time to belt it right out: *"Ohhh, baby,/You make me feel so goood!/Lemme take you by the hand . . . ."*

Singer and lyricist Jon Hendricks, whose first record was a vocalese duet rendition of Stan Getz' instrumental, "Don't Get Scared," has told me how shocked he was to go into the studio with Pleasure to find out that Pleasure hadn't written words for Hendricks to sing. On that recording, Pleasure sings Getz' tenor solo and Hendricks sings baritone saxophonist Lars Gullin's. But when Hendricks had asked Pleasure where were the lyrics he'd have to sing, Pleasure had to remind him that this was still jazz and that Hendricks was going to have to write his own.

I don't know whether Blossom Dearie had to do the same thing for the passionate but cool response to Pleasure's wolfish plea on "Moody's Mood for Love," and we didn't even think about anything like that back in Hutchins. All 6 or 10 of us would simply shift from baritone or tenor into falsetto register and gurgle out the girl's part too. And who can ever forget how she opens? Perhaps Dearie's coyness suggests what we were all probably too macho or unconscious to accept or understand: namely, that the seducer and the seduced are always in cahoots, and usually there isn't much question as to which has the upper hand, not in "Moody's Mood" anyway. Dearie, taking Swedish pianist Thore Swanrud's piano part, sings: *"What is all this talk/About loving me,/My sweet? . . ."*

And, on that sly note, just when they're off to find "a place where we can use a loving state of mind," Pleasure, like all good Victorian storytellers, draws the curtain on the ensuing scene, leaving to the imagination what didn't need to be said anyway. Then, telling James Moody that he can come on in there, man, and he can blow now, "we're through," the song ends as breathlessly as it began.

Most of us didn't really know who James Moody was, but there was a kid at school named James Moody, a rather prominent gang leader himself; he was the neighborhood head of the Shakers, a hardball pack of youths, ranging in age from 13 to 30, that terrorized Detroit in the early fifties. The story of how I, who belonged to no youth gang, managed to coexist on turf that both the Shakers and their rivals the Ooloos warred over regularly, and yet steer clear of both gangs diplomatically, would make a novella in itself. James Moody happened to like the song, though. He basked so completely in the reflected glory of this musical salute that he actually grew to believe that he'd composed it, or something.

The truth is that we were all composing it, over and over, every time we sang it. Even now when I listen to Aretha's version, still regarded as offbeat and too jazzy to be commercial, I remember how it was played over the rhythm and blues station, WJLB, on "Rockin' with Leroy"—a show upward-looking Negro parents didn't want their kids listening to, even though an awful lot of grown-ups' auto radios were glued to that 1400 spot on the dial. Leroy Holmes, the deejay, spun out a powerful line of jive, and when he put on "Sixty Minute Man" by Billy Ward and the

Dominoes or "Baby, Don't Do It" by the Five Royals or Hank Ballard and the Midnighters doing "Work with Me, Annie" or their outrageous sequel, "Annie Had a Baby (Can't Work No More)," my folks would voice concern about what the world was coming to, but they were fascinated all the same. Only the most daring of white kids at school knew anything at all about it.

"Are you guys making that up?" one kid asked us in the locker room one morning while we were doing a round of "Moody's Mood for Love." "No," some wisecracker told him, "James Moody wrote it."

"Oh," the curious kid, onlooker and listener, said, pulling up his sweat socks, "I didn't know he did anything but fight."

It was all about territory, I suppose; physical and mental, cultural and emotional; what was pure versus the adulterated and the adult, you might say. But, above all, it was still about square versus hip. Mainly, our feeling about what we sang and how we sang it and where it came from was this: It wasn't nobody else's business.

Lester Leaps In

Nobody but Lester let Lester leap
into a spotlight that got too hot
for him to handle, much less keep
under control like thirst in a drought.

He had his sensitive side, he had
his hat, that glamorous porkpie whose
sweatband soaked up all that bad
leftover energy.

How did he choose
those winning titles he'd lay on favorites

—Sweets Edison, Sir Charles, Lady Day?
Oooo and his sound! Once you savor its
flaming smooth aftertaste, what do you say?

Here lived a man so hard and softspoken
he had to be cool enough to hold his horn
at angles as sharp as he was heartbroken
in order to blow what it's like being born.

Topsy: Part 2

How overwhelming
that Lester tune
heard just out of the rain
early one night
in a cafe bar
full of African students
midtown Madrid
September 1963
young & dumb & lonesome
a long ways from home
amazed at my tall
cheap rum & coke
patting the wetness
from my leathered foot
to that Lester tune
cut by Cozy Cole
blown from a jukebox
right up the street from where
Quixote's Cervantes once died

Dance of the Infidels

in memory of Bud Powell

The smooth smell of Manhattan taxis,
Parisian taxis, it doesnt matter, it's
the feeling that modern man is all youve
laid him out to be in those tinglings & rushes;
the simple touch of your ringed fingers
against a functioning piano.

                              The winds of Brooklyn
still mean a lot to me. The way certain chicks
formed themselves & their whole lives around
a few notes, an attitude more than anything.
I know about the being out of touch, bumming
nickels & dimes worth of this & that off
him & her here & there—everything but
hither & yon.

              Genius does not grow on trees.
                                        I owe
you a million love dollars & so much more than
thank-you for rewriting the touch & taste & smell
of the world for me those city years when I could
very well have fasted on into oblivion.

                                        Ive just
been playing the record you made in Paris with Art
Blakey & Lee Morgan. The European audience
is applauding madly. I think of what Ive heard
of Buttercup's flowering on the Left Bank & days
you had no one to speak to. Wayne Shorter is
beautifying the background of sunlight with
children playing in it & shiny convertibles
& sedans parked along the block as I blow.

Grass
grows. Negroes. Women walk. The world, in case
youre losing touch again, keeps wanting the same
old thing.

You gave me some of it; beauty I sought
before I was even aware how much I needed it.

I know
this world is terrible & that one must, above all,
hold onto the heart & the hearts of others.

I love *you*

—AL YOUNG

The Depression

Charlie Green was a member of Fletcher Henderson's
Orchestra, played trombone, cut 38 sides with Bessie
Smith, froze to death on the doorstep of a Harlem
Tenement during the depression. The snow keeps coming
Down. Well, let it come down. The city gets
Kind of white. Your body is cool.
I forget when I look in your face how far back.
Details, standing around. Everything goes out.
Face back. Heat eases
Up. Suspended. You bring wine, you talk. I like
To hear you talk, the way you talk.
I get nervous, anyway. Follow me up, through
The clocks, Mister B.
B for boss. *The book I toss.*
She who longs for the red hot songs of Robert Johnson.
And so the bread is baked by you now, maybe draw
Some beer & sit for hours, you had it spaced wrong.
Saturn a bromide & Irish cream & footsteps on Sullivan
Street & Burgundy from the mountains, the mountains
Of romance, talk to me. Fat chance.
Tight wire risk.
The onion & onion.
Umbrellas from you, all broken.
Drunk & stoned & crazy 3 in the morning phone ringing.
The most difficult a relationship
Of air & what is wrong.
Trying to remember where the wall is.
Margaret Johnson came in from Kansas City &
Played piano on one record date with Billie Holiday,
Buck Clayton, Dickie Wells, Lester Young,
Freddy Greene, Walter Page & Jo Jones.
& Lester Young said, "I have eyes & I can see."

Lennie Tristano, No Wind

Waves: applause, fathoms above, calm air
Lets in fur rainbow bruise, layered light
Without a name yet, bluesy sweet lozenge
Of no sleep, tint: a young Monk sweeps up
Fragments of the living dream, Danube
Suction rides the Rhine clean & smooth
Jaunty, Yang is beginningless, dawn star
Echoes atonal nudge: applause, not the
Slightest ripple pushed so far as to
Dissolve these desires, tiny aches

Birthplace of waves, bottomland quivering
Bargain basement riches of sound, hydroponic voices
Stage left gorge evaporation, sizzling satin
Needles that pierce & don't try, pins locate
Density of longing embargoes each kiss, seaward
Rushing expendable charms, moods that light
Drifts in & out of, a popular treatise
On food, the lesser weirds unscrew

These blues are the streets themselves, heat
Rises throwing distortions off, lingering
Resonances feathers of applause, tremors
& awful salads dot the attention we pay
To surfaces, what's below disorder
Love plays no part in, vacant yawn
& plush air, waves swim through
Golden dawn teeming with earlobes

16. Lennie Tristano. Photograph by William P. Gottlieb, © 1979.

Little Light

for Eric Dolphy

> "He was like an angel
> that came down to Earth
> played his saxophone
> incredibly, and passed
> too quickly."
>
> —Clifford Jordan, 1966

There's
A
Little
Light
Over
The
Con Ed
Tower, Eric, and it's you. Too bright
to be a star, total capacity
brightens a still-raining sky, & I'm
on standby, waiting for your horn
to come crashing down on Manhattan.
            Tonight, in the bathtub,
Listening to your ancient sides, rolling over, scrubbing
my back with your delicate clarinet breeze, oh so blue,
the rain beating on my eyelids, big drowsy drops shaped
like coins, that lay their own tattoo on my palms as I,
too heavy to rise beyond as you do in your uniqueness
while the soot-tinted noise of too-full streets echoes
and I pick up the quietly diminishing soap & do
myself again.
            And, right now, it's noon in the tropics, as
a great big hand fondles the cherubs that cruise this ashen light,

one big whooshing sigh knocks a fleshy heave toward what snow
glides in on a severed tongue still singing, so beautifully
deranged, and squeezing some more difficult light
to dry my glazed flesh with
                    some of your happy brilliance.

—Jim Brodey

DAVID HENDERSON

Sonny Rollins

sonny rollins seeking
peace in the city
jamming with
the subway train
a free rhythm section
coney island beach on the bridge
of hart crane /
"the most important thing to me
is my sanity"
refrain

A Coltrane Memorial

my first day in new orleans
               home-house of jass
coltrane dead
            in my dreams
among marching creoles
among marching blacks
                  bojangling jass parade
in *le quartier*
as a resident of a black theatre thru southland
i laid upon carver's grave   lingered in his laboratory
                       in tuskegee
i kissed Laly   an ancestor
                of booker t.

she wore her hair afro
& played coltrane all night   slow
where the southern cross
the yellow dog

long caravan speeding thru alabama
then georgia red clay
black theatre of an albany backwood church
and then
                the long convoy stretch to new "o"
to find coltrane dead
amid the rubble
of newark negroes

i would want my favorite things
in summertime ritual
have coltrane
                the medicine man
of my ancestral journeys
toward my favorite moments

energy dies
energy dies
                tumult or riots
                            die
            the way of escape
            the underground rails
                        the trains
                            train
the freight
                                    coltrane
                            cargo of fate

            as we ride on
up
        the way

Thelonious
Sphere
Monk

loud niggers talkin more than shit
the blue monk swirling rainbows
in count basies lounge
with his people he dont show up late/
big tooth smile
homeboy home again
amber lights orchestras bassoons and lady sopranos
in chorus in cocaine johns slow motion zen space
face of the count over the dead piccolo
iridescent suit in day-glo shimmer
with the music and the space white saddle shoes
skip in space off and on the pedals
chandelier ring on the trill pinky
talmud cap bopping bebop beard

he lay in de cut
he dont talk loud
but he talk that talk
just the same

blue monk
on the island of the blue dolphins
all over the bronx
and upper manhattan
showing up
by the dozens

my man knows
he knows
when he knows /

letters from mama
the calling
come home son
before I die

—DAVID HENDERSON

Giant Steps

I

To want to be a saint to want to be a saint to want to
to want to be a saint to be the snake-tailed one to want to
be snake-tailed with wings to be a snake-tailed saint with wings to
want to be a saint to want to awaken men wake men from nightmare.

To go down to raise to go down to raise to go to go down the
ladder to go down as taught as dance steps taught by the master as
taught to dance to step-dance to dance with giant steps to go to dance to
step-dance to dance with giant steps as taught by the master to
dance to go down the ladder to go down to raise men from nightmare.

2

To want to be a saint to want to be a saint to want to
to be snake-tailed with wings to be a snake-tailed saint with
wings to leap upon the horse-headed woman the blue-eyed woman
who chokes the throat to want to be a saint to wake men from
    nightmare.

To go down to raise to go down to raise to go to go down the
ladder to go down as taught by the master as taught to dance to
step-dance to dance with giant steps to dance with giant steps
down the ladder to dance down as taught by the master to dance
    down the
ladder to obtain possession to go down to raise men from nightmare.

3

To want to be a saint to want to be a saint to want to
to want to be a snake-tailed saint with wings to leap upon the horse-
headed woman the blue-eyed woman the woman with the little moon
who chokes the throat to want to be a saint to wake men from
    nightmare.

To go down to raise to go down to raise to go to go down the
ladder to go to dance as taught by the master to dance to step-dance to
dance with giant steps to dance with giant steps to dance down the
ladder as taught by the master to obtain possession to dance down to
raise men with a horn to go down to raise men from nightmare.

4

To want to be a saint to want to be saint to want to
be a snake-tailed saint with wings to leap upon the horse-headed the
blue-eyed woman with the little moon the woman with nine shadows
who chokes the throat to want to be a saint to wake men from
    nightmare.

To go down to raise to go down to raise to go to go down the
ladder to dance as taught by the master to step-dance to dance with
giant steps to dance with giant steps to dance down as taught by the
master to obtain possession to dance down to raise men with a horn a
tenor horn to go to go down to raise men from nightmare.

—John Taggart

Coming Through Slaughter

[An excerpt]

*

So in the public parade he went mad into silence.

This was April 1907, after his return, after staying with his wife and Cornish, saying *sure* he would play again, had met and spoken to Henry Allen and would play with his band in the weekend parade. Henry Allen snr's Brass Band.

The music begins two blocks north of Marais Street at noon. All of Henry Allen's Band including Bolden turn onto Iberville and move south. After about half a mile his music separates from the band, and though the whole procession is still together Bolden is now stained untouchable, powerful, an eight ball in their midst. Till he is spinning round and round, crazy, at the Liberty-Iberville connect.

By eleven that morning people who had heard Bolden was going to play had already arrived, stretching from Villiere down to Franklin. Brought lunches and tin flasks and children. Some bands broke engagements, some returned from towns over sixty miles away. All they knew was that Bolden had come back looking good. He was in town four days before the parade.

On Tuesday night he had come in by bus from Webb's place. A small bag held his cornet and a few clothes. He had no money so he walked the twenty-five blocks to 2527 First Street where he had last lived. He tapped on the door and Cornish opened it. Frozen. Only two months earlier Cornish had moved in with Bolden's wife. Almost fainting. Buddy put his arm around Cornish's waist and hugged him, then walked past him into the living room and fell back in a chair exhausted. He was very tired from the walk, the tension of possibly running into other people. The city too hot after living at the lake. Sitting he let the bag slide from his fingers.

Where's Nora?
She's gone out for food. She'll be back soon.
Good.
Jesus, Buddy. Nearly two years, we all thought—
No that's okay Willy, I don't care.

He was sitting there not looking at Cornish but up at the ceiling, his hands outstretched his elbows resting on the arms of the chair. A long silence. Cornish thought this is the longest time I've ever been with him without talking. You never saw Bolden thinking, lost of people said that. He thought by being in motion. Always talk, snatches of song, as if his brain had been a fishbowl.

Let me go look for her.
Okay Willy.

He sat on the steps waiting for Nora. As she came up to him he asked her to sit with him.

I haven't got time, Willy, let's go in.

Dragging her down next to him and putting an arm around her so he was as close to her as possible.

Listen, he's back. Buddy's back.

Her whole body relaxing.

Where is he now?
Inside. In his chair.
Come on let's go in.
Do you want to go alone?
No let's go in, both of us Willy.

She had never been a shadow. Before they had married, while she worked at Lula White's, she had been popular and public. She had played Bolden's games, knew his extra sex. When they were alone together it was still a crowded room. She had been fascinated with him. She brought short cuts to his arguments and at times cleared away the chaos he embraced. She walked inside now with Willy holding her hand. She saw him sitting down, head back, but eyes glancing at the door as it opened. Bolden not moving at all and she, with groceries under her arm, not moving either.

*

The three of them entered a calm long conversation. They talked in the style of a married couple joined by a third person who was catalyst and audience. And Buddy watched her large hip as she lay on the floor of the room, the hill of cloth, and he came into her dress like a burglar without words in the family style they had formed years ago, with some humour now but not too much humour. Sitting against her body and unbuttoning the layers of cloth to see the dark gold body and bending down to smell her skin and touching with his face through the flesh the buried bones in her chest. Writhed his face against her small breasts. Her skirt still on, her blouse not taken off but apart and his rough cheek scraping her skin, not going near her face which he had explored so much from across the room, earlier. When Cornish had still been there.

They lay there without words. Moving all over her chest and arms and armpits and stomach as if placing mines on her with his mouth and then leaned up and looked at her body glistening with his own spit. Together closing up her skirt, slipping the buttons back into their holes so she was dressed again. Not going further because it was friendship that had to be guarded, that they both wanted. The diamond had to love the earth it passed along the way, every speck and angle of the other's history, for the diamond had been earth too.

*

So Cornish lives with her. Willy, who wanted to be left alone but became the doctor for everyone's troubles. Sweet William. Nothing ambitious on the valve trombone but being the only one able to read music he brought us new music from the north that we perverted cheerfully into our own style. Willy, straight as a good fence all his life, none to match his virtue. Since I've been home I watch him and Nora in the room. The air around them is empty so I see them clear. They are for me no longer in a landscape, they are not in the street they walk over, the chairs disappear under them. They are complete and exact and final. No longer the every-second change I saw before but like statues of personality now. Through my one-dimensional eye. I left the other in the other home, Robin flying off with it into her cloud. So I see Willy and Nora as they are and always will be and I hunger to be as still as them, my brain tying me up in this chair. Locked inside the frame, boiled down in love and anger into dynamo that cannot move except on itself.

I had wanted to be the reservoir where engines and people drank, blood sperm music pouring out and getting hooked in someone's ear. The way flowers were still and fed bees. And we took from the others too this way, music that was nothing till Mumford and Lewis and Johnson and I joined Cornish and made him furious because we wouldn't let him even finish the song once before we changed it to our blood. Cornish who played the same note the same way every time who was our frame our diving board that we leapt off, the one we sacrificed so he could remain the overlooked metronome.

So because Willy was the first I saw when I got back I pretended to look through his eyes, the eyes Nora wanted me to have. So everyone said I'd changed. Floating in the ether. They want nothing to have changed. Unaware of the hook floating around. A couple of years ago I would have sat down and thought out precisely why it was Cornish who moved in with her why it was Cornish she accepted would have thought it out as I set the very type it was translated into. *The Cricket*. But I shat those theories out completely.

There had been such sense in it. This afternoon I spend going over four months worth of *The Cricket*. Nora had every issue in the bedroom cupboard and while she was out and the kids stayed around embarrassed to come too close and disturb me (probably Nora's advice—why doesn't she still hate me? Why do people forget hate so easily?) I read through four months worth of them from 1902. September October November December. Nothing about the change of weather anywhere but there were the details of the children and the ladies changing hands like coins or a cigarette travelling at mouth level around the room. All those contests for bodies with children in the background like furniture.

I read through it all. Into the past. Every intricacy I had laboured over.

How much sex, how much money, how much pain, how much sweat, how much happiness. Stories of riverboat sex when whites pitched whores overboard to swim back to shore carrying their loads of sperm, dog love, meeting Nora, marriage, the competition to surprise each other with lovers. *Cricket* was my diary too, and everybody else's. Players picking up women after playing society groups, the easy power of the straight quadrilles. All those names during the four months moving now like waves through a window. So I suppose that was the crazyness I left. Cricket noises and Cricket music for that is what we are when watched by people bigger than us.

Then later Webb came and pulled me out of the other depth and there was nothing on me. I was glinting and sharp and cold from the lack of light. I had turned into metal at my mouth.

⋆   ⋆   ⋆

Parade (5th Morning)

Coming down Iberville, warm past Marais Street, then she moves free of the crowd and travels at our speed between us and the crowd. My new red undershirt and my new white shiny shirt bright under the cornet. New shoes. Back in town.

Warning slide over to her and hug and squawk over her and shoulder her into the crowd. Roar. Between Marais and Liberty I just hit notes every 15 seconds or so Henry Allen worrying me eyeing me about keeping the number going and every now and then my note like a bird flying out of the shit and hanging loud and long. *Roar.* Crisscross Iberville like a spaniel strutting in front of the band and as I hit each boundary of crowd—*roar*. Parade of ego, cakewalk, strut, every fucking dance and walk I remember working up through this air to get it ready for the note sharp as a rat mouth under Allen's soft march tune.

But where the bitch came from I don't know. She moves out to us again, moving along with us, gravy bones. Thin body and long hair and joined by someone half bald and a beautiful dancer too so I turn from the bank of people and aim at them and pull them on a string to me, the roar at the back of my ears. Watch them through the sun balancing off the horn till they see what is happening and I speed Henry Allen's number till most of them drop off and just march behind, the notes more often now, every five seconds. Eyes going dark in the hot bleached street. Get there before it ends, but it's nearly over nearly over, approach Liberty. She and he keeping up like storm weeds crashing against each other. Squawk beats going descant high the hair spinning against his face and back to the whip of her head. She's Robin, Nora, Crawley's girl's tongue.

March is slowing to a stop and as it floats down slow to a thump I take off and wail long notes jerking the squawk into the end of them to form a new beat, have to trust them all as I close my eyes, know the others are silent, throw the notes off the walls of people, the iron lines, so pure and sure bringing the howl down to the floor and letting in the light and the girl is alone now mirroring my throat in her lonely tired dance, the street silent but for us her tired breath I can hear for she's near me as I go round and round in the centre of the Liberty-Iberville connect. Then silent. For something's fallen in my body and I can't hear the music as I play it. The notes more often now. She hitting each note with her body before it is even out so I know what I do through her. God this is what I wanted to play for, if no one else I always guessed there would be this, this mirror somewhere, she closer to me now and her eyes over mine tough and young and come from god knows where. Never seen her before but testing me taunting me to make it past her, old hero, old ego tested against one as cold and pure as himself, this tall bitch breasts jumping loose under the light shirt she wears that's wet from energy and me fixing them with the aimed horn tracing up to the throat. Half dead, can't take more, hardly hit the squawks anymore but when I do my body flicks at them as if I'm the dancer till the music is out there. *Roar.* It comes back now, so I can hear only in waves now and then, god the heat in the air, she is sliding round and round her thin hands snake up through her hair and do their own dance and she is seven foot tall with them and I aim at them to bring them down to my body and the music gets caught in her hair, this is what I wanted, always, loss of privacy in the playing, leaving the stage, the rectangle of band on the street, this hearer who can throw me in the direction and the speed she wishes like an angry shadow. Fluff and groan in my throat, roll of a bad throat as we begin to slow. Tired. She still covers my eyes with hers and sees it slow and allows the slowness for me her breasts black under the wet light shirt, sound and pain in my heart sure as death. All my body moves to my throat and I speed again and she speeds tired again, a river of sweat to her waist her head and hair back bending back to me, all the desire in me is cramp and hard, cocaine on my cock, eternal, for my heart is at my throat hitting slow pure notes into the shimmy dance of victory, hair toss victory, a local strut, eyes meeting sweat down her chin arms out in final exercise pain, take on the last long squawk and letting it cough and climb to spear her all those watching like a javelin through the brain and down into the stomach, feel the blood that is real move up bringing fresh energy in its suitcase, it comes up flooding past my heart in a mad parade, it is coming through my teeth, it is into the cornet, god can't stop god can't stop it can't stop the air the red force coming up can't remove it from my mouth, no intake gasp, so deep blooming it up god I can't choke it the music still pouring in a roughness I've never hit, watch it *listen* it *listen* it, can't see I CAN'T SEE. Air floating through the blood to the girl red hitting the blind spot I can feel others turning, the silence of the crowd, can't see

Willy Cornish catching him as he fell outward, covering him, seeing the red on the white shirt thinking it is torn and the red undershirt is showing and then lifting the horn sees the blood spill out from it as he finally lifts the metal from the hard kiss of the mouth.

What I wanted.

—MICHAEL ONDAATJE

Four and More; for Miles Davis

I

a carrier of incandescent dreams this
blade-thin shadowman stabbed by lightning
crystal silhouette
crawling over blues-stained pavements his life
lean he drapes himself his music across edges
his blood held tight within
staccato flights

clean as darkness & bright as lightning
reversed moments where the sound is two cat eyes
penetrating the midnight hours of moon pearls lacing
the broken mirrored waters
mississippi mean as a sun-drenched trumpet/ man
holding dreams held high on any wind/ light

voice walking on eggshells

2

& time comes as the wrinkles
of your mother's skin shrinking inward
fly toward that compelling voice
light calling since time began
on the flip-side of spirit
you shed placentas at each stage of your music
then go downriver exploring new blues

the drum skin of young years wearing down

the enigmatic search of your music
now your autumn years of shadows creeping twilight
dancers wrapped tight in cobwebs hold on
to one another
beneath fractured light cracking the floor
their lives now prismatic poems at the point where the sun
disappears with every turning of the clock hands
spinning towards the death of light
there in the diamond point
of the river beyond the edges

the light glows smaller
grows inward becomes a seed to grow
another light illuminating the shadows
crystalline as this trumpetman

voice walking on eggshells

phosphorous as truth or blue
as luminescent water beneath the sun's eye

3

O Silent Keeper of Shadows
of these gutted roads filled with gloomy ticking
of time-clocks/ razor-bladed turnings of hairpin corners
of these irreducible moments of love found
when love was sought
iridescent keeper of rainbow laughter
arching out of broken-off gold-capped teeth

blues man holding the sun between his teeth

soothsayer of chewed-up moments
shekereman at the crossroads of cardinal points
talisman hanging from dewdrops singing deep
sea diver of transparent rhythmic poems

trumpet voice walking on eggshells
your shadow is as the river snake-thin
man at flood-time blood lengthening in the veins
coursing through the earth's flesh

shaman man gone beyond the sky's limit

music sleeps there in the riverbed
mississippi where those calcified shining bones sleep
deep reminding us of the journey from then to now
& from now to wherever it is we have to go

so pack your bags boy
the future is right around the corner
only a stone's throw from yesterday's/ light

as is this carrier of afternoon dream music
trumpet voice walking on eggshells

this eggshell-walking trumpetman
voice hauntingly beautiful lyrical music man
gold as two cat eyes penetrating the midnight hours
as blood blackening the pavement mean music man
shadowman holding the night in the bell
of his trumpet singing

mississippi river pouring from roots of his eyes

4

shadowman holding the night in his music
shekereman at the crossroads of cardinal points
elliptical talisman hanging from dewdrops singing
deep sea diver of haunting magical tones

trumpetman walking on eggshells

your shadow as the river at flood-time
snake-thin shaman man blade-sharp gone beyond
the sky's limit music sleeps there in your coursing
river veins curl around the bones
clear as diamond points on waters of sunsets

there where light grows inward
your genius moving out from that source
trumpetman walking on eggshells

afternoon dreamcarrier of blues in flight
steep night climber of haunting magical poems

juju hoodooman conjuring illuminating darkness

Snake-Back Solo

for Louis Armstrong, Steve Cannon, Miles Davis & Eugene Redmond

with the music up high
boogalooin bass down way way low
up &n under eye come sliding on in mojoin
on in spacin on in on a riff
full of rain
riffin on in full of rain & pain
spacin on in on a sound like coltrane

my metaphor is a blues
hot pain dealin blues is a blues axin
guitar voices whiskey broken niggah deep
in the heart is a blues in a glass filled with rain
is a blues in the dark
slurred voices of straight bourbon
is a blues dagger stuck off in the heart

of night moanin like bessie smith
is a blues filling up the wings
of darkness is a blues

& looking through the heart
a dream can become a raindrop window to see through
can become a window to see through this moment
to see yourself hanging around the dark
to see through
can become a river catching rain
feeding time can become a window
to see through

while outside windows flames trigger
the deep explosion
time steals rivers that go on & stay where they are
inside yourself moving soon there will be daylight
breaking the darkness
to show the way soon there will be voices breaking music
to come on home by down & up river breaking darkness
swimming upriver the sound of louis armstrong
carrying riverboats upstream on vibratos
climbing the rain filling the rain
swimming upriver
up the river of rain satchmo breaking the darkness
his trumpet & grin polished overpain speaking
to the light flaming off the river's back
at sunset snake river's back
river mississippi big muddy up from new
orleans to alton & east st. louis illinois
cross the river from st. louis to come on home by
upriver the music swims breaking silence of miles
flesh leaping off itself into space
creating music creating poems

now inside myself eye solo of rivers
catching rains & dreams & sunsets solo

of trane tracks screaming through night stark
a dagger in the heart solo
of the bird spreading wings for the wind
solo of miles pied piper prince of darkness
river rain voice now eye solo
at the root of the flower solo leaning voices
against promises of shadows soloing of bones
beneath the river's snake-back solo
of trees cut down by double-bladed axes
river rain voice now eye solo of the human condition
as blues solo of the matrix mojoin new blues solo
river rain voice now eye solo   solo

& looking through the heart a dream
can become a raindrop window to see through
can become this moment this frame to see through
to see yourself hanging
around the dark to see through this pain
can become even more painful as the meaning of bones
crawling mississippi river bottoms snakepits beneath
the snake-back solo catching rain catching time
& dreams washed clean by ajax

but looking through the dream can be
like looking through a clean window crystal
prism the night where eye solo now too be-
come the wings of night
to see through this darkness
eye solo now to become wings & colors
to become a simple skybreak shattering darkness
to become lightning's jagged sword-like thunder
eye solo to become to become
eye solo now to become to become

with the music up high
up way way high boogalooin bass down
way way low
up & under eye come slidin on in mojoin on in
spacin on in on a riff full of rain
river riff full of rain & trains & dreams
come slidin on in another riff
full of flames
leaning & gliding eye solo   solo
loopin & sliding eye solo now   solo

Leaving Los Angeles

leaving on the freeway eye thought
of complexity forming los angeles
molding sun shaping rhythms of movements
in streets   sounds
sun on the people
dazzling beauty of women driving music through
new blues dues smog burning the sun hours leaning
dark against mountains in the distance
eternally powerful embracing
the valley carved from stone & stretched out
over colors images freaks unknown & spaced out
hollywood tinsel town wilshire
the beverly hill-billies of feeling
east of fifth street
death hopes
of hobos dripping from wine-slashed faces
freeways wrecked with cars holding the foundation
of rhythm driven by salt of the ocean

forming the scope of the possible
that can be beautiful
as the bird
calling dolphy wondrous flute
song shining amongst the lyrical
sea fingers
spraying water sounds airy
dancing rhythms painting trances
blending sweet new juba spells leap
into weaving sounds of hoodoo mystery
drummed into skies of distance
of vibrations spinning
& gliding

—QUINCY TROUPE

17. Bill Evans. Photograph courtesy of Fantasy records.

To the Pianist Bill Evans

When I hear you
play "My Foolish Heart"
I am clouded

remembering more than
Scott LaFaro's charred bass
as it rested

against a Yonkers wall
in its transit
from accidental fire

like a shadowy
grace note
exploding into

rhythms of Lou
insanely driving
"Man, we're *late!*"

his long curved bass
straining the car
interior, a canvas swan

my hand clutched,
fingered, refingered:
steel strings as

of the human neck
the vulnerable neck
the neck of music

squeezed by hands
the fragile box
of song, the breath

I crushed out of music
before I killed
by accident

whatever in me
could sing
not touching the keyboard

of terrible parties
and snow
           snow

falling as canvas and
wood and hair flamed
behind a windshield

I imagined being
trapped inside, still
see it in my heart

our terror magnified
note by note
purified each year

the gentle rise
and circle of
cinders in

February air
in their transit
from fire

into music,
into memory, a space
where heroin

does not slowly wave
its blazing arm,
like smoking ivory

teeth and fingers
scorched by the
proximity

of cigarettes laid
on anonymous piano
lips that crush

our function, in-
transigent wire,
inanimate wood

of another century
we must save by song!
for which we are paid!

continuing to be
used, insisting
our hands present

themselves
and keep
on taking our hands

—Bill Zavatsky

Tampa Red's Contemporary Blues

we are stranded here against a dark blue and shaded night
peering into these intelligent rooms
                                        through the forested eyes
of thirteen great atlantic owls
conjuring while conceived in the original blue bottleneck
of Tampa Red

black-inked leaves teardrop and fall toward
the unbearable street or sit dumbfounded
                                        in corners
of chimerical ceilings
where we place our three eyes
                                under the melting pot
of ludicrous passion
and await that rude performance called the initiation
of the world, the opening of blistered and boiling water,
the translucent floodgates of incorrigible time
engaged in a dialectic
                        of wheatstraw and steel
or riding the australian crawling logs down market street,
speed boats contending
                                in the black plum trees, huge and scuffling
feet tangled in the buckling and bladed blood
of steaming and involuted roots

the initiation of the world, dark hands moulding charcoal
into the artifice
                        of bleeding stars, the mouths intent
and drawn-out
against the still life impression
                                of our own navels

where innumerable fish owls seek the obscure identity
of woman

the initiation of the world, absolute and libertine fisherman
dying
                    of freedom, their ox heads sighted beneath carnivals
of shitty peasant women, rancorous and fucked-up mules thrown
into a fulcrum
                    of wild nuts
and beaten under composition
                                    into a primeval cross
of woodcut carbon

the initiation of the world, perspiring and yellow moons
amid a sad procession of trees, through the sad night
an innocent man's blood caught in the sun
against the crucifixion
                            of evil and sad women, in the sad night
an alchemist composing cold and erotic ducks, under a sad tree
of the night we are waiting for a report
from Charlie Parker
waiting tables in Spain, 1939
or Diego Rivera, upside down scratching his ass
while beginning the construction of the new
and profoundly imaginary world, between shadows and mountains,
between drunken women and hod carriers, between some silver
altar piece and the portrait of a miserable stable
hoarding the angelic and allegorical eyeballs
of the heroic Zapata
we are waiting for Bud Powell
and the corn stalk
                    of nude prisoners
fleeing his persecuted and percussive piano
we are waiting for horses and their vestige, the child-figure
who will come out
                    of his solitary egg dancing
and bringing us an essay concerning the moon

we are huddled and waiting, western and cowboy drunk
between the one colour of our malleable landscape
to see if this poem just rides off into the sunset
or really succumbs to a frightening and logical end

—K. Curtis Lyle

LORENZO THOMAS

Wonders

I know where I belong
But I been away so long.
Sometimes I wonder.
Will I ever hear
Nostalgia In Times Square
Again, in some Avenue B
Break-in 1/2 bath flat
Will I ever sit
In the sun, high
On a Lenox terrace
And watch the Harlem River run
Away from the dope
And the crime
To the gray East
Again? And me
With some Boone's Farm
Meaning no harm
On anybody
Sitting there digging
Eddie Palmieri's
Hip conversations
With Obatala.
Sometimes I wonder
About that.
Or to be freak again
Be in the Bronx
Stoned on the rocks
As Jr Walker strain
His voice and young girls'
Credulity. Again?
Oh girls I can hear

Your radios
Loud at midnight
In Harlem or Elmhurst
And the smog a gangster
To ask proud
Stars to give it up.
Girls
Check it out
When you pout and talk bad
Think of me, exiled
Almost a year
From the life
Lord, and don't be so hard
Sometimes I be distracted
When I think how you style.
Hold it. I sound like
The Browning of America!
I feel so simple to be thinking of Harlem
New York, the apple
Where we had our own Adam
And damn near all
The wonders of the world

Saigon, VNCH

Historiography

"Bird is a god of good graciousness".
—Ted Joans

I

The junkies loved Charles Parker and the sports
And the high living down looking ones
Those who loved music and terror and lames
Who in Bird's end would someday do better

As the Bird spiralled down in disaster
Before the TV set some would come to prefer
Out of the sadness of Mr Parker's absence
Never again hearing the strings of Longines

Symphonette

Without hearing the keening cry of the Bird
Nailed to the wax they adored. In the memories
And warmth of their bodies where our Bird
Stays chilly and gone. Every cat caught with

A white girl wailed Bird Lives! And the dopies
Who loved Charlie Parker made his memory live
Those who loved music made his memory live
And made the young ones never forget Bird

Was a junkie

2

We lost others to pain stardom and
Some starved at vicious banquets
Where they played until the victuals
Was gone. Pretty music. For all that

Pain. Who made the young ones remember the pain
And almost forget the dances? Who did that?
Steal the prints and the master and burn down
The hope of his rage when he raged? It was

Not only pain

There was beauty and longing. And Love run
Down like the cooling waters from heaven
And sweat off the shining black brow. Bird
Was thinking and singing. His only thought

Was a song. He saw the truth. And shout the Truth
Where Indiana was more than the dim streets of Gary
A hothouse of allegedly fruitful plain America
Some will never forgive the brother for that. Bird

Was a junkie

3

According to my records, there was something
More. There was space. Seeking. And mind
Bringing African control on the corny times
Of the tunes he would play. There was Space

And the Sun and the Stars he saw in his head
In the sky on the street and the ceilings
Of nightclubs and lounges as we sought to
Actually lounge trapped in the dull asylum

Of our own enslavements. But Bird *was* a junkie!

LINER NOTES

Because it is conceived as a tonal evocation of the spirit of Charles Parker (1921-1955), "Historiography" is a poem designed for oral recitation. It is a solo constructed in the bop saxophone style. The poem was written to be performed with a jazz orchestra of 3-7 pieces, using traditional 1940s bebop instrumentation. In its own way, the poem is an investigation of the sonic developments pioneered by Parker and his associates.

"Historiography" has been performed in New York City sittin' in with the Wes Belcamp group at the Village Door (1972) and with the Ric Murray Trio on a poetry and jazz program entitled *Union* at Sir James's Pub (April 18, 1974). The piece has also been performed with Lanny Steele and the Texas Southern University Jazz Ensemble at the Westheimer Art Fair in Houston, Texas (September 1974).

—LORENZO THOMAS

Cousin Mary

goes way back to the days/my father a young man

central avenue his pride that tore down cobalt blue
plymouth struggle buggy and mom slave
to the sewing machine

pops used to babysit me/take me for rides everywhere
beside him staring out the window at all the black faces
making tracks
that was where the cotton club used to be
and the bucket of blood. do you remember when nat king cole
played on the avenue and the dunbar hotel where all the high steppers
went
saturday night like after the joe louis fight or on leave
from washing down the latrines of world war two
at the chicken shack greasin' down
with the black stars

that was before "we" had tv and pops was hot stuff
selling insurance. used to take me everywhere
i was *his* little girl (till baby brother got big enough)

we used to climb stairs/big stairs at golden state insurance
and my dad important, suit and tie—would prop me
up on his desk and the office people would
come around and say how pretty i was
all done up in pale pink organdy with taffeta ribbons to match
pink thin cotton socks and white patent leather shoes

she goes way back/those days/wide-eyed impressions

pops would take me to visit
her dancing with the gi's/boogie-woogie'n to
some dap daddy ticklin' ivories on the spin of a 78
playing cards and talking that talk

me a little bundle of grins
looking up at all those adults/trying to swallow it all
with my eyes. she was so fine
a warm friendly smile making her home mine

years later done in—arthritis and bad men
doing for those who can't help themselves and barely able
to help herself. selfless. a beauty so deep
gift of inexpensive ashtrays to be remembered by/gold

her song to me across years

but, ruby my dear

he hikes those narrow chords one more time
to a dingy walkup on the outskirts of ecstasy
he knows every note of her
down to that maddening musky treble
from between her dusky thighs
even as he raps twice to let her know
he means business
and hears her singeful "who's there?"
as she unlocks the double bass count
he's gonna put hurt on her
he's gonna love her like winter loves snow
he's gonna make her
beyond that scratchy 78 whining dreary days and
whiskey nights
beyond that too sweet smoke andante
beyond that hunger for impossible freedom
to the heart of melody
where they will go to steam
in the jazzified mystical sanctity
of discordant fusion

scaling

—Wanda Coleman

Capricorn Rising

for Pharoah Sanders

I wake up mumbling, "I'm
    not at the music's
mercy,"   think damned
     if I'm not, but
     keep the thought
           to myself.

Sweet mystic beast on the
    outskirts of earth,
  unruly airs, an awkward
              birth
    bruises the bell of its
            horn . . .
Life after life each like it
    was endlessly yet
        to arrive yet
      already there, a
      thin bread of duress,
                 a
sea-weary drift of boatlifted
      Haitians . . .
          The hiss of
               the sea
      whispering words of
             power,
    pinkish kef-pesh tools
   part the lips of the
         dead.

Lacking teeth but licking
the air for some
taste of Heaven,
hungered by
its name, what of
it I refuse
forks an angel's tongue,
what of it I refuse awakes
the wide-eyed
stone

"John Coltrane Arrived with an Egyptian Lady"

—belated prayer—

no sheet of sound enshroud
the Fount of this fevered
Brook becoming one
with God's Eye, not
a one of these notes

come near to the brunt
of the inaudible
note I've been reach-
ing toward

To whatever
dust-eyed giver
of tone to whatever
talk, to whatever slack
jaws drawn against bone

                    To whatever
        hearts abulge with
unsourced light, to whatever
        sun, to whatever moist
        inward meats
                        of love

        Tonight I'll bask
    beneath an arch of
                        lost
        voices,   echo
        some Other place,
Nut's nether suns
                        These
        notes' long fingers gathered
        come to grips of gathered
cloud, connected lip
                        to unheard of
        tongue

Bedouin Hornbook

[An excerpt]

6.XII.80

Dear Angel of Dust,

Your letter arrived this morning. Thank you for your encouraging re-
marks. I'm glad you like "Meat of My Brother's Thigh." I especially took
to what you say about "outward embrace compounded of inbred refu-
sals." Funny you should ask about the Crossroads Choir. I've been
meaning to update you on my attempts to make contact with them, to
let you know that I in fact did so the other night. Not that it was the
easiest thing in the world to do. I spent several weeks asking around
regarding their whereabouts, only to be told again and again that they'd
"gone underground." No one I talked to was willing to discuss it any
further than that. But two nights ago I received a phone call from some-
one who refused to identify himself. He said that if I wanted to meet with
the Crossroads Choir I should go alone, on foot and carrying the horn of
my choice to the summit where Stocker, Overhill and La Brea come
together. This I should do, he said, at half past midnight and once I got
there blindfold myself and wait. I would be picked up and from there
taken to where I'd, as he put it, "be allowed the audience you so deeply
desire." I tried asking what the point of all the cloak-and-dagger business
was, but he cut me off by emphatically repeating, "Alone, on foot and
with the horn of your choice!" And with that he abruptly hung up.

I suppose it's a measure of a lack in my life that I went along with this
arrangement. In any case, I did. I decided on bass clarinet as the horn I'd
carry along and once I got to the summit I blindfolded myself as in-
structed. I turned my coat collar up to the wind but the wait turned out
to be short. Before I knew it I was being helped into the back of a van
which had just pulled up. Once inside, I made a move to take the blind-
fold off but was told to leave it on. The van pulled away and I was given a
tasteless, odorless liquid to drink. The trip took maybe an hour and a half
I'd say, though it's hard to be exact as to how long. We seemed to move

across an undulatory terrain in which ups were immediately followed by downs and vice versa. It was hard for me, in fact, to keep from getting sick. The liquid I'd been given to drink induced a sense of immersion, a watery submission to the elements at large in which every wrinkle of wind, however slight, fluttered like wings or splashed like a swimmer's limbs. There was something baptismal about it, an invoked or in some other way sought-after thirst for shipwreck, a sense of having sunk. There was something Brazilian about it as well, a Bahian fisherman's tenuous truce with the sea. My sense was not so much one of having run aground (the van was clearly moving along smoothly), but of a "diet" I'd embarked on whereby my stomach fell into the pit of itself, its would-be floor falling away in an abrupt, breathtaking onslaught of vertigo.

The airiness of every previous disposition now made itself felt. It was as if the collision course or crash diet I'd embarked upon deserted me at the edge of a body of thought whose bitter, lawless beauty only led me on. Shunning every eventual advance, the road ahead brought me to the realization that I had never actually seen or heard the Crossroad Choir as such. My knowledge of their music, I couldn't help seeing, had to do with its having always been, as the expression goes, "in the air." It was with a merciless, missionary clarity I saw now that the Choir was an anonymous, axiomatic band whose existence had always been taken for granted. I suspected this was the only way it could be "taken" at all, even though to see it so made my pilgrimage seem absurd. Moist with the sweat running down my face, the blindfold projected an illusory pool of reflection in the seemingly sunlit distance ahead. The asphalt ribbon we'd set out upon, pursuing a watery promise without aid of an actual sun, brought the night to life with a kind of furry moisture (a feathered moisture in fact). Every pinpoint droplet of mist interacted with sweat, making for a velvety, somewhat salty compartment of blind, irretrievable flight.

When we got to wherever it was we'd been heading the van came to a stop and I was helped out and led thru a number of doors, the blindfold still in place and my horn, in its case, still in hand. We went from the damp outside air into a place whose air was warm, dry but oddly humid at the same time. It was the humidity of breath and bodies I knew at once, hearing the collective, incoherent murmur of what was obviously a crowd. My escorts sat me down at what turned out to be a table, one of those tiny round ones one sits at in nightclubs. It was alright, one of them told me, to remove the blindfold now. Having done so, my first impressions of what I saw were mixed and, in a certain sense, without definition. Whether this was the effect of the odorless, tasteless liquid I'd been given to drink I can't say for sure. What I can say is that I was struck by the indeterminate character of my surroundings, the variable aspects of which refused to settle into any solid, describable "take." One moment it seemed I was in an intimate nightclub, the next a domed arena with a seating capacity of thousands. One moment it seemed I was in a cramped garage (the sort of place Ornette's band used to practice in during those early days in Watts), the next a huge, drafty warehouse in Long Beach or San Pedro or some place like that. One moment it seemed I was in a cathedral, the next a storefront church. The possibilities seemed to go on without end. I was "everywhere," which, I now knew, was nowhere in particular, a blank check drawn on a closed account

In keeping with this, the crowd was faceless and of a variable aspect all its own. I looked around, a bit disconcerted by the blank, laconic stare I met on every rounded, "metaphysical" head. It was as though I'd stepped onto a de Chirico canvas, the crowd composed of hairless, mannikin-like men and women, each of whose faces wore itself like a tight, tautological mask. The smooth, more or less featureless flesh which enveloped each head contrasted dramatically with the faces of the band which had begun making its way onto the stage up front. The band's faces appeared to suffer from a surplus or an overcharge of features—etched, it seemed, with every crow's foot or expressive crease to which flesh had ever been prone. Fold upon fold, line upon line and wrinkle upon wrinkle gathered, one moment suggesting the Assyrian god Humbaba, whose face was built of intestines, the next the Aztec raingod Tlaloc, whose face consisted of two intertwining snakes. The band, which could only have been the Crossroads Choir, partook of an elastic, variable aspect equal to if not greater than that of the audience and the structure (whatever and wherever it was) in which we were gathered. Their entrance threatened to go on forever—a slow, numberless stampede, as it were, of musician after hyperbolic musician which made me wonder whether the stage could hold them all. It seemed they were every band I'd ever heard or even dreamt I'd heard all rolled into one.

Their rolling entrance did at last come to an end. They were a motley group of an uncountable constitution, one moment seeming as intimate as a trio, the next as large as eight orchestras combined. The audience had been applauding throughout the time they took coming onstage, the applause subsiding once the entrance came to an end. At that point one of the bass players, the apparent leader of the band, stepped forward and spoke into one of the microphones. He thanked the audience for their applause, then announced that the first number would be a piece he'd written called "Head Like a Horse's, Heart Like a Mule's." He described it as an Indo-Haitian Sufi nocturne based on a line from the *Upanishads*: "The pressing stone of the soma press is the penis of the sacrificial horse." The band came on with a somewhat tortured but robust keening, reminiscent of the choked, almost Korean insistence of the opening ensemble passage in Joseph Jarman's "Song for Christopher." It was a wild, inordinate avalanche of spirit which caught me off guard. I was suddenly ridden by the band's capitulation to ancestral fury, a horseheaded sleeper robed in cardiac stitchings who stubbornly brayed as if begging for love in a pirate's world.

Such a sense of myself I'd nourished only in private (or what I thought was private), unassailable, or so I thought, within the vascular walls of a fool's paradise. But the band had wasted no time going for the audience's jugular, laying claim to blood and to kinship ties as though they mined us for gold. It was risky turf on which they staked their claim, veins liable to be loaded but most likely yielding only fool's gold, as they themselves must have known. "Better fool's gold than no gold at all," they seemed to insist—a conviction after my own quixotic heart. Still, there was a thread running thru much of what the flute had to say which took a much more tentative approach. "Fools rush in," it warned, entering into an exchange with the rest of the band. Disregarding the equestrian character of the band's obsession with bittersweet sevenths, the flute insisted on referring to them as birds. "Dear Birds," I heard it say, my head cocked at an angle, "See sun in the shadow, yes, but also turn it around. Be alert. Beware." On a less obvious level, of course, the exchange was no more than a setup, a rigged appropriation of any would-be rider's misgivings or doubts given the feathered horse the band had become. Nevertheless it was the unobstructed body of love their exchange addressed, a pneumatic equation whose antiphonal factors each exacted an abrupt, unlikely gift of itself.

After several bars had passed and the rest of the band pulled back the flute continued on, a cappella. It was a solo whose impromptu structure somehow built upon the rags of its meager technical resources. Slaptonguing the lip-plate while fingering the keys, the flutist resorted to certain percussive effects whose goal seemed to be to do away with themselves as such. It was a technique Rahsaan used to make use of, but here it seemed condemned to cut its teeth on longing. In fact, the flutist went on to quote from "Serenade to a Cuckoo," the piece Rahsaan did on *I Talk with the Spirits*, giving it a veiled, agitational touch as of an Islamic perfume, humming and even talking as he played. Though it insistently announced its theme to be the "bliss of eternal becoming," the solo, with equal insistence, veered toward complaint. An extended note of regret having to do with "wasted youth," once admitted, took root like a dragon's teeth.

Just as I began to weary of a sloganizing strain which had crept into the solo (a syllogistic bent betrayed in advance by a host of "sculpted," "architectonic" preparations), the flutist did something which brought the crowd to its feet. At the end of a warbling, birdlike run reminiscent of Dolphy, he leaned forward and whispered across the lip-plate into the mike. "As for me," he muttered, "who am neither I nor not-I, I have strayed from myself and I find no remedy but despair." With that all hell broke loose. Everyone immediately rose, some of the crowd even standing up on their chairs, applauding, yelling, whistling, pounding tables and stomping their feet in approval. Off to my right I saw one man break two glasses on the edge of his table, set them up again and bring the palms of his hands down on their jagged rims. He then held his hands up for everyone to see, moving toward the stage to stand directly below the flutist, his bleeding hands up in the air and the blood running down his arms—a token, he seemed to be suggesting, of his appreciation.

It took me a while to realize that I too was standing. The flutist, egged on by the audience's response, for one extended instant fulfilled the most radical, far-reaching dreams of the otherwise oppressed. Opting for folly on the one hand and philosophy on the other, he extracted a barebones, hungry sound from the flute. An almost clandestine appeal, its claim was that were there no call the response would invent one. It was at this point that numerous bits of broken glass imbedded themselves in my forehead, each of them the seed of a low, breathy growl which seemed to emanate from the stars. The bits of glass had all the feel of something heavensent, but an angular, trigonometric intrigue born of airtight recesses gave rise to a traumatic, anticlimactic unpacking of the fact that it was the windshield of my mother's car when I was eleven which was, after all, their source. In a flash, I heard the screeching of tires and felt myself thrown forward, the car ramming the rear of the one in front of us, not having stopped in time. I went weak in my legs for a moment, the people on either side of me taking hold of my arms as I began to go down, easing me very gently back into my chair.

The bits of glass went on to instigate a prolonged, problematic meditation on a theme which up until then had been only tangentially touched upon. Could it be, each and every laserlike sliver of light gave me reason to wonder, that the pinpoint precision of any breakdown of the tribe made for an obsessed, kaleidoscopic rift in sound, the audible harmolodic equivalent of a certain impingement or pungency? Could the piercing, punchy use of brass one hears in salsa bands be the proof of this or at least a usable case in point? How would one then, I went on to ask, build outward from "pointillisticity" so as to account for the dry waterfall effect of what was at that moment coming out of the flute? And what about rescue? What, that is, could free the future from every flat, formulaic "outcome," from its own investment in the contested shape of an otherness disfigured by its excursion thru the world? My thoughts then took a somewhat different course. The fertile bed of glittering bits of glass had become an oasis, an agonizing mirage whose momentary splendor threw me back upon myself like a gun going off. A shadowlike report which, as it turned out, was the band coming in as the flute solo ended, inducted me into a dance whose disjointed aspects embraced an untested need I felt to investigate fear.

It was evidently a need I shared with others, for at that moment the tenor player stepped forward as the band made a quick transition into one of the most dangerous standards around, "Body and Soul." If you know the expression "teardrop tenor" then you've got some idea of what the sound was like. It was a rendition filled with a vulnerable regard whose rhetorical supports telegraphically "fell" so as not to be seduced by a possibly naive, no longer available eloquence. These rhetorical supports, meant to bolster up an unforced, freestanding truth (or what purported to be one), made for what I can at best only approximate by the phrase "liturgical ambush"—a self-inquisitive instrumentality which feasted on sorrow. On one level at least, the band arraigned every attempt to make a virtue of sorrow, not only plumbing the depths of an allegorical exhaustion but unwinding a parable, more or less, having to do with first and final things. The tune, as you know, is a showpiece for tenor, and the tenor man rose to the occasion with an almost lethal brilliance. To say that he chewed it up and spat it out, as the expression goes, doesn't even come close. There was a New World extravagance to what he came up with, an endlessly caressive ritual of adoration, a grammatology of touch. What came to mind was the way Shepp does Ellington, or Sonny Rollins on, say, "Everything Happens to Me." Then again, there was some altogether other stuff he mixed in with it which absolutely blew me away.

The bed of glass just behind my brow again began to throb as the piece went on. A rippling sense of *surge* complicated by *sway* had made its way into the music. The tenor man continued on in what had become an essay (a manifesto even) assaulting the notion of "everyday life," concocting a long, breathy, sinuous line whose hoarse exuberance he thinly laced with a sort of erotic dismay. I leaned over and asked the man sitting next to me (the crowd was now sitting again) were my ears playing tricks or did I hear something Egyptian running through the solo. He whispered back that he heard it too, going on to attribute it to what he referred to as the tenor man's "herbal sanction," saying that backstage between sets he'd seen him puffing on a "sherman"—which, he went on to explain, noting my puzzled look, is a joint soaked in embalming fluid. This might also explain, I suggested at once, the vicarious octaves he'd apparently added to the tenor's range, the solo's "phantom" reach. "Precisely," he whispered in agreement, nodding his head, as we both turned our attention back to the music.

The tenor man's face had become a sweating mask by now. A tight-lipped howling nursed an otherwise awkward ascent whose ritual insistence took us under its wing as if rooted in threadbare follicles of light. At the height of its powers—part rant, part psalm, part put-on—the solo took an abrupt yet understandable turn, its eventual cadences hissing and flaring like sodium dropped into water. A chemical wedding whose unlikely fruit bore the brunt of an exquisite, disquieting cross between Albert Ayler and Jr. Walker, the lyrical bridge the tenor embarked upon immersed us deeply in a sirenlike, wide-eyed whine. Possessed of an unkempt sandpaper texture suggesting a monochrome rainbow, each line invested itself in variegated gradations of black, each esoteric thread belatedly managing to harvest the raspy nothingness of a comet's tail. The crowd by this time had begun chanting one of the lines from the song, crying over and over, "My house of cards had no foundation." It was a chant whose edgy confession became a fleeting wisp of nothing so much as the wish to be there as well as elsewhere, everywhere at once.

I opened my mouth to join the chant but no sound came out. For some reason I couldn't get beyond the title, on which my thoughts locked as on something so axiomatic it left nothing more to say. At the same time, though, it was the very wellspring of what was being said. The realization hit me that here was the sweet, sour, somewhat acidic hollow in which what was spoken belied the mootness of what might better have been intoned, as if certain prohibitions against belaboring essentials made for an ulterior permission. "Body and soul," I muttered under my breath, taken aback by the relevance of these words yet again, but the abrupt renewal of such an apparently pristine relevance formed a lump in my throat. Building up to become a faint, unpretentiously drawn sadness, it was a lump which ironically confirmed my vocation, the vacated premise of an image of change I thought I'd one day grasp. But such a skeletal body of hope was not to be taken hold of nor taken lightly, even though the wildest, farthest reaches of spirit ran like an engine thru the blank but eloquent chambers of the heart. "Body and soul," I managed to mutter again, as though intoning a prayer too close to the heart to be put into words. No matter how much I cautioned myself against it, I couldn't shake the feeling that the lump had become a lozenge, so soothing and at the same time so sweet it gave my mumbling the sugared, ethereal sound of a children's choir.

As I began to muse on the borrowed voice I'd somehow contracted I became aware that I was being escorted toward the stage. I hadn't been able to help noticing the leader of the band pointing toward me from behind his bass, this evidently being a sign to the invisible ushers who helped me out of my chair. Still weak in the knees from the bits of broken glass, I instinctively grabbed hold of the case containing my bass clarinet as I began to move forward. It took me no time at all to realize that I'd been summoned, that I was now being given a chance to sit in. The opportunity both excited me and gave me cause to be wary. The tenor man was still deeply into his solo, blowing an insanely beautiful tremolo figure which, as did everything else, made his "act" an almost impossible one to follow. It was then that it occurred to me that the emotional cramp I'd felt in my throat might very well have been a dowry. I saw myself as a "bride" by way of whose wedding what had been confirmed was—how can I put it?—a vocation for longing. It was nothing less than a calling brought about in such a way that one nursed a sweet-tooth for complication.

Now I knew for sure that my heart cried out for obstruction, a realization which evolved into warnings I fought against in vain. It was as though it did so in order to exercise itself, to assert its beauty (a muscular beauty it seemed) in relation to resistances the world put up. However simplistic it seemed to put it so, I felt as though longing had long ago wearied of its ostensible objects, keeping itself alive by way of the obstacles it met. There were other sides to my meditation, of course, but by this time I was already onstage, horn in hand, trading fours with the tenor while trying to make sense of the tempo changes the leader introduced. I'd begun with a sly, breathy phrase which, however gruffly it started out, ended up as a sigh. It was a begging off from the possible hubris of going on, as if I shrugged my shoulders by way of asking, "What more can I say?" The sigh was an ode, an elegy and a confession all at once. I felt depleted and put upon. I rummaged around in the horn's lower register, buying time, though I knew that wasn't getting me anywhere. It wasn't ideas or feelings I lacked so much as a focus, a door by way of which to broach what I thought and felt. "Body and soul," I reassured myself, keeping close to the head but unraveling a line which progressively tutored itself on hope.

It was shortly after the tenor man pulled away and left me all to myself that a plea I'd have never predicted could issue from the horn did exactly that. A paradoxical plea, it had the quality of a koan, lecturing all who'd listen on the hopelessness of hope while at the same time indicting the presumptuousness of despair. What had taken place was that I'd had no other recourse but to resort to my recurrent appeal to a long lost, distant love, my memories of whom, to this day, refuse to fade. With infinite, greedy tenderness I embroidered the line with the tale of this obscure love affair, a seven-day romance I had ages ago with a woman I met halfway around the world. It was a whirlwind affair, love at first sight, proposing impossibly wide horizons and laying claim to only the most unlikely prospects. With painstaking patience I sketched every detail of our initial encounter, thrown back upon that oldest, ever-available sacrament—rites of seduction. The featurelessness of the crowd before me made my recollection of her face all the more poignant. Sounding as much like Dolphy as I could, I tried to suggest the gamy brightness of her eyes, the freckles to the inside of her cheekbones, the dimples below the corners of her mouth. I went on to elaborate as best I could, filling in the portrait with such details as the tiny star of an earring she wore, the curliness and cut of her hair, the generous pout of her slightly jutting mouth to which I'd been so drawn. Wrestling with the limits of the horn, I did what justice I could to the press of our bones and the snug, thrusting fit of our flesh, the enduring, wicked sting of the carnal rites whose plunge we took. I resorted to a melismatic bending of notes by way of evoking the gamma flood we felt in one another's arms.

The basses, appropriately enough, sustained an ominous, throbbing ostinato, the ironic donor of a heartbeat, growl and sob whose message was unmistakably clear. It had been a love, they reminded me, doomed from the very start, condemned to the crib and crypt of its promise (as love perhaps always is), an aborted or stillborn flight whose foreboding their throb so insisted on. They softened their line somewhat to allow that we'd been victims of circumstance, our love a case of mistaken identity perhaps (though they couldn't resist throwing in that such was almost always the case). I instantly ratified their suggestion, finding it the basis for the beautiful, squawking eloquence to which the bass clarinet's upper register lends itself. I admitted that, yes, we had both no doubt felt orphaned by the circumstances we attempted to flee, the inert familiarity of the lives we were doomed to return to, half an unmoved world apart. It was an image of global anguish, global desire and global ennui I resorted to, the meeting of promise with paradox, universal deadend. It was apparently an image which got to the crowd, for at that moment something miraculous happened. Not only did the audience come to their feet, as they had during the flute solo, but their heads all of a sudden acquired features, welcome wrinkles and expressive lines they hadn't had before. I went on playing, amazed and encouraged by what I saw, even though many of the faces appeared grotesque and distorted, recalling the twisted, misplaced eyes, teeth, noses and lips of New Guinea masks. A gambler against my will, I'd gone for broke and won.

Still, the brevity of our seven-day romance all but made me weep. It took every mystical consolation I could muster to keep from breaking down. I attempted, for example, to think of our week together as the seven days of Creation, recalling Messiaen's idea (come upon in some liner-notes I'd recently read) that the seventh day, God's day of rest, prolonged itself into eternity to become an eighth, a day "of unfailing light." The seven days had gone by so swiftly, I reflected, but the eighth, which we now inhabited, would never end. The last day we'd seen one another now returned, but with a new sense of lingering access—once a day of parting, now a day of repose. I relaxed into such a sense of it, deepening its consolation with a meditation on the number eight. "Upright infinity," I whispered into the horn. It occurred to me now, as though I'd never seen it before, that the eighth note of every octave is a return to the first, both end and beginning. It made me think of Lébé, the last of the eight Dogon ancestors, also said to be the oldest, which would make him the first. I reflected on his having died and become a snake, a fact I referred to with circular breathing in a run which also brought Ouroboros to mind.

The crowd had started singing again. "My life revolves about her,/ What earthly good am I without her?/ My castle has crumbled,/ I'm hers, body and soul." The band came in on the chorus and as the audience sang a ball of light bounced from syllable to syllable as in the sing-along cartoons we saw at the movies when I was a kid. I couldn't help thinking of it as a ball of cabalistic light our week-long courtship had sparked, a promise of one day overcoming division. It was both a ball of cabalistic light and the blank, bouncing check I'd gotten inklings of earlier. I knew I'd come home to the heart. I opened my eyes just in time to see that the ball was in fact a balloon the crowd was batting among themselves, each person tapping it ever so lightly to keep it aloft. It was a white balloon on which, written in black, were the words "Only One." Finally a woman tapped it with a sharp flick of her finger, sending it toward the ceiling. It rose with ever-increasing speed, taking my breath away, only to come down even faster.

Yours,
N.

—Nathaniel Mackey

okra to greens

a historical perspective of sound

i thought i might be in slug's
pharoah waz singin
though he didnt beat his
chest
carnival rolled outta brooklyn   thru the snow
& soho/ right up 7th avenue south
with our wintry american version of the jump-up
pharoah did know the sun
& tabo screamed over & over
6 tenor players filled the front row
the battles of the horns to commence
but i know this isnt slug's
cuz lee morgan's blood doesnt dot the sawdust
ayler's echoes cant be heard in the john &
sun ra doesnt work here mondays
i'm not 19 years old/ in tie-dyed jeans
& pink satin/ watchin 3rd street burn down lil by lil
while the yng ones with mouthpieces & brushes
wait to sit in/ this isnt slug's cuz death seems
so far away/ not boomer's where death is sold in packages
it's ten years later/ & the changes are transcribed

Rite-ing

for Oliver Lake, Anthony Davis, Michael Gregory Jackson,
Paul Maddox, Leonard Jones and Buster Williams

hold til there is not a breath to
    take
and i take the moment
imagine how you would sing
    song
if you had a right to gold with
    wings & sing
i can be every whenever in a
    while
real melody is unpredictable

see yellow unicorn with blue
    horn
red unicorn with yellow mane
a great white gallopin stallion
    of a unicorn
braized in a sea of orange
3 emerald women rolling shells
    in aqua waves
nineteen quartermoons dance/
    the sea is orange
the sky is orange

a chinese lady fans
with the wings of a scarlet
    butterfly
two lovers hold the fantasy
two lovers undone
two lovers in paradise with a gun
a woman laughing from a

redwood tree
eight faces smiling from the
idol's secret space

an arched man with a
saxophone
misted
the disappointing thing about
artists is that they die

wednesday is the favored day
for blk people to kill themselves
not monday/ not friday/ not
sunday
a holy day
but wednesday in the middle of
so much
we have not paced it

my shawls are not bones i wrap
myself in
not bones i throw to the dogs
my shawls are not bones to bury
in palm roots
they are shrouds—my shawls
commemorate the old one
when she was young

hold til there is not a breath to
take
and i take the moment
imagine how you would sing
song
if you had a right to gold with
wings & sing
i can be every whenever in a
while

real melody is unpredictable
with spells to shed
if touched
with the manners of a witch the
    ivory unicorn watches
the sunrise/ a sorrel
wades by the waterfall
a felon writes his poems
an ebony woman her arms filled
    with flowers
lays memory in the soil
that we might dig out
our beginnings

—Ntozake Shange

XAM WILSON CARTIÉR

Be-Bop, Re-Bop

[An excerpt]

BE-BOP, RE-BOP & ALL THOSE OBBLIGATOS

The liquor was flowing, everyone had a plate, folks had visited all the way back to the kitchen. . . . We were just settling into the spirit of Double's funeral wake when Vole took it in mind to drive all the guests from the house.

For some reason of crisis insanity and because my first reaction to mayhem is to staple down the madness to some detail of order, I've begun to take stock of the folks in the room, to estimate the number of floating mourners who've made their way past the living room rut to the recondite sanctum in the rear of the house. There are twenty-four people posed at candid angles as far back through the room as the eye can see, including five men: two family friends and three co-workers of Double's whom I've seen two or three times. The women, role models around me, are fine-feathered birds flown from flighty Saks and Montaldos, the haute couture rooms. We're all, all of us are musing over inscrutable chalices of highballs, including me in spasmodic sweet-six-teenhood, thanks to the blessing of mother-gone-from-the-room, but now Vole's back, so here's my solo, about to be crimped. . . .

Vole had been resting in the bedroom away from it all when Mona threw out, "Some folks might've called him irresponsible and impulsive, but one thing about Double is, he might have been practically back down to where he started when he died, but now there was a man who could keep going when the chips were down no matter *what* it took. If it took a Tom, he'd be one, and he has his own good reasons too, he must have, considering what he stooped to just to hold on to that trifling job in parcel post. It was the best thing he'd ever lucked up on."

She sucked her teeth and shook her head.

"Truth is the light," somebody said.

"Let it shine," somebody else said.

"Now *some* folks might have said Double was a dreamer with no firm sense of direction;" Mona went on, "they'd have said he was good for nothing but dead-end dreams . . . but I know better! though Double *had* him some dreams, at least till Vole started to stay on his back—she rode him all the time you know, though let it be said, Double needed some get-up and go. Don't talk about the dead, but you all know what I mean, you can't live a man's life for him; you've got to let him breathe. Vole knows that—maybe she's got another opinion—but well, you all know the story: You don't miss your water till your well runs dry!"

She raised her glass to the tune of the assents around her.

"Well, well, well." Vole appeared in the doorway looking store-rack crisp in her undefiled black dress, faille skirt riding impossible curves of her paragon legs. She raised that tight tan face, angled those high-carved cheekbones, fast-focused those radar eyes from their dusty socket-shadows. Her fingers draped the knob of the door like a mannequin's hand but for the fingernails, which she trimmed stoically in ruthless crescents. We're all looking over at her, ruffled in our own different ways, with reactions ranging from bitterness to outrage. Where are Vole's tears anyway? I'm thinking—and where's the crash of her gloom? There she stands, intact and unacceptable as usual. Her sometime pal Mona is one juror in particular who gives Vole the eye; Mona's response to Vole at the moment is disappointment that the convicted widow's alive and well.

"Having fun?" Vole flings at Mona over undermusical silence and rustling nudges, just as Mona's in process of leaning her emerald suède vested chest toward the woman beside her, in bracing gesture of *uh-oh.* . . .

"Now Vole, just calm down, honey," Mona dodges, the defense is pushed out of her instantly and she rolls on automatically: "Death is always hard, we know that, and it's hardest on the widow, yes, it always is, it's the shock, and—"

"What do you know?" Vole cut her off at the pass of her sass. "Just what in the *hell* do you know?" And I tense, since I feel Vole building to an open storm of her closet feelings; already she's lapsed into what she calls *vulgar language in public,* brazenly defying the Salt Away Box (this being a cylindrical empty salt box that we keep family fines in; whoever cursed had to pay). "I'm tired, but I ain't crazy," Vole goes on with further indication of no-holds-barredness, her lapse into "slang" as she calls it. "I'm tired but I ain't crazy enough to think you actually give a damn about anybody's grief, least of all mine, or do I *look* like a fool? Tell me anything!" Vole's leaning forward now with arms crossed across her chest, a hanging judge, waiting....

"Uh—" starts Mona....

"Yeah, 'uh,'" says Vole relentlessly, leaning further toward the defendant—"Come on, tell me anything, just front me right off. I'm supposed to be under the influence of widowhood, so you can't go wrong. Come on, don't let me stop your show since you know so much. Knock yourself out, come on; make like I'm not here.

"Look at you," Vole sneers on, "in your weep motif. You never did a damn thing for Double while he was alive, or for any of the rest of us" (here she gestures maternally toward me), "and you know it. But you take plenty time to rake us through with your mouth, mouth almighty, fatmouth queen, brilliantine—"

("Good*damn*" goes someone's hushed catharsis; all of us onlookers had been swept into the spirit of Vole's testimony)—

"Well, surprise, fools"—Vole turns to the room at large—"I can read you like a book. But don't let that throw you—" With this last you can hear a crew of voices arming with mumbles for self-defense just in case, be prepared, but look! There's Vole, on everyone's case already . . . here she comes, snatching plates of food and drinks from visitors ("Here, I'll take that"), rushing out of the room mechanically, then back again now with armloads of hats and coats which she flings in a heap on the couch and returns for the rest.

"If it took a Tom, he'd be one. . . ." It's this I consider during the following frantic interval; I try not to, but can't help but think it, this peanut butter thought that sticks to the roof of my immature mind . . . I think of the time only last week, when Double had lost his post office gig and Vole and I had passed him talking on the wallphone in the hall....

"Well, do you take colored?" Double has mouthed this then in mealy manner, or so it seemed to the both of us, Vole headed one way and I another, so that *What?* we stop and stare at each other, then both jump in at once—

"Do they do what?" Vole challenges Double and then walks away with no further display, a mystery to teenage me at the time, and I stay on to follow her words with a cop-bust frown of disgust aimed at Double, this at know-all black-and-white stage of analysis development, righteous adolescence. To tom or not to tom—seemed perfectly clear to me. . . .

Aw Double, I thought at the wake then that day, there it is, so my hump of shock and letdown can sink to its rest in the pit of my stomach—Was our case really so critical then that we were all the way down to our tommery? I asked myself again and again all through that week, near the time of your seemed-to-be sin when I thought I knew the answer, one answer: *Hell no! You can be down to death, and not down to tom!* Yet—this I know now—what could you do, standing limp with livelihood soon to be lost, as you knew, to the rake of unfeeling circumstance? What's more I'm human too and've whipped out my own slave-kerchief in time of distress, "It's reflex survival," I fibbed to myself until then when that day at your wake all your contrivance (just venial connivance, not mortal!)—all your contrivance comes floodingly clear and wet comprehension, it courses a trail through the heat of my face.

Militant memories: For months, years after his passing Double would appear through my sleep to bump a lesser dream, still bopping with the armed resistance of his dedication to "jazz"—which he said was "two, say three broad crooked jumps off to the side of the mainstream straight and narrow, out to where sound becomes sight, as it should be!"

When I think of Double that day at his wake, I see him standing beside the radio with his forefinger crooking for me to run over and check out this riff or those taps or that vamp or these changes. This I'd casually stroll up to do with cool beyond my childish years; my thumbs would be tucked in pinafore straps under fat kinky braids that laid on my chest.

"And how's Daddy's masterpiece comin along?"

"Aw, I can't kick."

"Well say hey, watcha know?"

"Aw, you got the go!"

"So tell me, what's to it?"

"Nothin to it but to do it!"

"Mean to say you can do the do?"

"Can Ella Fitz cut a scat? . . . Then, don't hand me that!"

"Can Eisenhower dance? Say HEY—not a chance!"

"Hey now. And how!"

My smallfry face at Double's knee. Abracadabra afternoons! And every day, on the way home from kindergarten at Booker T Washington School, there's hopeful harmony of Double and me, two hipsters vocaleesing to wide-angle sound up front in the Studebaker.

"Oop bop shabam buh do bo do,
We like to boogie, woogie, re-bop and be-bop it too!"

Yet Double has died. But why call it *death*, when in the scheme of simple reality, I should be and am convinced by the age of sixteen (time of no questions) that his passing, like his music, is more process than product by nature—that Double's demise has the matrix-free flow of an on-the-spot bop change. So since I know he's still bopping nearby in time to the tune of temporality, while Vole's handing out the coats and hats at his wake, I shake the scheme of my dream and seize the opportunity to come up with a note of relevant reality for the mourn-watchers.

"A side of Fats, anyone?" I call out, surrounded by scotchsippers' eyebrows jumping like spastic grasshoppers. "Ain't Misbehavin" has popped into mind like the miracle of the gramophone. So *apropos!* Talk about chromatic consciousness—why it's the final flipside! Besides, it was Double's favorite jam, so I put on the hi-fi and turn it to crescendo. Then's when Vole turns to face me so suddenly that distress bends distended in our corner of the cosmos—rapport needs no words in light of the sight of Vole rushing toward me with her hand upraised, the hand which she uses to spin me for a heartfelt lindy hop, steps of which I fall into by rote due to Double's diligent teaching—and Vole and I, hey, well we dance past all woe for a whirlaround while!

DOUBLE OR NOTHING AND ALL THAT JAZZ

Double's death was a personal nuclear disaster that radiated negative energy in all directions, from was-peaceful past to fallout-filled future. For one thing, death hit Double so all of a sudden that it seemed too contaminating to absorb. I found myself starting to envy folks whose folks had died of lingering cancer or any other dress-rehearsal disease; at least they'd had a fair cool-down period: Death had said *All right, here's the cue for my solo*, and the grieved-to-be had been able to say, *"Goddamn! Why him?"* till they wore themselves out in a natural way. All their guilt and blues had had a chance to sift around till it settled in place, not like me and my lump that still pulsates, oozing poison gas at random.

Yet Double/dear Papa was dead all right—though his death began my siege of dreaming for months, years after his passing that he still was standing beside the chifforobe with one foot resting on the radiator, singing the "Monkey Song" as I called it in kidhood, about one of the world's perennial agitators, this one anthropoid and clinging to the back of a wily buzzard who, pragmatist that he was, was bent on devouring the monkey dead or alive.

> *. . . Loosen up, said the buzzard,*
> *you're chokin me. . . .*
> *Loosen up your grip*
> *and I'll set you free.*
>
> *The monkey looked the buzzard*
> *right dead in the eye:*
> *"Your story's very touchin—*
> *but I know it's a lie!"*

When I think of Double, I hear him tapping his feet in time to the beat of developing melody, humming or scat-singing, winging his way through music of process, running through tonal tongue-to-tooth changes with curled fingers striding, flying off ivories in thin air. He'd turn to me in mid-riff with a question in the movement of his eyebrows—

"Young Fats," I'd answer with head cocked to doubledare side. "Young Fats, early Stride!"

Then came a pause, and next, his applause for diligent growth on the part of a smallfry. *"Whoo-whee! The kid's on the ball! What say! SKIN me, my friend!"*

And I'll do it again! I'm kneehigh at the time and filing the bulk of Double's sagacity for future reference, though already I've soaked up weight enough to hold my own in our name-that-tone champion finals. Fact is, I'm still spongy with pride when Double takes me aside to show me a dog-eared copy of a nineteenth-century abolitionist's knotted dialectic on the "marvelous complication" and "curious rhythmic effect" of a "strong musical network" which defied all due deployment of whitefolks' wit.

"See?" Double said then. "They never can manage to hook up our music to its source in the ghetto, be it concrete or cotton. Their bright idea has always been to rip up our music and chop it off at the roots, grimreaper style, just like they do their turnips. They keep the leaves and scrap the soul of the taste in the turnip!"

Our music. It's Double's top doctrine. And by default and devotion, I'm his ace apostle. Which is why later that same afternoon near the noon of it all, when Double's working his graveyard shift so's my daily caretaker while Vole social works her days away, Double and I've been jitterbugging up a storm all over the front room and now we're seated respectfully on the throw rug in the corner, watching the combination radio, a dome-shaped mahogany Mahal for the sounds coming through. We're as intent as if we can see through to the carrier crystal inside the box, major and minor soul-sensors that we are—watching as if the animated armoire is a TV, which is further down the line of dreamed-up illusion. But movement seems to materialize suddenly from the radio bowels, and a wildroot-dampened lilliputian, dapper ofay dollhouse doll, steps up to a miniature microphone between two fat black vacuum tubes.

"You said it!" he enlightens, as we look on unamazed. "That was 'Scrapple from the Apple'!" Then he turns to flash a bright white turnip smile at all of us here in the jimcrow balcony.

But look! Here comes wonder-worker Lady Day, tipping onstage from the wings, wearing her wiltless gardenia and sizzling sequins and mellow phantom pain, pulling free for a while from her private prison with grief disguised as a series of croons:

. . . I don't stay out late . . . (Yeah, Billie!) *. . . don't care to go . . . 'm home about eight . . . just me an my ray-dee-oe . . .*

She knocks us out. Kills us. Absolutely! And Double's now in process of snatching me up into a topheavy foxtrot, with his scratchy cheek to cheek. . . . We're riding out on a riff, right on up to the rickety railing in the redbrick hallway, don't-give-a-damn gliding right on down to the front door with its held-back reality demons. Then back we swing

18. Dizzy Gillespie. Photograph by William P. Gottlieb, © 1979.

toward the tune, in a serious gravity sweep to the source. A dip; we part. Brief shadow of a simple separation.

Why is it that time is so upbeat discreet, cuts no slack in its tempo for our schemes unredeemed? The illusion of endings in the world. Addictive fantasy.

Wait, Time, don't you see? At just 43 he was kicked into infinity by an off-the-rack/black/heart attack/and I was only/I'm still trying to improvise/to finishingtouch-up the rest of his life/in the riffs and the runs (BOPBOP/A-REE BOP!) of the chase through the (BOOGEDY/BOOGEDY/BOPBOPBOP) neo-blue/everblack/labyrinth life

of my dreams!

—XAM WILSON CARTIÉR

Expandable Language

Everybody knows that
the elder was watching
seen us coming from way far
you could hear his music
over six decades if you lived
that long but you didn't
not then he would say
you wanted him to say
but he wouldn't
he knew what you wanted

I watch the reflection
he said of the bridge
in the painting of the bridge
when the sun sets
his back turned
to the bridge even now

I haven't heard no music
since Kansas City
and I fear God
but I have heard 'em cook!
And I am crazy thank god
for that, I am no one
I'm 50 people I once knew

He could see us from way far
he only spoke looking through
your hair past your brain
to your safe zone
where you can be trusted

had no need to talk to you
of time you did not live

I could indulge you
but you can hear me
playing behind Lady Day
I know nothing
'bout slavery
I was born free
and heard the blues
when they asked me
was the Count colored
all I could say was very

You see I played music
with folks who could stand up
with nothing but the rhythm!

C.T.'s variation

some springs the mississippi rose up so high
it drowned the sound of singing and escape
that sound of jazz from back
boarded shanties by railroad tracks
visionary women letting pigeons loose
on unsettled skies
was drowned by the quiet ballad of natural disaster
some springs song was sweeter even so
sudden cracks split the sky / for only a second
lighting us in a kind of laughter
as we rolled around quilted histories
extended our arms and cries to the rain
that kept us soft together

some springs the mississippi rose up so high
it drowned the sound of singing and escape
church sisters prayed and rinsed
the brown dinge tinting linens
thanked the trees for breeze
and the greenness sticking to the windows
the sound of jazz from back
boarded shanties by railroad tracks
visionary women letting pigeons loose
on unsettled skies
some springs song was sweeter even so

Rogue & Jar: 4/27/77

the players: David Murray, Hamiet Bluiett,
Chas. "Bobo" Shaw, Fred Hopkins
poet: Ntozake Shange

the "Iron Man" sat with gone eyes/ a witnessing body
& a bad case of sky high low cold cerebral blues
the lady in orange came lit up with love and night blueness
David came with a gold horn/ a copper suit
& Joann's Green Satin Dress
Fred came to do bizness/Bobo came disguised as the Black
Knights
Drum & Bugle Corps
& Hamiet Bluiett came from Lovejoy, Illinois 62059
the truth came down twice and i was caught in the middle
when it catches me i'm tasty & dangerous like one more for
the road
it laid me out/ it buried me after it worried me
it put ice to my temples & spewed out steam
it was rough/like playing with crackers in Cairo
like playin hard to get on Cottage Grove
it was rough like making love in wet grass
a heat that leaves a chill of remembrance
when the bottom dropped & the floor sank to the metro
i fell in David's bell/where melody is personal
the drum skin began to sweat burlesque
i heard it plead: please the ghosts/cast the flowers
the poem asked what it is to be a man
it was a rough blues/the truth came down twice
& squeezed me like a lemon/ skinned me
& left a tingle there to taste
after such music there is only the quiet shimmer
the glow of eyes being handed back their sight.

—THULANI DAVIS

Solea

there are rapists
out there

some of them
don't like asian women
they stab them
and run off to lake tahoe
in search of more pussy
in casino parking lots

thelonious monk
reminds me of you
and i forget
about this place
it's nice

but then
i have to put in
an appearance
at family dinners
and listen to other voices
my blood
in the warm gravy
and the kiss i reserve
only for little children

i can't play
those records
all the time
thelonious monk
is only joyful

in a hurting kind
of way

there are sad men
out there
some of them
don't like me
they like to talk
about corpses and dirt
and how life used to be
so good
when they were young
in the war

i like to kiss you
like i do
little children
it tastes good
but i have to leave
the room sometimes
is deep
wanting to be crazy
and painting my toenails
gold
and seeing universes
in my colors

there are killers
out there
some of them
smile at me
they dream
about snipers on the freeway
aiming machine guns
and conga drums
at innocent drivers
in their volvos

and mustangs
and dodge darts

new york
reminds me of you
so do the locks
on my door
and the way i look
sometimes
when i feel
schizophrenic

there is real beauty
in my eyes
when i lose my mind

i understand you better
this way
and it doesn't hurt
so much

anymore

—Jessica Hagedorn

Like Cities, Like Storms

Like cities, like storms

these alto and tenormen
blow back cool legato or a rope of cries
against a world pouring down
so hard and fast

the bass and drums are about to fly
off the beat
and lose the soloist orbiting
round it

but don't, somehow
thirty, forty years ago at the Royal
Roost, Five Spot or studio
in Hackensack

With the owner counting heads
and the kid
down from Yale working his way up
his girlfriend's thigh

the rhythm men keep holding on

a foot off the ground,
but holding

Love Poem

As long as the cat comes home
and the skinheads keep
to their concrete shell, over the fence
screaming   *break your face*,   smashing empties

what need is there to worry or come undone
so the wolf slips in,
cutting through us like cheese, soft cheese
an emulsion of blood and cheese

except for the radio tower close by
blighting "Ruby, My Dear"
till you shift in your chair and it's right,
both speakers, all there . . .

Poor Monk, dying at the Baroness's
on the hill above Weehawken
night after night
cars sluicing into the tunnel below

into the city, fanning lights
across the broad river,
the West Side throbbing
across black water

out of notes, dying.

The Coming of John

(the evening and the morning are the first day)

it is friday
the eagle has flown
4 years before the real god Allah shows
before we know the happenings
we eat the devils peck
mondays hotlinks with porkenbeans
hear "newk" on dig and "bags" on moonray
see desolation in the dark between the buildings
our front view of bricks of the adjacent kitchenette

Pat riffs in a babyfied key
slips on the green knit suit
with the silver buckle at the belly
and we slide out into that wintertime
the last lights of day
with an uncanny clarity for chi town
the shafts behind the clouds popping them open
and the rust on the el grids
clashing and blending strangely
against the rays like hip black art
heaven about to show itself
above the ghetto holiday shoppers
the 1954 brand fragments of people on the walks
Hadacol on her way north
after officer driseldorf has stomped her on the street
and crushed her finger on a golden ring

the hipster in the tivoli eat shop
deals single joints after the commotion
dusk baring his first meal
with us streaming and talking about the guns
getting so mad and so frantic we sweat
get on to cool
go on home
make love and nod
then it is the new year
and the guns are going off across the alley

10 days or so hes still "on this end"
only Edwardo Harris knowing his name
John Coltrane (as he was called then)
in a big hat
gouster pleated pants and all
before metamorphosis miles plugs cotton in his ears
and philadelphia thunders in babylon
a shake dancer follows the set
and it seems a whole sea of black faces are out on "six trey"
a holy nation peeping and poor
behind the red oblong bulb of a highlife sign

Ohnedaruth the mystic has already blown and hypnotized us—
making us realize right then
THAT WE ARE LIVING IN THE BIBLE (HOLY KORAN, CABALA)

the konateski girl sets there frozen
shes followed her lifelong scent of judea
from the rich north shore township
all the way into the crown propellar lounge
into a blessed tenors bell
while we go "off into space"
peeping the dream of the old ladies of nipon
dragging the gunny sacks of brown smack across the dead battlefields
chanting "fun amelikaan" "fun amelikaan" "fun joe"
     And of course the bard says (from the corner of his mouth)

"Aw right na iss a party, ya dig that. Miles come in an be doin
alla right things. Ya understand! Takes the hord'overs from the
lazy susan with so much finesse, en be so correct when he be talk-
in to them big fine socialite hos. Understand. They be sayin
'Oh Miles' ya understand, En mah man leave the door open. Nah
here come Trane. He wrong from the get go. Ya understand.
Reach his hand down in the tray, say 'gemme one of them little
samaches.' He done pushed the mop out the way, en grabbed the
johnny walker red, way from one ah them ivy league lames. Un-
derstand! See en Miles he brought the man in there for that.
They working together. Understand. He his man. Yall been hearin
all of us. Jim! them intellectuals, all of um talk-
ing bout the new niggro. There he is right there. What he try-
ing ta tell yall with his horn, is that yall can't expect to
get nowhere bein what the gray call intelligent. If yall expect
to get somewhere in america, you gotta start bustin down dos an
shit, pitchin a fit, and poppin these lames upside the head.
Layin some ah these peckerwoods out across the room, is what
get you somewhere in america. If yall dont get just like me,
and start lettin yalls wigs grow wild and wooly and shit, and
starta setting all up in grays faces, yall aint goin another
futher. Cause this shit, in this here country right here is
coming down ta some shorenuff head bustin."
we stay till the lights
pull the covers off the room
showing the ragged carpet
in the great american tradition

'mayhap a manger'
make in in
fire up two thumbs and sleep
t. i. on a pallet in front of the bad window
and the hotel catches fire
and lobbys all smoking
the few steelworkers with their helmets
the several a d c families
the pimps, the hustlers and the chippies

are all milling around out of it
when the "konat girl" turns up in smoke
in just leotards and a mouton coat
now shes took the pressing iron to her slavic hair
(that morning is the second day)
A Love Supreme takes me in

i stretch my hands open to a sun of morning
and breezes are light that i encounter
in my handclasps with wind

your softness take me in
like a saharan morning taught it
an i hear all that ALLAH says
when i feel the universe about the miracle you are
there is the om of a morning sky
a herb tea and vegetable magic breakfast
you serve me
zodiac sister of the suns house

there are silks within the winds of autumn
and i do not feel the stench of close buildings
alive like smog
sometimes a blare of noon
enthralls me in a mystique
a heat of atoms love
and i am myself a 6 foot fire
a dynamo of afro-energy

there are gulls about the lake
and the sky like a big hip hat
guides them in compassed flight
then there is the small music
of these wise ghetto children
a symphony of innuendos on the street

we walk down six tray
down the line the day is endless
under the shadows of the el it triggers us
with the forces of the lions star
I AM—this love
lady a carbon copy of it
and somewhere over flat rooftops a moon is
so get it fire baby
our fluids will be celestial markings
cosmic clouds fluffed like creation

night will never harm you with its changes
were tuned into this purity of blackness
the gigantic spawn above just a part of it
that we must teach a nation
graces the lights of earth
and i pray while in your embrace
in this house

with the lion our protector
to keep the fruits above we bathe in

A Love Supreme . . . .

AWAKENING
we ate breakfast
with ohnedaruth the mystic
(when he was called john coltrane)
took him from the sissy pimps bar
still with shouters in the aisle
after the lights on set
dug him look up at the death room
in the strand hotel
the red marquee staining the perpetual dirt of the window facing six tray,
rode with him in his script blue chevie wagon
past the fake gothic architecture glowing
incomplete   in the nocturne of chalk and deceit

he was thinking of his death room
the prayers it took getting rid of
bad jones'/ plus a black mans paternity case set up
in a flick colorless chicago court room
the jaspers' sister cracking their sides

. . . .

evil in white
every day the nurse threw little joe out morphine caps

. . . .

. . . . . . it was the end of naima
that most beautiful melody . . . . . .
a dusty red crescent over the bell tower
and us fool enough to riff the head
Dedaaa daa daaaa dee daaaa daaaa daaaaaa
in the strangers madson park basement
with the mirrors helping the color explode
islamic feeling that is time to us/heaven to come
Allah everpresent/effervescent . . . . . .
we ate our last piece of pork bacon
heard ke ra give us the rundown on the evil
it definitely projected in the western world.
it was autumn 1961 . . . . . .
and john coltrane went to sleep
in the butterfly chair at the front of the room
under the color eruption caton had crucified himself on
with a trumpets bell stuck thru his head
with shango puts on african brass
the poet takes his cue
and john coltrane awakes
showing us the way to listen to his music . . . really
his head stiff/his round eyes freezing to the horns planetary trip
but he had to nod
only to awake again
to a half hour dialogue

ohnedaruth the mystic awoke smiling
to the term 'black power structure'
and the waving of the New West Coast magazine

—Amus Mor

Words & Music in America

Jazz poetry was not discovered by
Allen Ginsberg or Jack Kerouac
let alone Kenny Rexroth
Nor was it a literary invention of the
Beat(up) school, the New York School or
any other official institution of 20th
century AVANT-learning
It started if you really wanna know
(and you damn well should) in a white
whorehouse in East St. Louis, Illinois
in August 1928 where a bunch of drunken
unemployed Negro poets were sitting around
trying to sound like LOUIS ARMSTRONG as a
rickety Victrola ground out 1900 choruses
of "Tight like That" in the early mourning
hours of Eddie Jefferson's 12th birthday
It was Eddie's father who told the other cats
present that they should all donate their individual
stanzas to little Eddie as a birthday gift as Jefferson, Sr.
didn't have no money as usual to buy his wide-eyed son that
silver-grey saxophone he'd seen in the window of a weary
looking pawnshop called LIGHTS OUT in the "nigger section"
of town
The rest as they say is MYSTERY . . .

The Funky Butt Legacy Song
(An Epic in Progress)

for Louis Armstrong, Sidney Bechet and
Charles "Buddy" Bolden

I

It was 1918 and Louis and Sidney Bechet were walking
the streets of the French Quarter

James Reese Europe was in France with his wailing wall of sound
100 strong while the bewildered Parisian soldiers breathed German

mustard gas and wondered aloud where all that magical noise was coming
from. The fretful French lost in cartesian circles of thought could only

shrug and lift their shaking heads in awe as they emerged from the raging
bells of golden metal weapons wielded by celestial swingers in blackskin.

"Les Noirs!" the Parisians were heard to shout. "Les Noirs!" "Damn straight!"
cried the roaring choir of bluesteel blasters. The 369th regiment full of heroic

trumpet players and magnificent drummers. Full of courageous violinists
and daredevil clarinetists. Full of fiery trombones and leaping fusillades

of Joy. It was 1918 and Louis and Sidney Bechet were running along the nar-
row streets of the French Quarter. What's that I heard Buddy Bolden say?

"Swing it, Shake it, Take it Away. Funky Butt is here to stay!"

II

It was 1918 and Louis and Sidney Bechet were flying high above the streets of the French Quarter. King Oliver sitting on his throne in Savannah, Ga. What

a glorious cacophony! This supercharged symphony! "Give me five strong niggers with something to say and the nerve to say it and

we'll change the world forever!" the King was heard to pray. It was 1918 and Louis and Sidney Bechet were screaming high above the streets

of the French Quarter. James Reese Europe in Paris a jet-stream layer of notes cascading from the Benin lips of tone-happy Dada coons

from Harlem, Detroit, Mississippi and St. Louis, Illinois (not to mention Missouri). But what's that I heard Bunk Johnson say:

"Swing it, shake it, take it away. Funky Butt is here to stay!" O yes it was 1918 and Louis and Sidney Bechet were singing beyond the creole-covered

streets of the French Quarter. Jelly Roll Morton hustling sentimental cornhuskers in piano poolrooms all across the U.S.A. While millions come

back in freshly hewn wooden boxes as industrialists discuss the "terms" of Armistice. It was 1918 and Louis and Sidney Bechet were dancing on the

frenzied streets of the French Quarter. What's that I heard Willie "The Lion" Smith say? "Swing it, shake it, take it away. Funky Butt is here to stay!"

—KOFI NATAMBU

Fire Parcel

Postal authorities in New York City were worried about the shipping of Eric Dolphy's old alto to his mother, Mrs. Sadie Dolphy. For some time the inside of the horn had been burned out, but not far back enough to preclude the mischief of embers that sent packing crates up in smoke, stuffings and all, three times in a row! If they had stamped Eric Dolphy's forehead "CANCELLED," that would have been hitting the nail on the head, in 1964 anyway. But no one thought of that. Eric's music must have been the soundtrack for all of those fires, turning New York for a while into Nero's Rome. And that's how this story ends: with the drunken cluster of notes on "Epistrophy" and a fire ball. If you expected scenes of a firebird arrested and booked by the cops for arson, you were dreaming.

The Circle with a Hole in the Middle

"How long it has been since I ceased
to resemble myself!"

Lautreamont

A twitch stung from above face

        I make a fever pitch
of $25 in coin
           to help the large mammal

building
              Ornette my lorgnette

     I watch more than
     an alto   for alto wings

TOO LATE
        221 species extinct since 1600
don't budge

     . . . Flightless blue
       rail   (got no shadow)

(no soap)   Absurd giant
   tortoise

     Badlands bighorn   (no horn)

     Fiji bar
(made to take nightcap)
        winged rail . . .

   So many leave holes in

          the heart
    and what of Green dolphin
     street heroic
       rare

  and gone
     Homo sapiens spoon   stuck in

primate by genius erected   your mouth

Pithecanthropus erectus

　　　It's a window mirror
　　　fronted by iron bars   I gaze into

　　Lincoln Park Zoo
　　　　　　A sign reads

　　　"you are looking at the
　　　most dangerous animal in the world"

worse than the

　　　　　Dog pound
　　　　　　in flight

　　　you G. I. Joe outfitted duckling

　(Question)   Do you expect predators
　　　　　　　　　　　　　　　　to observe a meat boycott?

I can't tell foghorn
from leghorn   (Answer)

　　TOO LATE

　　　darkling I reach for
　　　　the aerosol can of dust
　　　to brush up mutability

　　　　　　　　odes   ·

　　　　　　Primate by madness infected
sun singes
　　　　　　a cigarette burns through blue sky

　　　　　and who can see wings on anything anymore

　　　　　　wingéd
　　　　　　　or not at all

YOU DON'T KNOW WHAT LOVE IS

—PETER KOSTAKIS

A Fine Line

Clear cedar air and
cold wind polish
tired trees of heavy

leaves. Very
predictable. But what
elements of thunder

are plastic, and
what are pain? Rain
remains a tedious

option which we
dismiss sans discussion.
Hanging from the ledge

of the window I'm
looking out wouldn't mean
much as it's only

one flight up. Didn't
Dexter Gordon record that
tune? Now I'm

confused—it was the title
of one of his LPs
but not a song

on the album per se. He
did record "Second
Balcony Jump" and, on

19. Dexter Gordon. Photograph by W. Patrick Hinely, ©.

a separate occasion,
"Stairway To The Stars," but
neither on that

particular record. Nor
is this a trivial
issue. He's dying now,

faster than most that
is, though it's a fine
line to draw, I

suppose. Not that
he's one of my
heroes either, yet there's

a resiliency and tough
tang to his work one
can't help but admire, aside

from those rhythmic
quirks which always bugged
me. No escaping

his lyricism—as hard
as it is for anyone
to truly *sing*—especially

ballads, bared
nerves balancing on crafty
breath. Like Billie

Holiday brooding "I Can't
Believe That You're In Love
With Me," as casual

as breathing and as surprised
at the outcome. But that's
too easy; it's rocky

comfort to consider
the self that should
shoulder such simple whims

and still fevers,
raging. A trace replaces
dull memories of loss

or longing with vital
statistics of art and
commerce, as if

they mattered. Most
meteors strain instead of
sizzle as they worry

their way across
the stratosphere—a bad omen
to medieval astrologers

who give consul to the
king—as on this date two
heads of state meet

to see if we
have a future. Or will
burn for another's

stupidity. No song
lasts long enough to make
measure of a man's

life. "Lover Man" was Sonny
Stitt's swan song, as I
heard it at Carnegie

Hall our sour summer
night; blown through a bent
hammered shiny sheet

of metal fingered a thousand
or hundred-thousand
flights of alternating fury

and fancy, flirting
with disaster
and finding . . . what? Not

salvation but sheer
self-amazement that it could
be done, as this last

one sung with
compunction and total
resolve. It gets

no easier, but has to be
done and done right
if it kills you. And it might.

Mbizo

Johnny Mbizo Dyani, 1946-86,
expatriate South African musician

Berlin, a bust
of Lenin, graffiti'ed,
Manfred mans the bar,
congenially, *auf*
deutsch, naturally.
"Ein brandy." "Zwei
marks, bitte." Bitter
pieces of All Soul's
Night clutter the musty
Quarter Latin, insouciance
made audible, when
the word—like licking
a live wire—comes, spread
by tongues of fire,
and the music is stilled,
momentarily, while
we wait for the spirit
in green shoes
and shades to escape
our somber waltz and consort
with other angels. It's
a long road to the Promised
Land—*immer, vielleicht*—
paved with fucking technology,
and where will he
rest, when we have turned
his homeland into a hologram?

A White Line

for Franz Koglmann

Hear, on any night
of near purple, palpable
empty hours, how

sound finds shape
in the ear; echo
absence, mirror no

oasis in us. Episodes
of moon newly
blue and white

wine help disguise
the dry sky's bitter
blur. Could clouds

be brittle, allow
moonlight enough to
trust without

music this riddle?
Some rain may
sober the streets, on

film or closer,
each frame a heart
beat away,

far from where we are,
were, regret
we're not there,

now (distance is cold
comfort at
best); rest, repetition

won't serve
as seduction, or torch
even alert

rhythms, rhymes.
Time is where
now is, was; a collage

of themes, quotations,
feelings—
as fallible as photographs—

can't contain
the debris of a grey
Autumn confused

with April, in any
city, in careful
consideration, in

secret, a mirage
of memory, a souvenir
of blue envious

of orange. We are heir
to endless shades
of indigo and ebony

impulses, an open
window of song
from which we watch

tipsy ghosts
waltz in unlikely
ecstasy. Soon calm

white chaos elicits
an inner urge, an
intoxication

of notes, a denial
of harmonies
that smack of rote.

In your favorite
cafe smoke
hangs sleepless, sour,

but speaks of
compassion, as phrases
like faces

whisper in paintings
we wear
on our walls. Who

without words defines
how fond
devices fade in delicate

disarray, or ache
in order
to explain the way

music shares
some truths, and others'
fiction, when music

means nothing, but life.
No relief.
No exit. Detour ahead.

—ART LANGE

JOEL LEWIS

To The Great Hard-Bop Pianists

Club cloakroom as soothing franchise, hats
for men lacking hats, and revise your face
as an authentic Mr. B. collar steps
onto the gum spot street.
I rap at the mystery door, nothing happens.
Phone ring: empty nest. "I have all these friends
who keep accurate time."

The tone scientists have returned
from the lab. The reports came straight out
of detective books. At home, Bobby Timmons' children
called him: "dear unpasteurized father of the depths."
At the Elysian Cafe's backroom, she told me
of Red Garland's last year of drunkboys' requests.

Crushed Marlboros. Good tip in ashtray.
Sports jacket in eye-blinking pattern.
Horace Silver counting Dead Presidents.
Wynton Kelly departing in a great dark jalopy.
The time machine's habit of summoning up Elmo Hope.
Everything can happen, including Ray Bryant.
Kenny Drew's itchy pulse across a Zildjian's rim,
used as the light bulb for the hewed volumes
of scrolls.

Author Biographical Notes

James Baldwin had written fifteen books and co-authored four others until his death in 1987. His widely acclaimed works include *If Beale Street Could Talk, The Fire Next Time, Giovanni's Room, Another Country, Go Tell It on the Mountain,* and *Going to Meet the Man.* His book of poems is titled *Jimmy's Blues.*

Amiri Baraka is a writer and political activist. His play *Bumpy: A Bopera,* with music by Max Roach is re-opening at the Aaron Davis Theater (CCNY) June 1993. Forthcoming are *Jesse Jackson and Black People* (essays) and a book of poetry *Whys/Wise.* He is the co-coordinator (with his wife, Amina Baraka) of Kimako's Blues People, an arts center in Newark.

Ted Berrigan was born in Providence, Rhode Island, in 1934. He moved to New York in 1960 where he founded the critically-acclaimed "C" Magazine, wrote art criticism for *Art News,* and taught now-legendary workshops at The Saint Mark's Poetry Project. He taught at Yale, the Iowa Writer's Workshop, Northeastern University, the University of Essex (England), and the State University of New York at Buffalo. His books include *The Sonnets* and *So Going Around Cities.* He died in 1983.

Paul Blackburn was born in Vermont in 1926. He attended NYU and the University of Wisconsin. He received a Fulbright Grant in 1954 , spent two years at the University of Toulouse in France, then lived in Spain. Upon returning to New York City, he made a living as an editor and translator. His translations included *El Mio Cid,* the work of Cortazar and Paz, and the entire canon of Provencal lyric poetry. He died in 1971.

Kamàu Brathwaite, born in Barbados, taught in Ghana from 1955 to 1962. Since that time he has been lecturing at New York University and the University of the West Indies. He has written many books, including *Rights of Passage, Masks,* and *Black & Blues.*

Jim Brodey was born in Brooklyn in 1942. His books and chapbooks include *Fleeing Madly South, Identikit, Blues of the Egyptian Kings: Poems 1962-75,* and *Judyism.*

Hayden Carruth, who lives in upstate New York, is the author of *Collected Shorter Poems, 1946-1991* (Copper Canyon Press) and *Sitting In: Essays on Jazz, Blues, and Related Topics* (University of Iowa Press).

Xam Wilson Cartiér was born in St. Louis in 1949 and currently lives in San Francisco. She has won an NEA grant, Millay Colony residency and California Arts Council grant. She is also a dancer, pianist and artist.

Wanda Coleman is a Los Angeles poet and essayist. Her most recent books include *A War of Eyes & Other Stories, African Sleeping Sickness: Stories & Poems* and a forthcoming volume of poetry, *Hand Dance* (Black Sparrow Press). She guest-edited "The Violence & The Verdict" summer 1992 issue of *High Performance* magazine (with CD) in response to the Rodney King beating trial.

Clark Coolidge's latest published books are *Odes of Roba* and *The Book of During*, both from The Figures. A volume of words free-blown to the music of the ROVA Saxophone Quartet (*The ROVA Improvisations*) will be published by Sun & Moon in 1993. And a sequence of variations on the music of Cecil Taylor (*Comes Through in the Call Hold*) continues. Meanwhile Coolidge has been known to play an occasional freebop clubdate on his Gretsch wood-shells.

Gregory Corso was born in New York City in 1930. A central figure among the Beats, he has travelled extensively when not living in New York. His most recent poetry collection is *Mind Fields*.

Julio Cortazar (1914-1984) was an Argentinian novelist and short story writer who emigrated to Paris in the 1950s and lived there until his death in 1984. He was an amateur jazz trumpeter whose books in English include the novel *Hopscotch*, short story collection *We Loved Glenda So Much*, and the essay collection *Around the Day in Eighty Worlds*.

Jayne Cortez lives in New York City. She is the author of 8 books and producer of 5 recordings of poetry. Her poems have been published in numerous journals, magazines and anthologies. She has read her poetry with and without music throughout the United States, Africa, Europe, Latin America and the Caribbean

Robert Creeley has published many collections of poems, among them *For Love* and *Collected Poems, 1945-1975*. Jazz was the initial grounding for his sense of serial order and phrasing both in his poetry and prose.

Thulani Davis, was born in Hampton, Virginia and currently lives in Brooklyn. Her journalistic work has appeared in the New York Times, the Village Voice and Washington Post. Her first novel *1959*, was recently released to widespread acclaim.

Fielding Dawson is the author of nineteen published books. The most recent is a new edition of his *Black Mountain Book*. He is at work on a new edition of his Franz Kline Memoir.

Henry Dumas (1934-1968) was born in Sweet Home, Arkansas, and died at the hands of New York policemen on a subway. He was one of the most promising writers of his generation as his two posthumously published volumes show. They are *Poetry for My People* and *Ark of Bones and Other Stories.*

Clayton Eshleman's most recent collection of poetry is *Hotel Cro-Magnon* (Black Sparrow, 1989); his most recent translation is of Cesar Vallejo's *Trilce* (Marsilio, 1992). He continues to edit *Sulfur* magazine at Eastern Michigan University where he is a professor in the English department. In 1991, Black Sparrow published Paul Christensen's *Minding the Underworld: Clayton Eshleman and Late Postmodernism.*

Jessica Hagedorn's novel *Dogeaters* was nominated for the National Book Award in 1990. Her latest collection of poetry and prose, *Danger and Beauty,* will be published by Viking Penguin in 1993. A limited edition, letterpress book from Coffee House Press entitled *Two Stories: Los Gabrieles/Carnal* is also forthcoming in 1993. She is presently editing an anthology of Asian American fiction, and is at work on a new novel.

Michael S. Harper is the author of *Dear John, Dear Coltrane, Hightmare Begins Responsibility, Images of Kin, Healing Song for the Inner Ear* and other titles, and is co-editor of *Chant of Saints* with Robert B. Stepto. He is Professor of English at Brown University, where he has taught since 1970. He is editing an anthology on Black American modern and contemporary poetry, with Anthony Walton, and two forthcoming poetry collections, *Honorable Amendments* and *Collected Poems.*

Robert Hayden was born in Detroit, Michigan, in 1913. He won a number of international awards for his poetry. His books include *A Ballad of Remembrance, Words in the Mourning Time* and *Angle of Ascent: New and Selected Poems.* He died in 1980.

David Henderson was born in Harlem in 1942. His poetry has been highly praised for its power and virtuosity. He has two collections, *Felix of the Silent Forest* (Poets Press, 1967) and *De Mayor of Harlem* (E.P. Dutton, 1970).

David Hilton, b. 1938 in Oakland, trained his ear on the saxophone bridges in early-'50s r'n'b, and has not attempted any new dances since the bop. He ended up an English prof, a trade he has practiced at Anne Arundel Community College in Maryland since 1971. His most recent book of poems is *No Relation to the Hotel* (Coffee House Press, 1990).

John Clellon Holmes has wrote three novels: *Go,* in which he immortalized the Beats; *The Horn,* an inside view of the bop jazz world; and *GetHome Free,* a stunning portrait of a modern love affair. He died in 1988.

Langston Hughes (1902-1967) left behind a wealth of poems, novels, short stories, plays, song lyrics, translations, children's books, and recordings. His book *The Weary Blues* might be considered the first serious attempt at confronting the range and mixture of poetry and jazz.

Evan Hunter has been publishing prolifically under pseudonyms, as well as his own name, since 1952. His best known novel, *The Blackboard Jungle*, was made into a successful motion picture. Two of his novels are jazz-oriented: *Second Ending*, the story of an addicted trumpet player trying to kick the habit, and *Streets of Gold*, the account of blind pianist Iggie Di Palermo's discovery of fame on New York's fabled 52nd Street. He is also the mystery writer Ed McBain.

Abdullah Ibrahim (b. 1939) is a world-renowned pianist-composer born in Cape Town, South Africa. He has recorded numerous records with labels such as Enja, Sackville, Blackhawk and his own record label Ekapa. He currently lives in South Africa after having lived several years in the United States.

Lawson Inada writes that his "biography is in the poetry: Bird died when I was a high school senior, Fresno, 1955; Clifford died the next year, and I saw Pres and Lady while a student at Berkeley, 1956-57; by 1962, I was teaching in New Hampshire, where "Blue Gene" and "Wintersong" take place, and where Dan Morin was a very good music friend; I've been in Oregon since 1965. My new book, *Legends From Camp* (Coffee House Press, 1992) includes many tributes to my jazz mentors."

Bob Kaufman, born in 1925, was known in the United States as "The Original Be-Bop Man" and in France as "The Black American Rimbaud." He has been noted as one of the chief architects of the Beat movement as well as its best poet. His three volumes of poetry are *Solitudes Crowded with Loneliness*, *The Golden Sardine*, and *Ancient Rain: 1956-1978.* He died in 1986.

Robert Kelly's latest poems are *A Strange Market* (Black Sparrow Press), and his latest stories are *Cat Scratch Fever* (McPherson & Co.). In the Newark piece, writing right in the middle of the time, he tried to make sense of the broken voices of our news, what we use for information. What he knew of a friend's heart was louder than what papers said, loud as another man's music. The time. Writing is listening. He has written a lot of books, still trying to hear.

Jack Kerouac, the father of the Beat Generation, was one of the most acclaimed (and criticized) writers of modern times. He was the author of eighteen books—including *On the Road, Dr. Sax, Dharma Bums, The Subterraneans*, and *Mexico City Blues*.

August Kleinzahler is the author of *Storm Over Hackensack* and *Earthquake Weather*, both published by Moyer Bell. He is the recipient of a 1991 Lila Wallace-

Reader's Digest Writers' Award, and lives in San Francisco.

Peter Kostakis has left the poetry fold (probably). But jazz and music will always matter. "Be at it ud," as is said in Arabic. He was born in Chicago, just north of the killing floors, in 1951.

Doug Lang was born in Wales in 1941 and came to the USA twenty years ago for the poetry and the jazz. He teaches at the Corcoran School of Art.

Joel Lewis' first collection of poems, *House Rent Boogie*, was the winner of the 1991 Ted Berrigan Memorial Award for poetry. His critical writings, reviews, and articles have appeared in *Wire*, *The San Francisco Chronicle*, *Sulfur, and American Poetry Review.*

K. Curtis Lyle was born and raised in Los Angeles, and currently lives in St. Louis, Missouri. He teaches at Lindenwood College in St. Charles, Missouri, where he is Professor of Cross Culture and Humanities. His academic areas of specialization are in the history, culture, music, poetry, art, religion, and philosophy of Africa, the Caribbean, and African America.

Thomas Mcgrath was born on a North Dakota farm in 1916. He was a Rhodes Scholar at Oxford University and served in the Aleutian Islands during World War II, before being blacklisted during the McCarthy era. The recipient of numerous prestigious literary awards he also worked as a documentary film scriptwriter, teacher and labor organizer. His final books, *Selected Poems 1938-1988* and *Death Song,* were published by Copper Canyon Press. McGrath died in 1990.

David Meltzer teaches in the Poetics Program at New College of California. His most recent works are: *Arrows: Selected Poetry, 1982-1992* (Black Sparrow Press) and an anthology, *Reading Jazz* (Mercury House).

Amos Mor (b. 1949) is an underground legend best known for his recitations on Muhal Richard Abrams's album *Levels and Degrees of Light* (Delmark Records) and the album *Black Spirits: Festival of New Black Poets in America* (Black Forum Records). He was last heard from in Chicago.

Kofi Natambu was born in Detroit in 1950 He has worked as an assembly line laborer, community organizer, university instructor, civil servant bureaucrat and free lance writer. He has a BA from Oakland University and MA from MIT. Since 1981 he has edited Solid Ground—New World Journal. His books include *Intervals* and *The Melody Never Stops.*

Larry Neal (1937-1980) was born in Atlanta, Georgia, and grew up in Philadelphia. He was one of the most important theoreticians of Black Arts movement, and brought to it a comprehensive analysis and knowledge of folklife. His books include *Black Boogaloo* and *Hoodoo Hollerin' BeBop Ghosts.* The Winter, 1985 issue of Calalloo was devoted to his work and his essays *Visions of a Liberated Future* were collected by Thunder's Mouth in 1989.

Frank O'Hara was born in Baltimore, Maryland, in 1926. He spent two years in the Navy, and later graduated from Harvard in 1950. A principal member of the New York Poets, he lived and worked in New York until he was killed by a car on Fire Island in 1966.

Michael Ondaatje was born in Ceylon and later moved with his family, first to England and later to Toronto, where he became a Canadian citizen. He has written four books of poetry, including *The Cinnamon Peeler,* and his newest novel *The English Patient,* won England's prestigious Booker Prize.

J. F. Powers' first published story, in *Accent,* "He Don't Plant Cotton," was written when he lived in Chicago, but is based on an incident he witnessed one night when the leader of the band was Jimmy Noone and Baby Dodds wasn't present.

Ishmael Reed numerous books include *Mumbo Jumbo, Yellow BackRadio Broke Down, New and Collected Poems,* and *The Free-Lance Pallbearers.* His honors include a nomination for a Pulitzer Prize in poetry, a NEA fellowship for creative writing, and a Guggenheim Foundation award for fiction.

James Schuyler was born in Chicago in 1923, grew up in Washington, D.C. and East Aurora, New York, and attended Bethany College in West Virginia. His books include three novels: *Alfred and Guinevere, A Nest of Ninnies* (with John Ashbery), and *What's for Dinner?*; and several collections of poetry: *The Crystal Lithium, Hymn to Life,* and *The Morning of the Poem,* which won the Pulitzer Prize. His *Collected Poems* were recently published by Farrar, Strauss & Giroux. Schuyler died in 1991.

Ntozake Shange is the author many books of poetry and prose including *Sassafrass, Cypress & Indigo, A Daughter's Geography, Spell #7, Three Pieces,* and *The Love Space Demands.* She also performs and records with her band Syllable.

Jack Spicer, born in Los Angeles, 1925, died in San Francisco, 1965. After many years in New York and Boston, he returned to San Francisco to develop his practice of poetry as dictation. His work has been published in *The Collected Books of Jack Spicer.*

John Taggart lives in Pennsylvania, where he teaches at Shippensburg University. Recent publications are *Loop* (Sun & Moon, 1991), *Prompted* (Kent State,

1991), and *Standing Wave* (Lost Roads, forthcoming).

Cecil Taylor is a renowned jazz composer and musician. His recording career started in 1957 and he has since recorded countless disks for Blue Note, Candid, New World, Impulse, Hat Art, FMP, Black Saint and other labels. He has recently issued a compact disc of his poetry entitled *Chinampas* (Leo Records).

Lorenzo Thomas was born in Panama in 1944 and attended Queens College and Pratt Institute. A poet, literary critic and writer on music and folklore, his books include *Chances Are Few*, and *The Bathers, Jambalaya, Sound Science*. He currently resides and teaches in Houston.

Melvin B. Tolson was born in 1900. He was an educator, poet, dramatist, columnist for the Washington Tribune, and mayor of Langston, Oklahoma. He was chosen Poet Laureate of Liberia in 1947 and his books include *Harlem Gallery*, *Rendezvous with America*, and *Libretto for the Republic of Liberia*. He died in 1966.

Quincy Troupe, author of nine books, including four volumes of poetry, the latest of which is *Weather Reports: New and Selected Poems*, (Harlem River Press, 1991), edited *James Baldwin: The Legacy* and co-authored *Miles: The Autobiography*, both published in 1989 by Simon & Schuster. Random House will publish in the winter of 1994, *Artist on the Cutting Edge*, a collection of personal essays on well-known and innovative artists. He is Professor of Creative Writing and American and Caribbean Literature at the University of California, San Diego. He lives in La Jolla, California with his wife Margaret and son Porter.

Jay Wright lives in Piermont, New Hampshire.

Al Young, born in Ocean Springs, Mississippi, in 1939, is primarily a poet and novelist. He has also written what he calls "musical memoirs," including *Bodies and Soul, Kinds of Blue*, and *Things Ain't What They Used to Be*. His novels include *Snakes, Ask Me Now*, and *Seduction by Light*, and his book *Heaven: Collected Poems 1958-1988* was recently published by Creative Arts Books.

Bill Zavatsky began music studies at age six and piano at age twelve. At fourteen he fell on his head after hearing the music of Charlie Parker. His books include *Theories of Rain and Other Poems* and his translations include *Earthlight*, poems of André Breton. He plays jazz with a seven-piece combo in New York, where he teaches English at the Trinity School.

Acknowledgements

"Sonny's Blues," Copyright © 1957 by James Baldwin, from *Going To Meet The Man* by James Baldwin. Used by permission of Doubleday, a division of Bantam Doubleday Dell Publishing Group, Inc.

"Answers in Progress" and "Now and Then" from *Tales* by Amiri Baraka. Published by Grove Press. Reprinted by permission of Sterling Lord Literistic, Inc. Copyright © 1967 by Amiri Baraka.

"In the Tradition" and "The Rare Birds" from *The Music*, by Amiri Baraka. Published by William Morrow & Co. Reprinted by permission of Sterling Lord Literistic, Inc. Copyright © 1987 by Amiri Baraka.

"String of Pearls" from *So Going Around The Cities*, by Ted Berrigan. Reprinted by permission of Blue Wind Press.

"Listening to Sonny Rollins at the Five Spot" from *The Selected Poems Of Paul Blackburn*. Copyright © 1989 by Joan Blackburn. Reprinted by permission of Persea Books, Inc.

"Clocks" by Kamau Brathwaite, used by permission of the author.

"Lennie Tristano, No Wind" and "Little Light" by Jim Brodey. Reprinted by permission of the author.

"Three Paragraphs" and "Freedom and Discipline" reprinted from *Sitting In: Selected Writings On Jazz, Blues, And Related Topics* by Hayden Carruth by permission of the University of Iowa Press. Copyright © 1986 by the University of Iowa Press.

From *Be-Bop, Re-Bop* by Xam Wilson Cartiér. Copyright © 1987 by Xam Wilson Cartiér. Reprinted by permission of Ballantine Books, a Division of Random House, Inc.

"Cousin Mary" from *Mad Dog Black Lady* by Wanda Coleman. Reprinted by permission of Black Sparrow Press.

"but, ruby my dear" is published in *African Sleeping Sickness: Stories & Poems*, Black Sparrow Press. Copyright © 1990 by the author. Reprinted by permission of Wanda Coleman.

"Of What The Music to Me" Copyright © Clark Coolidge, 1986, reprinted from *Solution Passage: Poems 1978-1981* (Los Angeles: Sun & Moon Press, 1986). Reprinted by permission of the publisher.

"Rhymes with Monk" from *Own Face* by Angel Hair Books. Reprinted by permission of Clark Coolidge.

"For Miles" from *Gasoline & Vestal Lady On Brattle*. Copyright © 1955, 1958 by Gregory Corso. Reprinted by pemission of City Lights Books.

Excerpt from *Hopscotch* by Julio Cortazar, trans. by Gregory Rabassa. Copyright © 1966 by Random House, Inc. Reprinted by permission of Pantheon Books, a division of Random House, Inc. "Louis, Super-Cronopio" from *Around The Day In Eighty Worlds*, by Julio Cortazar. Reprinted by pemission of Agencia Literaria Carmen Balcells, S.A.

"Rose Solitude," "I See Chano Pozo," and "Tapping" from *Coagulations*, Copyright © 1991 by Jayne Cortez. Reprinted by permission of the author.

"Solo Finger Solo" Copyright © 1992 by Jayne Cortez. Reprinted by permission of the author.

Index